The Economies of
Central America

The Economies of Central America

John Weeks

HM

HOLMES & MEIER

New York   London

First published in the United States of America 1985 by
Holmes & Meier Publishers, Inc.
30 Irving Place
New York, N.Y. 10003

Great Britain:
Holmes & Meier Publishers, Ltd.
Unit 5 Greenwich Industrial Estate
345 Woolwich Road   Charlton, London SE 7

Book design by Stephanie Barton

Library of Congress Cataloging in Publication Data

Weeks, John, 1941–
The economies of Central America

Includes bibliographies and index.
1. Central America—Economic conditions.   I. Title.
HC141.W43   1985   330.9728'052   84-10892
ISBN 0-8419-0914-8
ISBN 0-8419-0915-6 (pbk.)
Manufactured in the United States of America

for
Matthew and Rachel

Acknowledgments

As in the case of all books, this one benefited from the comments and suggestions of many people. I particularly want to thank Elizabeth Dore, who read the entire manuscript and gave countless helpful suggestions. Two other people provided me with invaluable insights: Francisco Vannini and Carlos Glower. Others who struggled through the manuscript and pointed out useful changes are Richard Feinburg, Richard Newfarmer, Margaret Crahan, and, of course, the editors at Holmes & Meier. While whatever errors remain are my responsibility, I thank all of these people for keeping those errors to a minimum.

Contents

The Economies of
Central America

Introduction

On his final voyage to the New World, Columbus encountered the Honduran coast, marking the European discovery of Central America. More than 450 years passed before the countries of Central America were rediscovered by the North American public.[1] Despite the U.S. government's political role in the area in this century, Central America has been a *terra incognita* to most North Americans. In medieval times, cartographers adorned unknown areas with exotic monsters and mythical and fantastic geographical features. Somewhat similarly, Central America until recently was perceived (by those who considered it at all) as a vaguely defined geographical area characterized by bananas, coffee, and dictators in costumes out of a Gilbert and Sullivan musical. Certainly no other area of the world has had to bear a generically descriptive term as derisive as the label "Banana Republics."

There is a certain irony in the North American ignorance of Central America. North American military intervention south of the Río Grande has a history of a century and a half, most of it occurring in Central America. Nationalistic Central Americans find it difficult to comprehend the fact that their countries have been dominated for over a century by the governments of the colossus to the north, yet even educated North Americans know so little of the twilight zone between Mexico and Colombia. The political turmoil that began in the mid-1970s highlighted rather than dispelled our ignorance of Central America. The fall of Somoza in 1979 in Nicaragua thrilled the left in the United States and filled the center and right with foreboding of more to come in El Salvador and Guatemala. Suddenly Central America was in the news, defined by North American policy makers as an arena of East-West conflict second in importance only to the Middle East. A presidential commission on Central America issued a report in early 1984 identifying the region as one of overwhelming strategic interest to the national security of the United States and dangerously vulnerable to Cuban-Soviet penetration and perhaps domination. While this book does not address itself explicitly to geopolitical issues, our discussion of the economic development of the region does provide insight into the political turmoil in Central America.

3

The purpose of this book is to describe the economies of Central America and to interpret the current economic developments in the region. The book presupposes no prior knowledge of the region, but does assume a basic knowledge of economics. A reader who has had a beginning course in economics or possesses functional knowledge of basic economic concepts will have no difficulty following the analysis contained in the book. The chapters that follow can be read by one merely interested in the salient economic characteristics of the region. We present a large amount of data on the five Central American countries and also for Panama. Although Panama is not, strictly speaking, part of the Central American region, certain aspects of its history and external economic relations link it to its five northern neighbors. It was therefore necessary to include Panama at points.

The book does not merely present information, but develops certain themes woven into the empirical discussion. The first theme, developed from the outset, is that the Central American region is extremely underdeveloped, perhaps the most underdeveloped area in the hemisphere. This underdevelopment manifests itself in many ways: social, political, and economic. The most important cause of this underdevelopment is the region's land tenure system, a legacy from colonial times which has been repeatedly adapted to changing conditions, but neither transformed nor reformed. The concentration of land ownership in Central America influences all aspects of society, and the failure of many attempts at land reform in the five countries gives Central America its particular underdeveloped character. If the reader takes one insight from this book, it should be the overriding importance of the land question in Central America.

Closely related to the underdevelopment of Central America has been the openness of the five economies to the international economic system. This openness with regard to commodity trade and capital flows relates intimately to Central America's historical domination by foreign interests. This second theme is tied to a third: the vulnerability of the economies to external stimuli. Economic growth has at times been rapid, but always fragile and easily reversed. A further theme of this book is that Central America is characterized by tremendous inequalities in the distribution of income and wealth, one aspect of which, the concentration of land, we referred to above. These four themes, underdevelopment, openness, vulnerability, and social and economic inequality provide the framework in which we organize the discussion that follows.

History in Central America casts a long shadow, and no understanding of the contemporary economies of the region is possible without first treating the past. In Chapter 1 we briefly survey Central America's past, with emphasis on the last one hundred years. Two central issues dominate the discussion, both of which relate to the themes of underdevelopment, openness, vulnerability, and inequality. The first is the relationship between the United States and Central America. No discussion of Central America, its economics, politics, or culture, is very meaningful without reference to this external factor. Second, the history of Central America is to a great extent the history of the power of landed property, and therefore, of the relationship between land tenure and sociopolitical development. This internal factor—land tenure—and the external—North American influence—are the axes upon which Central American history has turned.

The bulk of the book, Chapters 2–8, covers the decades of the 1960s and 1970s. This period coincides with the formation and evolution of the Central American Common Market (CACM). The issue of economic integration and disintegration plays a major role, interrelated with the four theses mentioned previously. Chapter 2 presents the basic social and economic indicators for the Central American countries. The evidence is depressingly indicative of economic and social underdevelopment and human deprivation. This chapter has two purposes: to document the similarities and differences among the countries of the area, and to compare the region to the rest of Latin America and the Caribbean.

Chapters 3 and 4 treat macroeconomic issues, growth of national income and trade, extraregional and intraregional. Consideration of growth performance in Chapter 3 brings out the instability of the economies. We also consider whether the economies of the region have tended to wax and wane in concert, a first approximation to a judgment about the extent to which the region can be viewed as having a common economic destiny. As we have already asserted, openness to the world economy characterizes these small economies, and the analysis of trade proves extremely important. Chapter 4 explores the two most important aspects of this trade—the development of the CACM and trade with North America. The pattern of trade, direction of trade, and terms of trade concern us in this chapter. Subsequent chapters deal with the production relations that underlie this trade.

Agriculture, the subject of Chapter 5, is the major productive activity in Central America. The changing pattern of production and land use in the last twenty years relates closely to the land-tenure system and the development of what is called "agribusiness." The trend toward large-scale capitalist agriculture has tended to modernize rural Central America and break down the almost feudal labor-land relationship inherited from the colonial past. It can be argued that developments in agriculture have been a modernizing element as strong and revolutionary as the growth of industry.

Indeed, the growth of industry has been connected to developments in agriculture, as shown in Chapter 6. A second major factor fostering manufacturing has been the emergence of a regional market through the CACM. In response to this regional market, tremendous growth occurred in production of nontraditional manufacturing products, but this growth has proved extremely unstable.

Although the organization of this book is not country-by-country, Chapter 7 deals exclusively with Nicaragua. The fall of the Somoza dictatorship and the fundamental changes that followed were the most dramatic political events in Central America in this century. We return to some of the historical discussion of Chapter 1 to account for the fall of this extraordinary, personalized regime, then describe the economic and political situation the new government faced. Of particular importance in determining the recovery of the Nicaraguan economy from a devastating war is the relationship between the public and private sectors.

The final chapter deals with the current Central American economic crisis, which has manifested itself in slow or negative growth rates, large foreign debt-servicing relative to exports, and persistent balance-of-payments deficits. The discussion of the previous chapters provided the background for considering the extent to which the economic crisis is regional (common to all of the countries) and the elements which are specific to each country.

As this book is being written, a general militarization of Central America is occurring. There is civil war in El Salvador and an undeclared war to overthrow the Nicaraguan government. The government of Honduras is significantly involved in both these conflicts, and the Costa Rican government tolerates the activities of a band of anti-Sandinista plotters which may draw it, too, into a regional war. The Guatemalan government is occupied by its own conflict. It is quite possible, even likely, that the result of these conflicts will be to turn Central America into a generalized war zone much like Indochina in the 1960s and early 1970s. Certainly, the recent invasion of Grenada suggests a willingness by the U.S. government to employ force in the region. If armed conflict escalates, economic policies will not be of first priority in the region. The limited and fragile economic development which has occurred in Central America will fall victim to the havoc of war. That the warfare in Central America is the result of "a mass revolt against the inequities of the past"[2] goes uncontested by any serious observer, and this book achieves its purpose if it shows concretely the nature of some of these inherited inequities.

NOTES

[1] In this book we use "the United States" and "North America" interchangeably. This follows Latin American practice.

[2] The phrase is from West and Augelli (1976, 481). This is the standard work on the geography and demography of Central America and the Caribbean.

1

The Political Economy of Central America

Conceptualizing Central America

Outsiders look at a map of the Central American isthmus and see between Mexico and Colombia a jigsaw puzzle of separate countries; Central Americans look at the same map and see a single country struggling to unify. This vision of a unified Central America even manifests itself in prosaic ways: automobile license plates in the region have included below the name of the particular country the word *Centroamerica*, a poignant manifestation of the unionist hope. Not a single country south of Panama includes on its auto plates *America del Sur*.

Writers of the north have generally taken a skeptical position on the unionist movement in Central America, even to the point of ridicule.[1] The judgment from afar is that the unity of Central America has been tried and has failed. The objective factors for disunity are in fact much stronger than the forces for unity, it is argued. Indeed, it does appear that at a political level the commitment to unification has been the form, and narrow parochialism the essence. The repeated attempts at political union, the last serious one being the announcement of a joint Guatemala–El Salvador state in 1945, have been judged from the north as manifestations of quixotic romanticism, doomed to failure (and fail they all have). Yet, while no middle-class Peruvian or Argentinian would consider himself or herself a "South American" in any sense but geographic, educated Nicaraguans, Guatemalans, Hondurans, Costa Ricans, and Salvadorans do fervently identify themselves as "Central Americans."[2] This vision is more than merely a subjective self-identification. Whether or not some or all of the Central American countries are ever unified, the perception of a common bond has been and will be a strong element in the social evolution of the region and has a real basis in the history of the isthmus.

South America also had its pan-national movement. Simón Bolívar dreamed of a united Spanish-speaking America, and various political parties took up his project at least in words. But a program for a united South America has never played any practical role in the politics of the continent. In Central America, however, the tension between separatism and political unification has been a continuous theme since independence from Spain in 1821. The strength of the unification sentiment reflects more than a perception of a regional bond. Since independence, the unionist dream in Central America arose from a perception of common nationhood. The distinction between a regional bond and nationhood is central to understanding Central America. The former involves the recognition of common problems based on a similar culture and geographic proximity. The latter goes beyond this, alleging a common culture, history, and inseparable destiny. South Americans feel a regional bond; Central Americans perceive a common nation.

This perception of a regional nation is not merely a subjective phenomenon. Ideas that enter the consciousness of a population and then are in part the motivation for actions are as real as governments and other formal institutions. The fact that Central America is divided into five countries does not contradict the existence of a sense of nationhood. The source of this sense of nationhood arises from the common historical experience of the five states and the late development of those states into country status. Formally, the five assumed their present identities and boundaries (with some minor adjustments) upon independence. The formation of the Central American Federation quickly followed. While the federation dissolved in 1838, five coherent and separate countries did not emerge from the dissolution. The process of country-formation took another fifty years. Our argument is that the idea of a single Central American nation has persisted strongly because of the late development of popular identification with the separate countries of the region. This, in turn, reflected that the five states were not countries in fact until into the twentieth century.

The late development of Central America into coherent countries with separate, independent governments was a consequence of colonial and postcolonial history. The region in colonial times was divided around provincial urban centers. This division continued after independence, though it was obscured by the formal creation of the present five countries. In the colonial period, the region was administered from Guatemala City. However, the extremely crude state of communications meant that local areas had considerable autonomy. Local elites, landowners and merchants, guarded their autonomy zealously and viewed the colonial authority in Guatemala City with considerable antipathy.

Elsewhere in the New World, wars of independence served to a certain extent to forge alliances among elites, which later provided the basis for national cohesion and identification. But independence came to Central America with virtually no struggle. This allowed the provincialism of the colonial period to carry over largely intact. With independence, the region divided into states, but this division proved essentially formal, a manifestation of provincialism, with sharp divisions within each state that contained more than one urban area of significant size.

The early postindependence years were extremely chaotic. The area of Chiapas, administratively part of colonial Central America and contiguous to Guatemala, entered the new Mexican union, permanently severing its regional tie. Shortly thereafter in 1823, a congress of merchants and landlords in El Salvador showed its suspicion of union with Guatemala City by voting to annex itself to the growing North American federation. While Nicaragua was nominally a single country, divisions ran deep between the elites of León and Granada, the two major towns. Open warfare broke out in 1825, and the conflict between León and Granada would dominate Nicaraguan politics until occupation by North American troops in 1912.

At independence, present-day Costa Rica and Honduras were areas of no economic consequence, sparsely populated and without exports. The population of Honduras numbered less than 150,000 and Costa Rica's half of that. The elite of Costa Rica formed a separate state to a great extent because the territory remained largely inaccessible to any who would dominate it. Honduras in particular had no coherent identity as a country in the nineteenth century. Guatemalan strongmen maintained it as a client-state for most of that century. This was also a status suffered by tiny El Salvador, both at the hands of Guatemala and Nicaragua.

The lack of national identity for these territories that masqueraded as countries reflected the absence in each of a cohesive elite with the power to assert its domination and establish its economic and political interests as the "national interest." Once production for the world market became important with the spread of coffee, this would change. But in the interim, economic interests remained parochial and extremely fragmented. Guatemala was an exception. Colonial rule had given the elite of Guatemala City privileges such as the monopoly of trade with Spain that warranted defending. Further, Guatemala was the only territory of the five to have a large indigenous population. The repression and control of this population united the merchants and landed aristocracy in a common project, since their wealth depended upon it. This gave Guatemala a stronger national cohesion than in the case of its neighbors, though the majority of the population was excluded by class and culture. The cohesion of the Guatemalan elite allowed it to dominate Central America from independence until the 1890s, and this domination further retarded the development of national identity in the region's other states.

The unionist vision of a regional confederation reflects an implicit view that a regional identity is more fundamental than the loyalties to the separate states. An analogy to Europe helps clarify the nature of this vision. Along with the formation of the European Economic Community has gone a hope for eventual political confederation. European union-ists, however, recognize that a move towards greater political integra-tion conflicts with the nationalism of the population of each country; that is, that the real basis of European politics is the division of the region into countries. Central American unionists, on the other hand, see the division of their region into countries as an historical aberration, an artificial barrier to the natural unity of the peoples which history itself has forged.

When Central American unionists speak of regional confederation, the implied vision is much broader than just a common government for the isthmus. The vision reflects the incomplete development of national-ism and national identity on the basis of the separate states. The nationalism is epitomized in the regional view of the infamous William Walker affair. In the late 1850s, this North American proclaimed himself ruler of Nicaragua. An army made up of soldiers from the various coun-tries of Central America delivered the crushing blow to Walker's designs on Nicaragua, designs interpreted as threatening the entire region. To this day that campaign, ending in the Battle of San Jacinto, is called throughout Central America "the National War."

Central America's Economic Backwardness

Colonial and Early Independence Economy

Throughout the colonial period Central America was a backwater of the Spanish empire, both economically and politically. In the sixteenth cen-tury various *conquistadores* had sought to establish fiefdoms in the area, leading to decades of feudal warlordism. The prize to be gained, how-ever, was not great. Except in Honduras there were no precious metals to be exploited in sizeable quantities given the technology available, and the quantity of gold and silver mined near Teguicigalpa was insignificant compared to production in Zacatecas (Mexico) and Potosí (Bolivia). The region's most serious drawback for the Spanish crown was its lack of population. Imperial Spain was a feudal society, and riches flowed from forcibly incorporating more toilers into the empire, not by raising the productivity of those who toiled or by expanding markets for the fruits of increased productivity. Only the area of the Guatemalan highlands provided a substantial population to be incorporated into a forced labor system, and this made Guatemala the most important area of Central America in the colonial period.

For the most part, the Central American population pursued subsistence agriculture in the colonial epoch, as a portion does to this day. The major crops were for local and largely subsistence consumption: corn and kidney beans, with wheat cultivated in the higher altitudes and rice along the Pacific coast. The region traded abroad through Mexico by royal monopoly, but was quite isolated. This isolation was caused in part by the particular geography of Central America. The region is split by the extension of the continental divide. While the mountains are not high by the time they stretch down to Central America, they effectively divide the region between a dry Pacific lowland and a wet, tropical Caribbean lowland. The Spanish chose to populate the Pacific side, its lowland areas and highlands, with virtually no population on the Caribbean (or Atlantic) side. The Pacific savanna stretches from Guatemala through Panama, with only Honduras excluded from this ecological zone. Even along the savanna communications remained extremely primitive and improved very little before the end of the nineteenth century. Thus, the provincial urban centers of the colonial period had little regular contact with the central administration in Guatemala City. This was partly due to natural obstacles, such as the Gulf of Fonseca which interrupts the savanna between El Salvador and Nicaragua, but primarily due to economic backwardness which made the construction of cart roads of dubious utility. The consensus in the literature is that the colonial administration in Santiago de Guatemala (and later Guatemala City) had little control over what went on elsewhere. The merchants and landlords in the other major centers, such as San Salvador, León, and Granada, managed their affairs much as they pleased within the general constraints set by the Crown.

In international trade Central America was marginal in the colonial period. The first export of significance, other than the trickle of precious metals from Honduras, was cacao, sent to Europe *via* Mexico. By late colonial times, Central America could not compete with production from South America and in the nineteenth century the region became a net importer of cacao. As the colonial period wore on, indigo dye from the *juguilite* plant replaced cacao as the major export. The area around San Salvador produced this commodity, and relatively prosperous merchant and planter classes developed. This trade peaked in the eighteenth century and then declined drastically. Even in the heyday of cacao and indigo, Central America never boomed within the Spanish mercantile system, and the wealthy families in the area enjoyed riches extremely modest compared to those in Mexico. The area of modern Guatemala in particular suffered from the decline of cacao. Even though it was the most important province in terms of population and administration, it contributed little to colonial export trade in the final years before independence. In the first decade of the nineteenth century, Guatemala began to export cochineal, a red dye made from insects. The modest revenues from cochineal disappeared when the European textile industry switched to synthetic dyes.

Central America stagnated on the periphery of world trade from the time of the conquest until the mid-nineteenth century. The areas now constituting Honduras, Nicaragua, and Costa Rica had virtually no exports of significance. Guatemala generated some exports, but these were more often in decline than ascendancy. El Salvador managed to maintain an export trade in indigo, which though in decline continued well after independence. Panama at this time was administered from South America, cut off culturally and politically from the isthmus, and without exports of significance. Taken as a whole, the region was one of subsistence production and self-sufficiency even on the large estates. It was during the second half of the nineteenth century that coffee would integrate Central America into the world economy.

Integration into the World Economy

Coffee brought Central America into the world economy. Settlers introduced it into Costa Rica in the 1790s, and forty years later exports began in small quantities. Major exports first came from El Salvador in the 1840s, and by the 1880s all of the Central American republics except Honduras exported coffee. From independence until the end of the nineteenth century, Central America was a land of "coffee republics," and the land tenure pattern associated with coffee largely determined political power. With the exception of Costa Rica, coffee production extended and reinforced a near-feudal system of land use. Where land was fertile, there stretched the great estates in coffee or livestock grazing. Concentration of landholding confined the peasantry to marginally productive land, frequently on the mountain slopes and hillsides.

This pattern would be further reinforced in the mid-twentieth century with the cotton boom. El Salvador is the extreme case, with coffee growing dominated by a few families. Estimates indicate that in the 1960s 80 percent of the land in coffee belonged to fourteen families, and this concentration reflects the pattern established in the nineteenth century. In Guatemala land concentration was less, but here, too, the coffee barons ruled in the nineteenth century. In Costa Rica the land tenure system associated with coffee growing also determined the political character of the society. Initially the small, independent peasants—concentrated in the central highlands—played a major role in coffee production. While there have always been large estates, it is this yeoman peasantry on the rich coffee lands that has given Costa Rica its political pluralism unique in Latin America. In accounting for the "Switzerland of Latin America" one need look no further than its land tenure system. Similarly, the antithesis of that tenure system in the rest of Central America goes far to explain the repressive nature of the governments in the other countries.

The relationship between land tenure and authoritarianism is quite clear-cut. The system of land tenure which developed in Central America required a supply of cheap labor, particularly for picking coffee, and later cotton. The colonial epoch had, of course, been characterized by forced labor not only in Central America but throughout the Spanish New World. This system was formally eliminated in the region when the Central American Federation was formed in 1823. In practice, however, rigidly institutionalized forced labor continued during the nineteenth century, though in different form. The founders of the federation in principle favored modernization and the wage labor system which characterizes capitalism. However, the land tenure system they encountered contradicted free wage labor and the development of pluralistic institutions. Had the peasantry enjoyed political rights, it hardly would have chosen forced labor.

Through most of the nineteenth century, forced labor took the form of debt peonage, in which the debtor was legally required to work for his creditor and was guilty of a criminal offense if he left that employer while still indebted. Since the authorities tended to accept the testimony of the employer on the issue of repayment, the system effectively tied peasants to their landlords. The entry of foreign capital into Central America in the last two decades of the nineteenth century tended to reinforce involuntary servitude. Just as the local dominant classes were based on landed property, so was foreign capital, most obviously the banana companies. Thus, the development of production for the world market in the nineteenth century strengthened rather than weakened the forced labor system. During the reign of Justo Rufino Barrios in Guatemala (1873–1885), vagrancy laws strengthened the system of debt peonage. These laws made it a criminal offense not to work a portion of the year as a wage laborer, and facilitated the incorporation of peasants into forced labor. The strength of the landed aristocracy and its demand for cheap labor was evident in the constitutions of El Salvador and Guatemala as late as the 1950s. In that decade the Salvadoran constitution read, "suitable measures shall be enacted to prevent and suppress vagrancy." The Guatemalan constitution is even more explicit (Parker 1965, 194): "Every person has the obligation to contribute to progress and well-being through work; vagrancy is a punishable offense."

The vagrancy laws characteristically required all males over a certain age to work a given number of days each year. The Guatemalan law of 1934, which formally ended debt peonage, required 150 days of work per year. In practice the law affected only the indigenous population. The law required workers to carry a passbook into which the employers entered their job records as evidence of legal compliance. Such a basic violation of personal rights was justified in Guatemala as necessary to bring the indigenous population into the modern economy. The actual function of the laws, of course, was to ensure a docile and cheap labor force for large-scale agriculture. In probably no part of Latin America in the twentieth century were individual rights more grossly sacrificed to the demands of landed property than they were in Central America.

Foreign capital entered the productive sphere in Central America *via* bananas. North American companies dominated banana production from the outset. Large-scale production and export began in the 1880s and in a few decades the world's most important banana-exporting countries were Honduras, Guatemala, and Costa Rica. Banana production requires vast amounts of land and initially developed in the unpopulated Caribbean coast, except in Costa Rica where United Fruit (UFC) began operations on the Pacific side. The banana companies were more than economic enterprises. Enormous landholders, they quickly became a law unto themselves, dominating governments from Panama in the south to Guatemala in the north. Indeed, in the heyday of the "Banana Republics" era, 1910–1940, it is doubtful that any governments in the hemisphere were so subservient to narrow corporate interest as those of Honduras and Guatemala. Writing of Guatemala, Parker (1965, 117) comments, "when Ubico was president [1931–1944], the government and United Fruit worked hand-in-hand, both profiting at the expense of the laborer in the fields." The economic interests and control of the companies went beyond their landholdings. In Guatemala the UFC owned the railroad to the Caribbean at Puerto Barrios (whose docks it virtually monopolized), and in Honduras and Costa Rica controlled major rail lines through long-term leasing contracts. The few laws that existed to regulate the abuses of the companies usually were written by the companies themselves. And when the legal framework was deemed unsatisfactory, the companies simply ignored it, as in Guatemala in 1948 when the UFC refused to obey a government order to enter into binding arbitration of a labor dispute. A few years later the UFC would successfully affect the overthrow of a freely elected Guatemalan government.

The entry of the fruit companies into Central America marked the first major North American economic interest in the region, and permanently altered relations with Washington.

Although the banana boom greatly increased the foreign exchange earnings of the states in the area, excluding El Salvador, the nature of banana production resulted in little modernization of the economies. Almost no skilled labor was required, so there was no spill-over training effect, and low wage and rather transient labor characterized the plantations until the emergence of trade unions in the 1930s.

The companies had a quite cavalier land-use policy. Because of the large land concessions and the cheapness of land, there was little incentive to economize on its use. This had two consequences, the most obvious being the huge tracts of idle land held by the companies. Closely related to the idle land was the companies' response to plant disease and blight. When the problem of plant disease would reach serious levels, the companies simply abandoned plantations. For the first part of this century Nicaragua was a major producer, but in 1935 the plantations in Bluefields were abandoned. By the end of World War II Nicaragua no longer exported bananas in significant amounts. The UFC pulled out of major areas of production in Guatemala, Honduras, and Costa Rica, though in these cases production shifted to other parts of the countries. Plant disease certainly presented a problem throughout the history of banana production in Central America, but the wholesale abandonment of plantations hardly reflects a sophisticated or technologically advanced response to the problem. But given the companies' ability to obtain virtually limitless land concessions, abandoning plantations was rational economic policy.

If the development of coffee and banana production pushed Central America into the world market, it was the boom in cotton after World War II that lay the basis for the capitalist transformation of Central America. Unlike coffee and bananas, cotton could not be profitably grown in Central America on the basis of servile labor or land-extensive techniques. In order to obtain high yields and exportable quality, large applications of fertilizers and pesticides must be used. The intensive use of pesticides, incidentally, has caused a major pollution and contamination problem. In addition to the human health consequences, this contamination has affected dairy and fresh meat production, resulting in occasional bannings of Central American exports by the North American and other governments. The need to apply modern inputs resulted in large capitalist estates, particularly in Nicaragua and El Salvador. To an extent, the cotton planters represented a new landed class, a class of capitalist farmers whose interests and values show more similarity to those of industrial capitalists than to the values of the old coffee aristocracy. As is discussed further on,[3] cotton disrupted the colonial land tenure system in a way neither coffee nor bananas had done, creating a class of landless wage laborers to complement the class of agricultural capitalists.

Coffee production had dominated Central America's export economy in the nineteenth century, and the great fruit companies had reached their peak of importance in the first half of this century. The post-World War II decades have seen a dramatic expansion of cotton production. Honduras, the least developed country of the isthmus, has yet to become a significant producer, and Costa Rica and Panama have been hardly touched by the cotton boom. But for Nicaragua, cotton became the most important export in the 1960s, and assumed second place in Guatemala and El Salvador behind coffee. In these three countries the emergence of cotton has heralded the capitalist transformation of the agricultural sector, and more than any other crop, it has placed the agribusiness stamp upon the region.

Strongmen and Intervention

The Federation and Its Aftermath

The economic development of any country or region is closely linked to its political development, and this link is clear in Central America. The history of dictators and foreign intervention in the region is an oft-told tale (Karnes 1961; Parker 1965; Rodriguez 1965). The postindependence political history of Central America divides itself into two periods, 1820 to 1910, and 1910 onward. During the first period, there was foreign intervention and meddling, but the great powers—Great Britain and the United States—were content to let the political stability or instability of Central America be determined by regional strongmen. In this period various Guatemalan dictators dominated the entire region, and at the turn of the century José Santos Zelaya of Nicaragua briefly continued this tradition. Then, with the coming of the banana companies and the building of the interoceanic canal, this period of the relative autonomy of Central American rulers came to an end. Coinciding with the fall of Zelaya in 1909, Washington established a de facto protectorate over the region, and subsequent governments would wax or wane to the extent that Washington nurtured them, with a few notable exceptions. This would be the golden age of North American influence in the area (LaFeber 1983).

Independence came to Central America in the context of internal division and conflict, with every major regional center at odds with and suspicious of the intentions of the others. That a Central American union was established at all in 1823 is remarkable. The founders of the Central American federation took their inspiration and model from the Spanish constitution of 1812, sometimes called the Cádiz Constitution after the city in which the drafting convention was held. This constitution, written in the context of a corrupt and collapsing monarchy and occupation of much of Spain by Napoleon's armies, embodied the political liberalism of the late eighteenth century. Indeed, the term "liberal" as applied to political ideology first appeared in the context of the Cádiz constitutional convention. The central tenets of the liberal ideology were the principles that government derives its legitimacy from the consent of the governed, anticlericism, and free trade. These principles gave the liberals an almost religious commitment to modernization and economic progress.

In this tradition the elite of Central America sent its representatives to Guatemala City in 1823 to draft a document that would be the basis for a united, prosperous nation. The contradiction between the liberal dream and Central American reality quickly forced the delegates into a series of compromises with the Cádiz model. Strong provincial rivalries within the five states as well as among them allowed only a loose federation with a weak central government. For example, throughout the brief life of the federation each state maintained its own army separate from the federal army. All five states ratified the new constitution in 1824, but the peaceful coexistence between the state governments and the government in Guatemala City lasted only two years. Conflict began between the federal army and the state army of Guatemala in mid-1826, and soon civil war raged throughout the federation. The financial cost of the civil war of 1826–1829 bankrupted the federal treasury, and the disruption caused by the war seriously affected economic life. Further, the civil war failed to unify the five states, and lesser conflicts continued up until the federation collapsed in 1838.

The most common explanation for the failure of the Central American Federation is that the liberal program that characterized it was premature given the social and economic conditions of the region. For example, the church in Central America exerted great power down to the village level. The anticlerical ideology of the liberals came into conflict with this mainstay of traditional values, particularly in education, which the federal government sought to secularize. Land policy proved even more controversial. Liberals sought to transform land tenure in order to commercialize and modernize agriculture. This involved not only a threat to the privileges of the large landowners, but also the peasantry. The alienability of land was a central element in the liberal program, and it necessarily implied the elimination of communal rights to land. Thus, the peasantry perceived the liberal program as an attack upon traditional rights granted in colonial times. The ideological hold of the church over the peasantry, combined with the threat to the established land rights, drove the rural masses into opposition. A peasant leader from eastern Guatemala, Rafael Carrera, capitalized on rural unrest and launched a popular insurrection in 1837. His military success inspired conservatives within the elite, who sought a postindependence order modeled upon colonial institutions: hierarchical, pro-church, and based in feudal Hispanic values. A conservative elite with a mass base proved the undoing of the liberal-controlled federation.

Carrera served as the instrument by which the federation was destroyed. In January 1838, his peasant army entered Guatemala City, and the federal era ended. Three months later the federal congress, now in San Salvador, formally dissolved the Central American union. The independence of the five states proved largely formal in the following decades. Carrera, nominally dictator only of Guatemala, formed a close alliance with the conservative ruler of Honduras and established a client as president of El Salvador. Carrera would dominate the northern three states of the isthmus until his death in 1865.

The period of union and Carrera's conservative rule marked the height of British influence in Central America. This influence manifested itself in the control of the region's foreign trade and the dependency of first the federal government and later the Guatemalan government upon loans from British banks. Frederick Chatfield, British agent in Guatemala City for twenty years, personified this influence. Chatfield delved repeatedly into the internal politics of Central America. British strategy was to maintain close, and if possible dominant, relations with whatever government controlled the region. When the federation was strong, Chatfield presented himself as a liberal federalist; when it collapsed, he championed Carrera and the separatist cause. Despite his period of federalist sympathies, Chatfield is remembered in the works of Central American historians primarily as a foreign intriguer who contributed to the failure of attempts to re-form the federation.[4]

For the most part, the British government restricted its imperial designs to Belize ("British Honduras") and the Caribbean coast of Nicaragua. The latter territorial claim had been formalized in 1786 in something called "The Kingdom of Mosquitia," which consisted of an alliance with a local indigenous chieftain. While the formal protectorate status of this amorphous kingdom in the jungle swamps did not last long, the British navy treated the Caribbean coast as its own until 1850. Indeed, it was not until the 1890s that the Nicaraguan government assumed effective control of its eastern shore. British domination of the Caribbean seas and Central American trade did not, however, involve the making or breaking of governments. But the presence of imperial agents and the Royal Navy was a continuous source of humiliation to the governments in the region, demonstrating the weakness of those governments individually or collectively to enforce their territorial integrity. A notorious demonstration of this weakness occurred in 1848 when the Royal Navy seized and occupied the Caribbean port of San Juan de Nicaragua.

The Rise of North American Influence

But events to the north would bring an end to British pretensions in Central America. The United States government had not been pleased with the British role, and with the California gold rush of the late 1840s the issue came to a head. The overland route to California was costly and slow, which stimulated interest in a transisthmian passage through Central America. Washington moved quickly to consolidate such a route. In 1848, a treaty was signed with Colombia (Nueva Granada) for transit rights across Panama (then a province of Colombia). Treaties were also signed with Honduras and Nicaragua. The Nicaraguan treaty was a direct challenge to the British. The relevant transit route involved the San Juan River and its Caribbean port, San Juan de Nicaragua, which the British considered to be in their sphere of influence. This challenge, which raised the possibility of an Anglo-North American war, prompted the Clayton-Bulwer Treaty of 1850. According to the treaty, the governments of the United States and Britain granted each other equality of interest in Central America and agreed to form jointly a company to transmit passengers and freight from San Juan de Nicaragua to the Pacific coast.

This treaty is important for two reasons. First, it was epoch-marking in that it formalized the end of British domination of Central America. While the agreement established formal equality between the two Anglo powers, Great Britain made all the concessions. Prior to the agreement, the British virtually monopolized trade in the region and the Royal Navy held de facto control over the Caribbean coast. The treaty in effect set in motion the decline of British influence. While that influence would continue for fifty years, it would now be a residual influence, its extent determined by the pace of U.S. expansion. The future status of the British as junior partner was indicated in the formation of the joint Anglo-American transit company, which was headed by a North American, Cornelius Vanderbilt. But a second aspect of the treaty was even more portentous for the governments of the region. This treaty—which determined foreign influence over Central America—was negotiated and signed in the absence of a representative from any regional government, without even an observer. The implication was clear: foreign powers need not consult Central Americans to determine the region's place in global politics.

For the next sixty years, the full consequences of this precedent would not be realized. Interventions there were, principally the Walker affair in the late 1850s and North American troops in Panama in the 1880s, but for the most part governments rose and fell according to the balance of internal power in the region.

The strongmen of Central America could with some justification see themselves as masters in their own land. The first of these was Carrera of Guatemala, who was the undisputed master of the region during the 1850s and early 1860s. He overthrew uncooperative governments, selected presidents, and maintained a political climate to his liking, particularly in tiny El Salvador. Indeed, the Walker affair was in great part the result of the frustration of Carrera's opponents in face of their weakness to confront him. In 1855, Nicaragua was ruled by allies of Carrera centered in the city of Granada. Their opposition, in León, hired William Walker, a North American adventurer, and invited him to Nicaragua. Walker and his mercenary army successfully took control of the country, but to the dismay of his hosts, he declared himself president. This tenure proved brief, however.[5]

After the death of Carrera, another Guatemalan dictator, Justo Rufino Barrios, assumed the role of Central America's overlord. While not as dominant as Carrera, he established a client in Honduras and maintained servile governments in El Salvador. These two dictators personified the conception of a united Central America. While Carrera was formally antiunionist, his extra-Guatemalan adventures reflected a view that national sovereignty counted for little in the region. Barrios was overtly unionist, announcing the formation of a federation in 1885, which his client in Honduras endorsed. Porfirio Díaz, the Mexican dictator, opposed the plan, wary of a united Central America, and sent troops to the Mexican-Guatemalan border. Shortly thereafter Barrios died in an attempted invasion of El Salvador, where his client president was proving uncooperative to the planned union. This period, particularly the Barrios epoch, can be characterized by unsuccessful attempts to unite Central America by force.

U.S. Hegemony and Intervention

The last of the great Central American overlords was José Santos Zelaya of Nicaragua, president from 1893 to 1909. Like Carrera and Barrios before him, he sought to impose unity of a sort on Central America, controlling the governments of El Salvador and Honduras for much of his rule. Interestingly enough, it fell to this autocrat to be extolled as a regional nationalist hero. In his domestic policies, Zelaya showed little to distinguish himself from previous Nicaraguan dictators or those in the other countries of Central America. Some writers characterize Zelaya as a "modernizer," since Nicaragua's transportation infrastructure improved and exports increased during his rule. However, these developments occurred elsewhere in the region at the same time, and in Nicaragua were more a sign of the times than the achievements of Zelaya. But his name was made in regional history in 1894, when he expelled the British from the Caribbean coast of Nicaragua. This alone would have made him a nationalist hero. He was to prove even bolder: in the early 1900s, Zelaya confronted Washington with the pretensions of an equal, something no Central American ruler would again do until Arévalo of Guatemala almost fifty years later. It would cause Zelaya's fall.

From the 1860s, the construction of an interoceanic canal had been a distinct possibility, a possibility with great economic and political ramifications. A French company actually received rights to a Panama route and began construction in the 1870s. When this attempt failed, opinion shifted, and until the early 1900s it was generally assumed that the transit route would be through Nicaragua. Shipping could follow the natural waterways of the San Juan River and Lake Nicaragua, leaving only a short canal to dig. At the turn of the century, Washington began negotiations with Zelaya for the rights to a Nicaraguan route. In these negotiations Zelaya refused to grant the North American government full legal control over the proposed canal route; in other words, he sought to maintain some degree of Nicaraguan sovereignty over its territory. He was supported by the Costa Rican government, which by two nineteenth century agreements had established rights to use the San Juan River. After long negotiations, the governments of Nicaragua and the United States reached an agreement by which Zelaya was paid $6 million for the concession. However, the limited sovereignty Zelaya maintained proved unacceptable in practice to Washington. Zelaya's conditions led to reconsideration of a Panamian canal route, and in 1903 the Roosevelt administration orchestrated secession of Panama from Colombia. The secessionist state received instant recognition, and the compliant government, installed with the aid of North American warships, showed none of Zelaya's qualms about signing over its sovereignty. Panama became a North American protectorate, with military occupation of the Canal Zone. Until 1978 this strip of land would be beyond the touch of any Panamanian government.

Central America seethed in conflict during the first decade of the twentieth century as Zelaya sought to establish his mastery over the region. He encouraged an invasion of Guatemala by opposition forces, which led to the fall of that government. Nicaraguan troops invaded Honduras, where Zelaya created a puppet regime. These actions and others continued the traditions of Carrera and Barrios and should be seen as yet another attempt by a regional strongman to dominate and perhaps unite Central America by force. Zelaya resented interference from Washington in his ambitious projects, arguing that outside powers had no right to intervene in the affairs of Central America. However, with construction of the Panama canal in progress and growing North American investment in the banana industry in several countries of the region, Washington was less tolerant of strong-willed Central American dictators.

With the purpose of blocking Zelaya's regional ambitions, the Roosevelt administration convened a peace conference on Central America in Washington in 1907. Formally, this conference sought to neutralize Honduras, outlaw the use of force among the five states, and establish a regional court to adjudicate boundary disputes. All participants recognized that the true purpose was to contain Zelaya within Nicaraguan territory. Though Zelaya was well aware of this, he reluctantly agreed to attend under great pressure from Washington and his anxious neighbors.

This conference is noteworthy, particularly compared to the second Washington conference on Central America in 1923. The conference was chaired throughout by Latins, and the Roosevelt administration took care to see that the government of Mexico played a major role. The participation of Mexico was particularly important, for at the time the Mexican dictator Porfirio Díaz was on friendly terms with Zelaya and could play a mediating role. While in 1904 Roosevelt had assumed the right for his government to unilaterally intervene in Central America (the "Roosevelt Corollary" to the Monroe Doctrine), the peace conference seemed to establish a framework of dispute settlement that would make intervention unnecessary.[6]

However, stability of a sort was to come to Central America by "the big stick" from the north, not by negotiated settlement. The canceling of certain preferential treatment of North American firms in Nicaragua and rumors that Zelaya was considering a Japanese company to build a canal led to a diplomatic break between Washington and Managua in 1908. In 1909 Washington tried to sabotage a loan Zelaya had negotiated with European banks for railway construction. The dictator's internal enemies took heart and revolted, and the North American secretary of state, Philander C. Knox, endorsed these rebels. Under great external pressure, Zelaya resigned. The U.S. Navy aided the rebels in overthrowing Zelaya's replacement, and all subsequent presidents of Nicaragua would serve with the blessing of Washington or not at all. Zelaya was not alone in falling victim to the new North American policy of unilateral interventionism. In 1917 Federico Tinoco Granados seized power in Costa Rica. Otherwise undistinguished, his independent policies incurred the wrath of Washington. None other than John Foster Dulles described policy toward Tinoco's government as "economic strangulation," and Tinoco fell in 1917, another unlikely martyr to Central American nationalism.

The fall of Zelaya ended an epoch in Central America. From that point onward, the region would be dominated from Washington in a way no South American country has ever been dominated. Intraregional conflicts and meddling would be significant only in as far as Washington prompted or supported them—such as the Honduran-based overthrow of the Guatemalan Arbenz government in 1954 or the present Honduran-based attacks on Nicaragua. From 1912 to 1933, the Marines occupied Nicaragua (see Chapter 7); this was only the most visible aspect of the new rules for the region. North American policy would be applied unilaterally, without the consultation of neighboring states such as Mexico, Venezuela, and Colombia. Previous accords among the five Central American republics would be ignored in the Bryan-Chamorro Treaty of 1916, which gave Washington "perpetual" rights to a canal route through Nicaragua. This treaty was made with a Nicaragua under de facto protectorate status (and militarily occupied), and without consulting either Costa Rica (with legal rights to the San Juan River) or Honduras (with legal claims to the Gulf of Fonseca).[7]

Overt North American military intervention occurred in Honduras as well in the 1920s, though not on the Nicaraguan scale. By the end of the First World War, the Honduran economy was, in the words of one writer, "virtually indistinguishable" from the three great banana companies that dominated all aspects of economic life (LaFeber 1983, 45). A conflict within the Honduran elite over presidential succession prompted Washington to land troops in 1924. The episode embodied a bit of black humor. Washington justified intervention on grounds of protecting North American property and enforcing the principle that governments would not be allowed to gain power by armed insurrection. But the expeditionary force discovered that the aspirant presidential usurper enjoyed the support and funding of one of the banana companies, United Fruit. The U. S. Department of State managed to avoid an embarrassing situation by sending a functionary to Honduras to negotiate the presidential succession in a manner agreeable to the banana companies.[8]

The new regional order was formalized at the Washington conference of 1923. The contrast to the 1907 conference was striking: Mexico was not invited, nor any Latin country save the five of the region; the conference was chaired throughout by a North American; and the agenda could be augmented only by unanimous consent (*ergo*, consent of Washington). The conference helped to lay the groundwork for repressive and long-lived military dictatorships in all of the republics but Costa Rica. Beginning in the early 1930s, the same men ruled El Salvador and Guatemala until 1944; Honduras until 1949; and in Nicaragua Anastasio Somoza García continued until his assassination in 1956, and was replaced by a son. This era of repressive, one-man dictatorships is often referred to as the period of *continuismo* in Central America.

Two major political events ushered in the period of extended, one-man dictatorships in Central America. The first was Augusto Sandino's six-year insurrection against the U.S. occupation of Nicaragua. In 1927 the US occupying forces reached an agreement with a faction of the Nicaraguan elite to continue military control of the country, which had already lasted for fifteen years. The new agreement excluded an important sector of the elite from power and sent it into armed opposition. The insurrection of the elite collapsed quickly, but in 1928 Sandino began a guerrilla war whose goal was to expel the foreign invaders. For six years, using the most advanced military technology of the time, including air power, the US military tried and failed to subdue Sandino's peasant army. Sandino's successful resistance would bring him recognition throughout Latin America as the continent's greatest nationalist since Simón Bolívar, and inspired his admirers to give him the middle name "César" for his military exploits.

Finally Sandino's resistance proved so costly that the US government encouraged its client government to seek an accord with the nationalistic rebel. Though the agreement involved no political power for Sandino nor his supporters, he accepted it. In 1934 Sandino was lured from his hideaway and murdered after dining at the presidential palace, probably on direct orders from Anastasio Somoza.[9] Sandino's successful resistance demonstrated the limits to direct use of force by Washington in Central America. The costs of direct intervention prompted a shift in policy toward creating professional, US-trained local armies to fulfill the task of domestic pacification and political stabilization. The North American government first implemented this new policy in Nicaragua itself, creating the National Guard and selecting Somoza as commander. In the years that followed, a military school in the Canal Zone and scores of US military advisers throughout Latin America worked to achieve the same success that the National Guard brought in Nicaragua. Direct intervention in Central America became the exception rather than the main instrument of policy, not in small part due to Sandino's insurrection.

The second major political event was the Salvadoran peasant revolt of 1932, which had a profound impact upon the governing elites throughout Central America. In 1930, Arturo Araujo, an upper class reformer influenced by Fabian socialist ideas, won election as El Salvador's president. Up to Araujo's presidency, Salvadoran politics had been characterized by intra-elite conflicts and intrigues to gain the advantages that governing could bring. The combination of Araujo's tolerance for dissent and economic hardship, particularly falling wages for coffee pickers, led to an upsurge in mass protest. When Araujo failed to repress this protest with sufficient force, the military replaced him in December 1931 with his vice-president, Maximiliano Hernández Martínez. With the popular unrest still on the rise, the tiny Communist party called for a general insurrection in the countryside. In the brief fighting, about thirty landlords and their overseers lost their lives at the hands of rebels. Martínez responded with the most violent reign of terror in Central American history. Government troops massacred about fifteen to twenty thousand peasants.[10] The insurrection and its bloody aftermath changed the nature of Salvadoran politics. Since then, the country's politics have reflected the landed elite's fears of a recurrence of the 1932 insurrection. As one writer put it, the insurrection changed the basis of politics from intra-elite rivalry to class conflict between the privileged and underprivileged.[11]

The authoritarian dictators that ruled all the Central American states except Costa Rica were the heirs to Sandino's rebellion and the Salvadoran peasant insurrection. The success of Sandino's movement showed that direct US intervention could call forth strong nationalist opposition and prompted a shift to reliance on local, North American-trained armies to maintain the traditional order. Salvador's 1932 uprising threatened, however momentarily, the rule of elites and prompted them to contain their internal conflicts and support military-based regimes that could enforce the status quo.

Reform and Reaction

World War II brought relative economic prosperity to Central America, particularly since many Asian suppliers of tropical products were occupied by Japan or had their sea lanes disrupted. The war also brought a wave of reformist politics, though not to Nicaragua where there would be no hint of this for another thirty years. Reform was most dramatic in Guatemala; less fundamental but also less tragically transitory in Costa Rica; and largely cosmetic in El Salvador and Honduras. Reform in Guatemala began with the presidency of Juan José Arévalo in 1945. As one quite pro-North American writer has said (Rodriguez 1965, 142), "[B]y our standards, Arévalo's reform program was moderate . . . but considering Guatemala's past, it constituted a real revolution. . . ." The most controversial part of the Arévalo program was the land reform. While the measure was considerably milder than that which had been implemented in Mexico decades before, it would bring down Arévalo's popularly elected successor, Jacobo Arbenz. Guatemala in the early 1950s was a semi-feudal society of a landed aristocracy, an aristocracy that had a powerful ally in the United Fruit Company (UFC). The land reform might have broken the power of this aristocracy in time and helped transform Guatemala into a modern capitalist country. Such speculation is idle, for in 1954 Arbenz capitulated in the face of a CIA-financed invasion from Honduras and vacillation by his army command (Schlesinger and Kinzer, 1982). With the fall of Arbenz, Guatemala entered a dark age of repressive dictatorships shocking even by Central American standards.

The land reform of the Arévalo and Arbenz administrations played a major role in stimulating the overthrow of Guatemala's only democratically elected regime, and the spokesmen of the UFC branded it as communist-inspired. Essentially, the land reform had two elements: the nationalization with compensation of unutilized lands, and a land-to-the-tiller program in which the landless peasants would receive title to property. In 1811, an organization of merchants in Guatemala City, the *Consulado Real*, had issued a document of recommendations to the royal governor on the economic development of the colony. Included in the document was a land reform program. The merchants decried the concentration of land ownership, arguing that a few families controlled the land of the colony, "with enormous prejudice to the many who form the mass of the State, and who do not have a palm of land where they can plant some corn."[12] The document recommended that the state take over the unutilized land of large property holders and sell it at concessionary prices to the peasantry. The strength of landed property in Guatemala is indicated by the reaction of the country's elite to a similar proposal 140 years later.

Reformism in Costa Rica was strictly political, not touching the distribution of income or wealth. In 1948 there occurred a civil war, with the sides divided in quite unexpected ways. Allied with the old order was the Costa Rican Communist Party and, from across the border, Anastasio Somoza. The unifying issue for the victorious rebels was honest elections and an end to corruption and nepotism in government. After the victory, a Second Republic was formed and the presidency went to the candidate who had lost the 1947 election by fraud. The new president, Otilio Ulate Blanco, was basically quite conservative, though his government is known throughout Latin America for taking the astoundingly radical step of abolishing the Costa Rican Army in 1950.

The otherwise conservative reformism of this government led to a split in the movement that had forged the rebellion of 1948. In 1953, the social democratic National Liberation Party won the presidential election and virtually swept the more conservative National Union Party from the national legislature. Subsequently, the two parties would alternate victories in the presidential elections, the National Union in 1958 and 1966, the National Liberation Party in 1962 and 1970. Thus for over twenty years, from 1948 to 1970, the opposition won each presidential election, and the governing party peacefully relinquished power—an impressive record for Latin America. The peaceful and legal transfer of power continues to this day.

In El Salvador, the long dictatorship of Hernández Martínez came to an end in 1944. His autocratic rule had alienated even parts of the oligarchy, and his pro-fascist tendencies branded him as unreliable from Washington's point of view.[13] A militant demonstration of workers in San Salvador precipitated his fall. While he momentarily crushed the popular uprising, continued unrest indicated that he could no longer control the population, which the oligarchy expected from its president. Contemporary accounts suggest that he finally offered his resignation upon the request of the US ambassador.

A mildly reformist regime followed Martínez, though without moves toward representative government as in Guatemala or Costa Rica. Indeed, in 1948, a military coup overthrew Salvador Castañeda Castro, who had been elected in a relatively honest fashion in 1945, and jailed him. A reformist period followed, bringing El Salvador's first social security law.[14] By the standards of the region, the military rulers of El Salvador proved progressive, though the most progressive sector of the military, which staged a coup in the late 1960s, fell under intense domestic and North American pressure after three months. As one author put it referring to the 1950–1970 period (Rodriquez 1965, 37), "Salvadorans have only a choice between rival military factions," and given the mildness of reform, "traditional societal patterns . . . have not been unduly disturbed."

Something akin to fair elections have been held in Honduras from 1924 to 1932, but the winner of the presidential contest of 1932, a military man named Tiburcio Carías Andino, suspended elections for sixteen years and ruled as a dictator. The regime that followed Carías instituted a number of mild reforms. But its most notable activity was to allow the 1954 right-wing invasion of Guatemala to be staged from Honduras. A major democratizing trend did occur in Honduras in the 1950s, but not because of government action. In mid-1954 the country was seized by a major strike on the banana plantations, and the strikers won significant concessions. This signaled that organized labor would play a significant, if intermittant, role in Honduran politics, counter to the situation in Guatemala where the labor movement was being destroyed by Castillo Armas, the dictator who followed Arbenz.

In Nicaragua the postwar period brought no reformism. Hopes for change rose with the assassination of the elder Anastasio Somoza in 1956, after over twenty years of one-man rule. His oldest son, Luis, and later his younger son, Anastasio Somoza Debayle, followed in the presidency and continued their father's autocratic rule. While not the most repressive regime in Central America, the Somoza dynasty was the most anachronistic, a type of personalized rule for family enrichment that was a thing of the past in almost all of the Western Hemisphere.[15] Fearful of reform in the region, the Somozas fostered several unsuccessful rightist invasions of Costa Rica in the 1950s, directly aided the overthrow of Arbenz, and Luis Somoza personally saw off the ship carrying the North American-backed invaders of Cuba in 1961. The rule of the Somozas did coincide with rapid economic growth in Nicaragua, at least until the mid-1970s. All observers agree that the benefits went to the dynastic family and its court.

Strictly speaking, Panama is not a Central American country, since its cultural ties are to South America and it was ruled as a province of Colombia until 1903. However, Panamanians, like it or not, were drawn into the maelstrom of Central American politics by the North American government. The very creation of Panama as a nominally independent country resulted from events in Central America: Zelaya's qualms about signing over Nicaraguan sovereignty for the construction of a canal. The governments of Panama, however, have never meddled in the internal affairs of Central America, and in that way Panama lacks one of the common historical characteristics of its five neighbors to the north.

At the time of Colombia's independence from Spain there was a Panamanian secessionist movement and briefly, in 1840–1841, an independent Panama. Among the countries on the isthmus, only Panama experienced direct North American intervention in the nineteenth century, excluding the Walker affair. In the early 1880s the U.S. government dispatched troops to safeguard the North America-built railway. US troops returned in 1902, much to the fury of the government in Bogotá. Despite or because of this show of force, Washington negotiated a canal treaty with Colombia in 1903. The Colombian Congress, however, showed some of Zelaya's qualms about sovereignty and refused to ratify the treaty. The legislators had in effect voted the independence of Panama.

The Roosevelt administration—having failed to convince two governments to surrender their sovereignty over a canal route—now abandoned diplomatic niceties. With aid from Washington, a French mining engineer and a North American lawyer conspired with Panamanian politicians to create an insurrection. North American warships moved into Panamanian (perhaps one should say, Colombian) waters and prevented Colombian troops from arriving to quell the provincial uprising. Washington recognized the new government and within two weeks negotiated a canal treaty. Until the signing of a new canal treaty seventy-five years later, Panama would be one of the few countries in the world without even nominal rights in a portion of its own territory.[16] Further, up to the outbreak of World War II, Washington maintained the right of unrestricted intervention. For almost forty years the entire country was a North American protectorate. Formal renunciation of the right of intervention in 1939 meant little in practice, since the North American government greatly expanded its military presence in Panama during the war. Only strong nationalist protests forced the abandonment of some of the bases (but far from all) after the war.

Panamanian postwar politics centered on the canal issue. After the war, dictator José Antonio Remón sought to renegotiate the canal treaty. The Panamanian government presented credible evidence that the tax revenues and income from the Canal Zone before the construction of the waterway exceeded the rent paid on the canal. A discriminatory pay policy within the Zone—one rate for North Americans and a much lower one for Panamanians—was also a bone of nationalist contention. The treaty was modified in 1955, though the issue of sovereignty went untouched. On the contrary, Secretary of State John Foster Dulles reaffirmed in 1956 the principle of unrestricted North American control over the Canal Zone and all within it. Even an agreement to fly the Panamanian flag in the Zone required a state visit to Washington by President Roberto F. Chiari in 1962. Demonstrations in Panama in 1964 over the sovereignty issue and related bloodshed led to a brief break in diplomatic relations. A decade later, Omar Torrijos would make himself a nationalist hero in Latin America by negotiating a new treaty with the Carter administration that finally made the government in Panama City legally the government of all of Panama.

A small group of oligarchic families dominated Panamanian politics until the late 1950s. But the overriding importance of the canal issue—the issue of national sovereignty—fueled the growth of a national populist movement led by Arnulfo Arias Madrid, a populism that exploded in anti-North American riots in 1947, 1959, and 1964, and took root in the National Guard in the 1950s. With wide popular support, Arias became president in 1968. His presidency was brief, however. An attempt by

Arias to reduce the political power of the National Guard led to a coup, and from the ranks of the *golpistas* emerged Torrijos, who governed Panama until his death in an airplane crash in 1981. Ruling with a personal style that often seemed modeled on that of his personal friend Fidel Castro, Torrijos implemented a mild but highly visible populist program. This program included a moderate land reform and greater rights for organized labor. In economic policy Torrijos was less populist than capitalist. His government promoted with considerable success the growth of international banking, so tiny Panama is now a major world center for large banks seeking to escape regulations in developed countries. Torrijos' government also fostered with considerable success a "duty-free" industrial zone, where multinational manufacturers can take advantage of relatively high productivity and low wage labor as well as tax concessions. It can be persuasively argued that foreign banking and manufacturing interests in Panama now outweigh the canal in economic importance.

Reaction and War

The 1960s seemed to offer Central America a new and more progressive era. President John F. Kennedy announced in 1961 a new hemispheric policy, the Alliance for Progress, and in his rhetoric he repeatedly used the term "revolution" and called for structural change in Latin America to redress historical inequities. In fact, the 1960s and 1970s brought reaction and war to Central America, as the strength of right-wing political forces increased thoroughly all of Central America. The reforms suggested by the Alliance, particularly land reform, heartened the moderate left and centrist political elements in the region, but their emergence prompted a powerful counteraction by the right which has plunged Central America into violence and war.

El Salvador provides the clearest example of this process. In 1960 a coup by moderate military officers against right-wing dictator José María Lemus seemed to offer the type of controlled modernization that the Alliance would call for a year later. The North American government's fear that the officers harbored sympathies for Fidel Castro prompted a decision to withhold diplomatic recognition. After a few months, right-wing military elements took back power with Washington's blessing and ruled through the 1960s. However, for the first time in El Salvador's history, a reform-oriented mass political party arose to challenge oligarchic rule, the Christian Democratic Party (PDC). Late in the decade the PDC made a strong showing in municipal elections, which included the election of its leader, José Napoleón Duarte, as mayor of San Salvador. In 1972, Duarte and his running mate Guillermo Ungo appeared to win the presidential election. But as the results came in, the military suspended counting and declared its candidate, Arturo Molina, to be the winner. This election fraud touched off an insurrection in the ranks of the army, which the government suppressed with the aid of Nicaraguan and Guatemalan troops.

The election debacle of 1972 set in motion a polarization of Salvadoran society which eventually turned to civil war. Moderates joined with the revolutionary left once elections seemed no longer an avenue to power. The terrorism of the right, particularly against the moderate and centrist political elements, stimulated the administration of Jimmy Carter to bring pressure on the Salvadoran government and actively seek an alternative to the right-wing drift of Salvadoran regimes. In 1979, the military formed a junta which included civilians (Ungo among them) and announced a broad land reform (see Chapter 5). However, continued right-wing terrorism against the middle-class parties brought the resignation of most of the civilians in the junta in January 1980. Ungo himself went over to the rebel cause shortly thereafter. During the subsequent four years the various governments of El Salvador have moved rapidly to the right, to the extent that an ultra-right politician closely associated with the death squads (Roberto D'Aubuisson) was the runner-up in the presidential election of 1984.

The crushing of the moderate opposition and descent into civil war in El Salvador has a clear cause. We have stressed that the power of the landed oligarchy is a major aspect of Central America's underdevelopment, and nowhere is it more powerful than in El Salvador. In the view of the Salvadoran oligarchy, politicians such as Ungo and Duarte are as dangerous as the far-left, since they would alter land ownership if given the opportunity.[17] For the large landowners it matters little who takes away their land, the communists or the Christian Democrats; the oligarchy would retire to Miami in any case, and some have done so already.

Much the same dynamic has ruled Guatemala. The fall of the Arbenz government had been orchestrated by an alliance of foreign and domestic landed interests, and Armas, who followed Arbenz, moved quickly to re-establish the power of the oligarchy. After the assassination of Armas in 1957, Miguel Ydígoras Fuentes held the presidency for six years. Compared to what would come later, Ydígoras's rule was only moderately repressive. At the end of his presidency some hope for liberalization seemed justified, for he allowed the return of Arévalo for the elections of 1963. Fearful that the progressive Arévalo might win the presidency, as he had done so overwhelmingly in 1945, the far right overthrew Ydígoras, and replaced him with a president who would tolerate no liberalizing trend.

Since the fall of Ydígoras, Guatemala has been ruled by a right-wing civilian-military alliance which a CIA report called "the most extreme and unyielding in the hemisphere."[18] Under the rule of this alliance, right-wing death squads have operated with freedom, and by the late 1970s moderate political parties no longer existed in Guatemala, their members either murdered or in exile. The repression became so extreme that in 1980, the vice-president of Guatemala, Francisco Villagran Kramer, resigned in protest and went into exile. As in El Salvador, the hegemony of the far right in national politics reflects the power of a landed property class which is an anachronism in the rest of the hemisphere.

The same rightward drift of national politics has occurred in Honduras in the last twenty years, though in less violent form. As in El Salvador and Guatemala, the early 1960s saw a hint of reform. Again, the land question was central. Ramón Villeda Morales assumed the presidency by election in 1957 and in 1961 introduced a land reform, in part encouraged by the rhetoric of the Alliance for Progress. However, strong pressure from United Fruit, including threats to reduce operations in Honduras, forced major reductions in the proposed program.

An army coup in 1963 brought Osvaldo López Arellano to power, and he ruled until 1975 with a brief interruption in 1971–1972. Lopez was convinced that political stability required a solution to the land problem, and his government implemented a successful program of land reform, though pressure from the oligarchy kept it to modest proportions. In 1975 evidence that Lopez had accepted huge bribes from United Brands (corporate successor to United Fruit) forced his resignation. Subsequent governments have been nominally civilian, but in practice the military has ruled.[19] The dominance of the land question in Central America is demonstrated by the fact that in the 1970s Honduras instituted the only significant land reform in the region and was the only country except Costa Rica to have no guerrilla movement of any importance.

In the 1960s Nicaragua and Costa Rica were the most politically stable countries in the region, one on the basis of a family dynasty,[20] the other on the basis of liberal democracy. But even in Costa Rica politics drifted to the right. The social democratic National Liberation Party (PLN) won four of the six presidential elections from 1962 to 1982, but took on a more conservative orientation with each victory, until there was little to distinguish it from its opponent, the National Union. For the most part this rightward drift of the PLN manifested itself in economic policy, not in any reduction of the political liberties so unique to Costa Rica. Whether this long tradition of democratic freedoms and peaceful transfer of power through elections can continue in the 1980s in the face of the general militarization of the region remains to be seen. The history of Central America suggests that none of the countries can long be isolated from the unrest and instability of the others.

Understanding Central America

From the foregoing economic and political history it should be clear that Central America cannot be conceptualized or understood as simply a part of Latin America. First, the modern history of most countries south of Panama can be written (and is written) such that North American influence and intervention enters in only a secondary or indirect way, with some exceptions. Such is not the case in Central America. Any book on Central America has continuous and extended reference to treaties, interventions, and other overt and covert manifestations of North American presence. All authors, whether pro-North American, anti-, or neutral (of whom there are few), feel called upon to pass judgment upon the relationship between the isthmus and the dominant power in the hemisphere. Woodward (1976, 191), for example, calls the relationship established with Central America after 1910 "The New North American Colonial Empire," and Parker ventures (1965, 307) that "no one can argue that Central America is well off today through her long association with rich neighbors."

The chapters that follow deal largely with economic issues (with the exception of Chapter 7 on Nicaragua). Treatment of what even moderate political observers call the "neocolonial" relationship between Central America and North America has been restricted to this chapter, except for passing allusions and our discussion of Nicaragua. Otherwise, the book would seem obsessed with the issue, for it has permeated all aspects of Central American life in the twentieth century. Certainly Central Americans are obsessed with it. As one historian has written (Rodriquez 1965, 117), North American policy in Central America "fostered a fund of hatred, or Yankeephobia, that has endured to the present day."

Second, the land question continues to dominate the politics and economics of Central America to an extent which is no longer the case in South America. The ownership and distribution of land is the primary political issue in Guatemala, El Salvador, and Honduras, still of major importance in Nicaragua after the fall of Somoza, and even key in the region's most developed country, Costa Rica. Economic development in the region, rather than diminishing the importance of this issue, has intensified it. Agribusiness has given the landed oligarchy a new and growing base of economic and political power, so that land ownership still determines the relationship between the privileged and underprivileged. The historical legacy of unequal access to land hangs heavily over Central America, the fundamental barrier to social peace in the region.

NOTES

[1] See Karnes (1961) for a typical treatment. Slightly more sympathetic is Parker (1965), who is British.

[2] I carefully say "middle class," because it is difficult to know the sentiments of the Central American poor, particularly the rural poor, on this issue.

[3] See Chapter 5 on agriculture.

[4] Rodriguez (1965, 80) discusses the role of Chatfield and the perception of that role by Central American nationalists. See also Woodward (1976).

[5] The Walker affair is treated in more detail in Chapter 7.

[6] On this important and soon-to-collapse agreement, see Rodriguez (1965, 110ff).

[7] "In the eyes of Central Americans, the United States' insistence upon the negotiation of a canal-option-treaty with a submissive Nicaragua was especially humiliating and offensive, an uncalled-for display of the might-makes right thesis in foreign relations." Rodriguez (1965, 120).

[8] For an account, see LaFeber (1983, 62–63).

[9] Sandino's rebellion is considered further in Chapter 7.

[10] Anderson (1971) is the definitive work on the insurrection of 1932.

[11] "One can say that the course of Salvadorean history changed . . . with the suppression of the rebellion of 1932, after which a new order of things was apparent. After this change, Salvadorean history has been above all else a series of moves or shifts made in relation to a basic conflict between the privileged attempting to maintain their privileges and the representatives of the interests of the underprivileged." Whyte (1973, 95).

[12] Quoted in Rodriquez (1978, 25–26). The original document is reprinted in *Economía Guatemalteca* (1970, 63).

[13] In 1934 Martínez recognized the Japanese puppet state of Manchukuo and in 1936 established diplomatic relations with Nationalist Spain.

[14] ". . . social security [was] approved not because of the plight of the people but because it is embarrassing to be listed in world reports as one of the few countries on the globe which does not have it." Parker (1965, 155).

[15] And repressive it was: "The Anastasio Somozas, father and son, . . . both stand accused of taking personal delight in the persecution of their victims." Parker (1965, 233).

[16] The 1903 treaty reads that Washington can have the rights in the Canal Zone that it "would possess and exercise if it were the sovereign."

[17] Duarte remains an anathema to the oligarchy despite having served as president with the blessing of part of the military after the counter-coup of 1980. The complexities of Salvadoran politics personify themselves in the career of

Duarte: in 1972, the military stole the election from him; in 1980, it chose him as its token civilian in the government; in 1983, he again was judged unacceptable by the military and in 1984 was elected president with U.S. support.

[18]This report is quoted in LaFeber (1983, 171).

[19]The de facto rule of the Honduran military stems in part from a unique arrangement by which the military command is not legally bound to accept orders issued by the president of the republic.

[20]The political evolution of Nicaragua in the 1960s and 1970s is treated in Chapter 7.

REFERENCES

Note: When sources are listed, the name of the relevant organization is given in the same language as the document or report. Thus, IDB and BID refer to the same organization, as do ECLA and CEPAL.

Anderson, Thomas P. 1971. *El Salvador's Communist Revolt of 1932*. Lincoln: University of Nebraska Press.

Bell, Patrick. 1971. *Crisis in Costa Rica: The Revolution of 1948* Austin: University of Texas Press.

Jones, Chester Lloyd. 1940. *Guatemala: Past and Present*. Minneapolis: University of Minnesota Press.

Karnes, Thomas L. 1961. *The Failure of Union: Central America, 1824–1960*. Chapel Hill: University of North Carolina Press.

LaFeber, Walter. 1983. *Inevitable Revolutions: The United States in Central America*. New York: Norton.

Martz, John D. 1959. *Central America: The Crisis and the Challenge*. Chapel Hill: University of North Carolina Press.

MacLeod, Murdo J. 1973. *Spanish Central America: A Socioeconomic History, 1520–1720*. Berkeley: University of California Press.

Martinex Palaez, Severo. 1979. *La Patria del Criollo: ensayo de interpretación de la realidad colonial guatemalteca*. Costa Rica: EDUCA.

Munro, Dana. 1974. *The United States and the Caribbean Republics, 1921–1933*. Princeton: Princeton University Press.

Nearing, Scott and Joseph Freeman. 1966. *Dollar Diplomacy*. New York: Monthly Review.

Parker, Franklin. 1965. *The Central American Republics*. New York: Oxford University Press.

Rodriquez, Mario. 1965. *Central America*. Englewood Cliffs, N.J.: Prentice Hall.

———. 1978. *The Cádiz Experiment in Central America*. Berkeley: University of California Press.

Schlesinger, Stephen and Stephen Kinzer. 1982. *Bitter Fruit: The Untold Story of the American Coup in Guatemala*. Garden City, N.Y.: Doubleday.

Seligson, Mitchell A. 1980. *Peasants of Costa Rica and the Development of Agrarian Capitalism*. Madison: University of Wisconsin Press.

West, Robert C. and John P. Augelli. 1976. *Middle America: Its Lands and Peoples.* Englewood Cliffs, N.J.: Prentice Hall.

Whyte, Alastair. 1973. *El Salvador.* London: Ernest Benn Ltd.

Woodward, Ralph Lee, Jr. 1976. *Central America: A Nation Divided* New York: Oxford University Press.

2

Social and Economic Profile of Central America

The accumulated inequities of Central America's past manifest themselves in the present in extreme underdevelopment by hemispheric standards. Since the Second World War, the economies of Central America have grown rapidly, but with the exception of Costa Rica, extreme poverty and great inequalities of income and wealth characterize the region. The data verifying this underdevelopment and poverty in Central America are cited below, but the detail should not obscure a general issue: why does most of Central America remain so underdeveloped and impoverished despite rapid economic growth?

First we should consider possible geographic or climatic bases for Central America's relative underdevelopment. Nineteenth century travelers' accounts of Central America frequently reported the alleged riches of the region and its great potential for prosperity. In fact, the region could hardly be considered generously endowed by nature. Mineral resources are few, and agriculture suffers from all of the debilitating characteristics of a tropical climate. To the casual observer, the tropical environment appears lush and fertile. In practice, the sweltering heat and dramatic difference between the rainy season and dry season make agriculture a constant struggle against erosion, depletion of the soil, insects, and plant blight. Natural conditions are not particularly favorable in Central America.

But while generations of Central Americans cannot be accused of failing to realize the potential bounty of nature, climate and geography cannot alone explain the region's underdevelopment. Costa Rica possesses no significant advantages over its neighbors in climate or geography, yet by some measures it is among the most developed countries of Latin America and the Caribbean. Cuba is another example of a tropical country with no mineral resources which nonetheless is much more developed than the Central American countries (excluding Costa Rica, of course).

A central theme of this book is the relative underdevelopment of

Central America, and derivative from this are other themes: the vulnerability of the economies; their relative openness to the world economic system; and the extreme inequalities of income and wealth. How are we to explain these characteristics? The explanation lies in the history of the region. In the previous chapter we saw that the states of the region achieved national cohesion quite late. This reflected, in turn, the late development of a modernizing elite, so that for much longer than the rest of Latin America, reactionary and autocratic dictators based on landed oligarchies ruled the Central American states. The term "reactionary" is used precisely: these dictators and the landed oligarchy they represented reacted negatively to pressure for reform and modernization. When commercialization of economic life occurred, it did so not through the transformation of archaic land-tenure patterns and labor control systems, but within or alongside them.

The reduction of poverty and underdevelopment is not merely the result of economic growth, but also the development of social institutions designed to mediate the distribution of that growth. In most of Latin America, trade unions and organizations of rural workers and farmers have played an increasing political role as economic growth proceeded. These institutions along with others affected the distribution of both political and economic power, altering the power balance between the privileged and underprivileged. The nature of economic modernization in Central America, "on top" of the old autocratic order, as it were, largely precluded political modernization. As a consequence, startling contradictions characterize the societies of Central America: contradictions between the development of the region's economic potential, on the one hand, and the inability of underdeveloped institutions to distribute the benefits of economic progress. These contradictions in turn manifest themselves concretely in the quality of life of the mass of the population.

Geography and Population

In land area Central America is relatively small compared to the continental countries of Latin America, only larger than Panama, Uruguay, Ecuador, and Paraguay (being roughly the size of the last). As Table 1 shows, the population of Central America is less than that of four Latin American countries, and approximately 6 percent of the population of Latin America and the Caribbean lived in Central America in the late 1970s (see Table 2). If Central America were one political unit, it would rank as a moderately populous underdeveloped country, but certainly not a large one.

Taken individually, the Central American countries have quite small

TABLE 1
Population of Central America and the Most Populous
Latin American Countries
1960 and 1980
(millions of people)

Countries	1960	1980
Brazil	70.8	120.3
Mexico	34.9	69.9
Argentina	20.6	27.7
Colombia	16.2	26.1
Central America[1]	11.0	20.7
Central America[2]	12.1	22.6
Peru	10.0	17.6
Venezuela	7.3	15.1
Chile	7.7	11.1

Sources: IDB 1981, and SIECA 1980.
[1] Excluding Panama.
[2] Including Panama.

populations. Costa Rica has the smallest population of any Latin American country with the exception of Panama. The distribution of the population within Central America reflects a complex interaction of social relations in the countryside and modern economic development. Over a third of the Central American population lives in Guatemala, which is densely populated compared to Costa Rica, Honduras, and Nicaragua. The relatively high density of population in Guatemala is in part explained by the large pre-Columbian civilization which developed social relations and land-use methods persisting in some areas to this day. However, the population density in Guatemala is modest compared to El Salvador, which has more people per square kilometer even than Haiti.

By any measure El Salvador is a highly populated country, but the extreme difference in population density between that country and the others of Central America is somewhat misleading. All of the countries except El Salvador stretch from coast to coast, and their populations are concentrated towards the Pacific side of the countries or in the centers. Nicaragua is a case in point. Ninety percent of the Nicaraguan population lives west of the range of low mountains that divides the country between what are called the "Atlantic Coast" and "Pacific Coast." The population density of the Pacific Coast is well over 50 persons per square kilometer. Indeed, culturally and economically, Lake Nicaragua and the mountain range above and to the east of the lake form Nicaragua's eastern border. East of the lake and the mountains stretches a vast rain forest and coastal swamp almost totally without population until one reaches the small and marginal coastal towns of Puerto Cabezas, Puerto Isabel, and Bluefields. The meagre population on this side of the mountains speaks English or native Indian languages, and until 1983 no road linked Nicaragua from coast to coast. Comparison to Nicaragua in part explains the extremely high population density of El Salvador. Squeezed in against the Pacific by Honduras and Guatemala, El Salvador lacks the vast flat eastern expanses which lower Nicaragua's average population density. In relation to its neighbors, El Salvador is a land of dense settlement and intensive cultivation.

Compared to the rest of Latin America and the Caribbean, Central America is rural. As Table 3 shows, in the Latin American and Caribbean countries two thirds of the population lived in urban areas in 1980, compared to 43 percent for Central America. Of the Central American

TABLE 2
A. Growth of the Central American Population
1960–1970
(Population in Thousands)

	Costa Rica	El Salvador	Guatemala	Honduras	Nicaragua	Panama	Total[1]
1960	1250	2430	3960	1900	1420	1060	10,960
1970	1730	3580	5350	2640	1970	1460	15,270
1975	1970	4140	6240	3090	2320	1680	17,760
1980	2210	4800	7260	3690	2730	1900	20,690
Rates of Growth (percent, annual)							
1960–1970	3.3	4.0	3.1	3.3	3.3	3.3	3.3
1970–1980	2.5	3.0	3.1	3.4	3.3	2.6	3.1
Area (Km²)							
(ooos)	51	21	109	112	139	77	432
Population Density per Km² 1980	43	228	67	33	20	27	48

[1]Excluding Panama.
Sources: IDB 1981, and SIECA 1980.

B. Distribution of the Central American Population
1960–1980

	Costa Rica	El Salvador	Guatemala	Honduras	Nicaragua	Total
1960	11.4%	22.2%	36.1%	17.3%	13.0%	100%
1970	11.3	23.4	35.0	17.3	12.9	100
1980	10.7	23.2	35.1	17.8	13.2	100

Sources: SIECA 1980.

TABLE 3
Percentage of Total Population in Urban Areas
by Country in Central America
1970, 1975, and 1980

Country	1970	1975	1980
Costa Rica	39%	42%	46%
El Salvador	39	42	44
Guatemala	34	36	38
Honduras	33	37	40
Nicaragua	47	51	54
Central America	37	40	43
Panama	49	51	54
Latin America and the Caribbean[1]	57%	62%	68%

[1]Excluding Central America and Panama.
Source: SIECA 1980; IDB 1981.

countries, only in Nicaragua was half the population measured to be urban. It is quite possible that the percentages in Table 3 overstate the degree of urbanization in Central America. In several of the countries an extremely liberal definition of "urban area" has been used for the last two decades in the census and, considering this, it may be that less than 40 percent of the Central American population was urban in 1980. Further, the measured urbanization rates among the Central American countries have quite different implications. To live in a rural area in Costa Rica is quite different than for the other countries. A majority of the Costa Rican rural population lives in the central highlands around San José, and the villages of this coffee-growing area are linked by paved roads and usually have electricity, a piped water supply, and benefit from the best rural social services in Latin America and the Caribbean.[1] In contrast, to be a poor peasant in the rest of Central America in the 1970s involves a life "mean, brutish, and short," to use a famous phrase of Hobbs.

The availability of public services in rural areas of Costa Rica means that the difference in the quality of life in rural and urban areas is less extreme in that country than elsewhere in the region. Measurement of this differential is quite difficult, but it can be approximated by what are called "material indicators," one of which is the access to piped water. In 1973 virtually 100 percent of urban dwellers in Costa Rica enjoyed access to piped water, compared to 66 percent of rural dwellers. While the difference is large, no country in Latin America or the Caribbean supplied a larger portion of the rural population with piped water. In shocking contrast, 87 percent of urban Guatemalans benefited from this basic public service and only 2 percent in rural areas. The statistics on water supply and other material indicators indicate a wide gap between urban and rural living standards in the other three countries of Central America also (World Bank 1976). The case of Central America's neighbor Panama is rather unique and interesting. In Panama the rapid development of the capital as a financial and commercial center has in recent years generated a stark urban-rural dichotomy of lifestyles, and the capital has grown to include 30 percent of the country's population. This concentration of both wealth and population has virtually transformed the country into two distinct societies, the urban-modern and the traditional-rural.

Social Indicators

We have repeatedly used the term "underdeveloped" without an explicit definition of it. Underdevelopment has two major aspects: the capacity to produce and the quality of life of the population. While these are related, they do not stand in perfect correlation to each other. A large number of studies in recent years, particularly by the World Bank, indicate that the per capita production (per capita income) of a country does not indicate the degree of poverty. This has prompted use of material indicators as a measure of the standard of living, one of which, piped water, we mentioned above. The purpose of these material indicators is to escape the ambiguities of using per capita income, which measures the capacity to produce, not the standard of living which that production provides. Even if measured accurately across countries, per capita income fails on a number of grounds, the most important being distribution. Two countries might have the same per capita income, but the country with the more equal distribution of income would have fewer people below any given income and thus fewer people in poverty (other things being equal). Also serious are the practical problems of measurement. Since inter-country comparisons of per capita income must be in a common currency, the ranking of countries is sensitive to changes in the exchange rate between the countries being compared (or sensitive to whatever assumptions are made when using an exchange rate other than the official one).

In recent years a summary measure of material indicators has come into common use, called the Physical Quality of Life Index (PQLI). This index employs a weighted average of three indicators: life expectancy at birth, infant mortality, and adult literacy. Table 4 shows the performance of the Central American countries and Panama on this index along with

TABLE 4
Per Capita Income and PQLI[1] for Central American Countries

	Per Capita Income (1976)	PQLI[1] (1977)
Costa Rica	$1040	87
El Salvador	490	67
Guatemala	630	53
Nicaragua	750	53
Honduras	390	50
Panama	1310	81
Latin America & Caribbean[2]	1250	75

[1]Physical Quality of Life Index
[2]Simple average of twenty-one countries, excluding those above.
Source: ODC 1977.

per capita income. A cautionary note is necessary when interpreting the PQLI. Per capita income is what is called a *cardinal* index: that is, a person with an income of $200 has double the income of a person with $100. But the PQLI is an *ordinal* index, which gives an accurate ordering of countries (in this case), but does not allow one to draw judgments about either the relative or absolute difference between the physical quality of life in two countries.[2]

As one would expect, Costa Rica performs best of the Central American countries on the PQLI. Its performance is particularly striking by comparison to other underdeveloped countries of the hemisphere: while twelve countries had higher per capita incomes, only four scored higher on the PQLI. For example, Venezuela's per capita income was two-and-a-half times higher, but the PQLI lower. At the other extreme fall Guatemala and Nicaragua, countries whose PQLI falls below what their per capita incomes would imply. In any case, the four impoverished countries of Central America have very low standards of living by hemispheric comparison. Only two countries, Bolivia and Haiti, score lower on the PQLI than Honduras, Guatemala, and Nicaragua, and only one more, the Dominican Republic, measures lower than El Salvador.

One obtains a clearer understanding of social conditions in Central America by considering separately the elements which make up the PQLI, and Table 5 gives these statistics. Inspection of these indicators shows that Costa Rica stands out dramatically from its neighbors; indeed, some of the numbers for Costa Rica are nothing short of astounding. For example, the US per capita income in 1977 was over six times per capita income in Costa Rica, but life expectancy at birth differed by only three years, 73 in the former and 70 in the latter. Among the countries of Latin America and the Caribbean only in Argentina, Barbados, and Uruguay was life expectancy higher (71 years in each case). And no underdeveloped country in the hemisphere had a lower child mortality rate, though the Costa Rican rate of 3 per 1,000 children is three times the level in any industrial capitalist country. One can also note that Costa Rica performed better or as well as Panama for all indicators, though Panama's per capita income was 20 percent higher.

Perhaps even more surprising is the performance of El Salvador. By per capita income El Salvador is the second poorest country in Central America, yet its performance on total mortality, life expectancy, and child mortality is considerably better than for Guatemala and Nicaragua. In fact, so above expectations are these social indicators that one cannot but be exceedingly skeptical of the data's reliability. A major determinant of the level of these social indicators is nutrition, and World Bank data indicate that the Salvadoran population has the lowest nutritional level in all of Central America.[3] Further, it is difficult to explain why infant mortality would be high (108 per thousand in 1970) and child mortality low (8 per thousand in 1970, below the Guatemalan, Honduran, and Nicaraguan levels in the late 1970s). With these considerations in mind, it can be concluded that the Salvadoran population probably had life expectancy and mortality rates similar to those in Guatemala, Honduras, and Nicaragua, and that there has been a systematic misreporting of the Salvadoran data.

With the exception of Costa Rica, one finds shocking levels of material deprivation in Central America compared to the rest of Latin America and the Caribbean. It is highly probable that in the late 1970s life expectancy at birth in the four poorest countries was almost a decade less than in the rest of Latin America and the Caribbean and that child mortality was twice as high. Only in Bolivia, Haiti, and Peru in the late 1970s did data on life expectancy, infant mortality, and child mortality indicate similar or worse material deprivation than in El Salvador, Guatemala, Honduras, and Nicaragua.

The social indicators in part B of Table 5 indicate a similar pattern of underdevelopment. Costa Rica performs better than the Latin American average in primary school enrollments and adult literacy and at the average for secondary school enrollment. In Panama school enrollment ratios were even higher. The other countries of Central America again display their backwardness. Guatemala is the most extreme case: in 1970 (the latest available data) no country in Latin America had a smaller portion of its school-age population under tuition and only Haiti in the hemisphere performed worse. In the late 1970s, only six countries in the Western Hemisphere had primary school enrollment rates of less than 90 percent; of the six, four were in Central America.

TABLE 5
Selected Social Indicators for Central America in the late 1970s
A. Demographic Indicators

	Costa Rica	El Salvador	Guatemala	Honduras	Nicaragua	C.A.	Panama	L.A. and Caribbean[6]
Crude birth rate[1]	28	39	41	47	45	41	31	32
Crude death rate[1]	5	9	12	12	13	11	6	9
Life Expectancy at birth[2]	70	63	57	57	55	60	70	65
Infant mortality rate[3]	38	108[5]	77	103	122	91	47	—
Child mortality rate[4]	3	8	15	14	17	12	3	8

[1]Per thousand.
[2]Years.
[3]Per thousand live births.
[4]Per thousand children aged 1–4.
[5]1970.
[6]Excluding Central America and Cuba.

B. Education (Percentages)

	Costa Rica	El Salvador	Guatemala	Honduras	Nicaragua	C.A.	Panama	L.A. and Caribbean[4]
Primary School Enrollment[1]	111	77	58[3]	89	85	77	124	101
Secondary School Enrollment[1]	43	21	11[3]	13	21	18	53	42
Adult literacy[2]	88	62	46	57	57	58	78	80

[1]Percentage of school age population enrolled; may exceed 100% because of students above and below official school age.
[2]Percentage of population 15 years of age and older.
[3]Early 1970s.
[4]Excluding Central America and Cuba
Source: World Bank 1980.

In summary it can be said that the four impoverished countries of Central America fell far behind the rest of the hemisphere's underdeveloped countries in the late 1970s in terms of health care, education, and meeting the basic needs of the population. Only the performances of Bolivia and Haiti kept El Salvador, Guatemala, Honduras, and Nicaragua from consistently claiming last place in rankings by social indicators. The extremely poor performances by the impoverished four to a great extent reflects inequality in the distribution of income and wealth in these countries.

TABLE 6
The Size Distribution of Income
in Selected Latin American Countries

Country and Date	Income Share of	
	Poorest 20%	Richest 5%
Argentina, 1961	5.1%	32.0%
Brazil, 1970	2.8	44.8
Chile, 1968	4.8	31.0
Colombia, 1970	2.9	33.7
Dominican Republic, 1969	4.3	26.3
Ecuador, 1970	1.8	43.0
Mexico, 1969	4.2	37.8
Uruguay, 1967	3.0	20.8
Venezuela, 1971	2.7	40.5
Costa Rica, 1971	5.4	23.0
El Salvador, 1961	4.3	34.0
Guatemala, 1970	5.0	35.0
Honduras, 1967/68	1.6	32.9
Nicaragua, 1970	3.1	42.4
Panama, 1972	4.6	22.2

Note: For Chile, Costa Rica, Dominican Republic, Honduras, and Mexico, these are
    household distributions. For the other countries, the percentages are for the eco-
    nomically active population or the economically active plus the unemployed.
Sources: Jain 1975; and World Bank 1980.

Just how unequal the distribution of income in the four countries is,
compared to elsewhere in the hemisphere, is difficult to say. In underdeveloped countries surveys of income distribution are rarely comparable
over time in the same country, much less among countries. It is fairly
clear, however, that in the 1970s income was distributed with a great
degree of inequality in Central America, with the exception of Costa
Rica. This inequality reflected in great part the high concentration of
land ownership. In El Salvador, the 10 percent of landowners with the
largest holdings controlled almost 80 percent of the land, while at the
other end of the scale, the smallest 10 percent of landowners had less
than one-half of 1 percent of the land (World Bank 1979, iii).

Some rough indication of comparative inequality can be obtained
from Table 6, which gives available data for Latin American countries on
the size distribution of income.[4] In the nine countries at the top of the
table, the poorest 20 percent of the population received from a low of 1.8
percent (Ecuador, 1970) to a high of 5.1 percent (Argentina, 1961) of total
personal income. The income share received by the poorest 20 percent in
Honduras was below this lower limit, while the share in Costa Rica was

above the upper limit. The poorest 20 percent in Guatemala appears to have received a relatively high share of total income, 5 percent, virtually the same as in Argentina. However, the Guatemala statistic is for urban areas only, and it is generally accepted that in Latin America income inequality is greater in rural areas than urban ones. Since two-thirds of the Guatemalan population was rural in 1970, we can assume that the poorest 20 percent of the population for the country as a whole received considerably less than 5 percent of total income.

At the other end of the distribution, income was quite concentrated

TABLE 7

A. Gross National Product
(millions of 1970 Central American *Pesos*)[1]

Year	Costa Rica	El Salvador	Guatemala	Honduras	Nicaragua	Total	Panama
1960	717	739	1304	555	480	3795	624
1965	919	1070	1717	704	863	5273	989
1970	1329	1281	2243	968	1003	6824	1471
1975	1726	1691	2905	1059	1309	8690	1716
1980	2380	1794	3803	1569	1390	10936	2140

B. Distribution of GNP by Country
(1970 Prices)

Year	Costa Rica	El Salvador	Guatemala	Honduras	Nicaragua	Total
1960	18.9%	19.5%	34.3%	14.6%	12.6%	100%
1965	17.4	20.3	32.6	13.4	16.4	100
1970	19.5	18.8	32.9	14.2	14.7	100
1975	19.9	19.5	33.4	12.2	15.1	100
1980	21.8	16.5	34.9	14.4	12.8	100

C. Relative Per Capita Income
(Central American Average = 100)

Year	Costa Rica	El Salvador	Guatemala	Honduras	Nicaragua	All	Panama
1960	144	91	108	72	94	100	156
1965	138	91	99	76	114	100	179
1970	160	81	100	77	111	100	201
1975	176	76	103	63	121	100	203
1980	214	77	106	68	76	100	230

[1]The Central American *Peso* equals one US dollar.
Source: SIECA 1980.

in Central America. In all cases but Costa Rica the richest 5 percent of the population received a third or more of total income. This is less than the concentration in Brazil and Ecuador, but more than for the other countries at the top of the table, particularly the Dominican Republic and Uruguay. Panama had a distribution similar to Costa Rica's, with relatively low concentration of income in the highest category.

We can conclude that in the 1970s extreme underdevelopment, absolute poverty, and great inequalities in the distribution of resources characterized Central America. Central America is, therefore, an area of concentrated economic backwardness in the hemisphere.

Economic Indicators

In the previous section we considered the underdevelopment of Central America in terms of the living conditions of the population. Now we turn to the growth and structure of production in the region and make two points: first, that the economies are quite small; and second, that performance in terms of growth of production has been considerably better than in terms of meeting the basic needs of the population. The small size of the combined economy of the five Central American countries is shown by the fact that total private consumption in the region in 1980 approximately equaled the sales of tobacco products in the United States in the year (about $15 billion).

Table 7 presents data on gross national product (GNP) in constant prices for the 1960s and 1970s. In the next chapter we consider growth performance in some detail and here are primarily interested in the relative sizes of the economies. Data for 1980, though more recent, is not as indicative as the figures for the mid-1970s. In both El Salvador and Nicaragua, war caused declines in GNP, so that output in 1980 fell below what it had been in 1977–1978. With this in mind, we see that the distribution of GNP among the countries remained more or less constant, with Guatemala generating about a third of regional GNP and Costa Rica and El Salvador each about a fifth.

In the last part of Table 7 we have facilitated comparison of per capita incomes by calculating each country's level as a ratio of the Central American average. In terms of this relative per capita GNP index, Panama stood well above all of the Central American countries. Throughout the 1970s the per capita income of Panama was twice the Central American average, though by 1980 its differential with Costa Rica's was small. Comparison of parts B and C of Table 7 shows that while the distribution of GNP among countries has changed little, income per person by country changed substantially in terms of the regional average. In 1960 the ratio of Costa Rica's per capita income to that

TABLE 8

**Gross National Products for Central America
and the Largest Economies of Latin America, 1970 and 1980
(billions of 1980 dollars)**

Country	1970	1980
Brazil	$86.1	$200.2
Mexico	62.1	107.3
Argentina	42.5	53.6
Venezuela	24.6	37.0
Central America	17.6	28.1
Colombia	13.7	24.1
Peru	15.4	20.9

Source: IDB 1981; and SIECA 1980.

of Honduras (the highest and lowest) stood at two-to-one, and by 1980 had risen to over three-to-one. While output grew at similar rates in all five countries during the two decades, population increased at a much slower rate in Costa Rica (see Table 2). As a consequence, income disparities increased among the five countries.

In 1975 the GNP of seven Latin American countries exceeded that of Guatemala, the largest in the Central American region. Taken together the Central American countries produced less than four Latin American countries, as Table 8 shows. However, the growth of real GNP (in constant prices) in Central America over the last twenty years has been

TABLE 9

**Rates of Growth of Gross Domestic Product
at Constant Prices, 1960–1979**

Country	1960–1970	1970–1979
Costa Rica	6.4%	6.4%
El Salvador	5.7	6.5
Guatemala	5.6	5.8
Honduras	5.7	5.1
Nicaragua	6.9	5.6[1]
Central America	6.0	5.8[2]
Panama	9.0	4.2
Latin America and Caribbean[3]	5.0	5.2

[1] 1970–1978.
[2] 1970–1977.
[3] Simple average, excluding Central America and Panama.
Source: SIECA 1980, and IDB 1981.

faster than for the rest of Latin America and the Caribbean taken together. Panama, too, grew faster than the rest and marginally faster than
the Central American average for 1960 to 1979. Among the countries of
Central America, Costa Rica grew fastest, at 6.4 percent in both decades.
The growth of output in Central America has been higher than the
average for underdeveloped countries of the hemisphere, but population growth has also been higher. As a result, per capita income for the
region did not rise compared to the rest of Latin America and the Caribbean during the 1960s and 1970s, and the relative poverty of the region
remains.

In the previous section we showed the social characteristics of Central America's underdevelopment. This underdevelopment manifests
itself in a number of economic indicators, one of which is the "openness" of the economies to the international economy. Openness to international trade has both a quantitative and a qualitative aspect. The
former refers to the importance of trade to an economy as measured, for
example, by the share of exports and imports in GNP. The qualitative
aspect refers to the restrictions placed on trade, such as tariffs, quotas,
and foreign exchange controls. Until 1979 when the new government of
Nicaragua instituted a wide range of controls and regulations, all of the
Central American economies were extremely open to the international
market both quantitatively and qualitatively.

The degree of openness is shown in Table 10, along with the comparison to the other countries of Latin America and the Caribbean. Central America as a whole exported a quarter of its GNP in 1970 and 1975,
in contrast to only slightly over 10 percent for the rest of Latin America
and the Caribbean. Further, the share of exports in GNP has declined
over time for the latter countries, while rising sharply in Central
America. This increase at the regional level manifests itself in each country. To an extent the increase of exports in GNP reflects the evolution of
the Central American Common Market (see Chapter 4). But even in the
early 1960s (before CACM became a major factor), the economies of
Central America were quite open compared to the rest of Latin America
and the Caribbean.

This openness to international trade reflects the underdevelopment
of Central America. Elsewhere in Latin America decades of import substitution policies (fostering domestic production behind tariff walls) has
resulted in broad-based production of consumer commodities and intermediate products. This type of strategy appeared in Central America
only in the 1960s and in a form considerably milder than elsewhere in
the hemisphere. As a result, Central American consumers and busi-
nessess must satisfy a large portion of their demand through imports.
This high import intensity for both domestic consumption and production must be roughly balanced by exports. Thus the high degree of

TABLE 10
Export Earnings
as a Share of Gross Domestic Product
1960–1980[1]
(constant prices)

Country	1960	1970	1975	1980
Costa Rica	20.2	34.2	36.4	37.8
El Salvador	20.4	21.3	24.4	53.9
Guatemala	14.6	19.3	21.2	20.9
Honduras	20.3	29.6	26.4	30.1
Nicaragua	24.0	30.1	33.7	—
Central America	18.5	24.8	26.6	—
Panama	30.6	40.7	32.9	38.4[2]
Latin America and Caribbean[3]	13.4	12.2	9.7	11.6

[1] Including non-commodity foreign exchange earnings ("invisibles").
[2] For 1979.
[3] Excluding Central America and Panama.
Source: IDB 1981.

openness reflects economies still based in agriculture on the export side and relatively backward in the development of domestic manufacturing on the import side.

This underdevelopment of manufacturing we show in Table 11. Agricultural production narrowly defined (crops and livestock) represented about 20 percent of Central American GNP in 1975, compared to about 10 percent in the rest of Latin America and the Caribbean.[5] The manufacturing sector contributed only 14 percent of the Central American GNP. Only in Nicaragua was the share over 15 percent, and the Nicaraguan proportion is misleading, since a part of "manufacturing" in Nicaragua is rural-based processing of primary products, such as coffee. If agroindustry were excluded from manufacturing, the sector's share might have been no more than 10 percent of regional GNP in Central America, half the share for Latin America and the Caribbean.

Further, the mining sector, which is so important in several underdeveloped countries of the continent, is totally insignificant in Central America. Only in Honduras is the mining sector more than one-half of 1 percent of GNP, and non-precious metals represented only slightly more than 1 percent of the value of Central America exports in the 1970s. While obviously mining production is dependent upon natural endowments, it is unlikely that an area the size of Central America would have no significant mineral resources. The more likely case is that modest mineral resources exist, but the region is so underdeveloped with regard to infrastructure that private capital finds exploitation (and perhaps even serious exploration) nonprofitable. This possibility has, in fact, been verified in the case of Nicaragua. On the Atlantic side of the mountains in Nicaragua there are sufficient gold reserves to make Nicaragua a significant, if not major, exporter of gold. However, the almost total lack of infrastructure (and population) in the area has kept gold production well below $10 million annually during the 1970s. While Central America will probably never be an important mineral producing area (with the possible exception of petroleum), the almost total absence of mining activity can in part be attributed to the general lack of development as well as to the whim of nature.

Central America and the Hemisphere

In presenting our profile of the Central American economies, we have stressed the absolute smallness of the five economies. While it would be a mistake to consider Central America as economically insignificant, it certainly cannot be seen as an area of economic weight in the hemispheric (much less world) economy. Table 12 indicates the rather modest economic role of the countries between Mexico and Panama. The countries of Central America had 6 percent of the population of Latin

TABLE 11
Shares of Agriculture, Manufacturing, and Mining in
Gross Domestic Product of Central America, 1975

Country	Agriculture	Manufacturing	Mining[1]
Costa Rica	14%	14%	—
El Salvador	17	13	—
Guatemala	24	14	—
Honduras	20	11	2%
Nicaragua	17	16	—
Central America	19	14	—
Panama	16	15	—
Latin America and Caribbean[2]	10	20	2

[1] A dash (—) indicates less than .5 percent.
[2] Very approximate.
Source: IDB 1981.
Note: These proportions are based on IDB data, and differ from SIECA figures given elsewhere in this book. They are used for purposes of comparison.

TABLE 12
Participation of the Five Countries of Central America
in Selected Variables for Latin America
and the Caribbean, 1978

	Percentage
Population,[1] total	5.9
urban	3.5
rural	10.5
Gross Domestic Products	4.2
Private Long-term investments (net)[2]	1.9
U.S. Direct Investment[3]	2.4
Exports and imports[4]	9.4
Agricultural Value Added	9.2
Mining Value Added	0.6
Manufacturing Value Added	3.0
External Public Debt	4.2
External Debt Payments	2.4
Imports of Petroleum	5.6

[1] 1980.
[2] Annual net movement of long-term capital.
[3] Book value of direct foreign investment, 1977.
[4] Commodities and services. Average of export and import shares.
Sources: IDB 1981; and USDC April 1981.

America and the Caribbean in 1978, and their shares for the other indicators generally fall below their population share. Two of the exceptions to this—the share of rural population and agricultural value added—are well-recognized indicators of economic backwardness. The same might be said of the third, share of exports and imports, for we argued that the openness of the economies reflects relative underdevelopment.

Another aspect of Central America's underdevelopment is its small share of foreign investment. In 1978, less than 2 percent of private long-term capital flows to Latin America and the Caribbean went to the five countries of the isthmus. More striking is the relative unimportance of the region for North American direct foreign investment; that is, investments in productive activities as opposed to mere financial holdings such as bonds and interest-bearing bank deposits. The Central American economies accounted for over 4 percent of the GNP in Latin America and the Caribbean, but only 2.4 percent of US direct investment. This is hardly what one would expect, since no countries of the hemisphere are more politically dominated by Washington than those in Central America. There are two reasons for the low foreign investment share. First, a large portion of US direct investments in Latin America are in mining and petroleum, and neither sector is important in Central America. If we consider only manufacturing investments, the Central American share roughly equals its share of the GNP. Second, because per capita income in Central America lies below the average for the countries of Latin America and the Caribbean, one would not expect the market for manufactures to be proportional to the share of GNP attributed to the region. As per capita income falls, the share of food and other necessities in consumer budgets rises, which in general implies a disproportionate decline in expenditure on manufactures. This, in turn, implies less investment to produce manufactures.

For whatever reasons, the fact remains that Central America is not an area of great importance to U.S. business interests. The total direct investment in the region represented $1.8 billion in assets, compared to $3.5 billion for Panama alone and $1.9 billion for nearby Colombia.[6] To put the figures in perspective, in 1977 the value of inventory investment in tobacco products (stocks held) in North America was almost twice the value of US fixed assets in Central America. The small absolute size of US direct investment in Central America has prompted most observers to conclude that the importance given to the area by North American policy makers reflects political and strategic considerations more than economic ones (LaFeber 1983).

Particularly in the last ten years, purely financial investments have taken on increasing importance for North American capital, as governments of underdeveloped countries have borrowed heavily from private banks to finance their balance of payments. The governments of Central America participated actively in this process, to a point where interest and amortization payments on their foreign debts reached crisis proportions (see Chapter 8). However, as serious as debt problems may be for the Central American governments, the total debt of the area pales in comparison to the rest of Latin America and the Caribbean. In 1979, the governments of Mexico and Brazil each made foreign *interest* payments which exceeded the total indebtedness of each Central American country by at least $1 billion: interest payments of almost $3 billion for both countries compared to Costa Rica's external debt of $1.9 billion (the largest in the region). Further, in 1979 the government of Mexico retired (paid off) more principal of its foreign debt than the entire contracted foreign debt of the Central American countries ($7.5 billion compared to $6.1 billion). As in the case of direct investment, US financial investment in Central America is relatively small.

These points are not to suggest that Central America has little significance to North American corporate interests. On the contrary, probably nowhere else in the hemisphere have US corporate interests so blatantly determined North American foreign policy. But these have been narrow, parochial interests, with the banana companies being the most obvious case. This tends to be the fate of small, underdeveloped countries: to be easily dominated by one or several foreign corporate interests. The history of Central America demonstrates this tendency.

NOTES

[1] In 1982 the new Costa Rican government (of the National Liberation Party, PLN) began to reduce social expenditure dramatically.

[2] This is partly the result of the nature of the items which make up the index and partly the result of the way they are measured. In the case of life expectancy, there is no objective basis for equating, for example, a two-year increase from 40 to 42 with the equal increase from 70 to 72, for it could be argued the former is more important since it occurs during the prime of life. The measurement aspect makes the PQLI and per capita income only comparable ordinally for a more obvious reason. While per capita income in principle has no upper limit to its value, the literacy rate cannot exceed 100 percent. Thus a country with a literacy rate of 60 percent could not double this rate no matter how many times its per capita income multiplied.

[3] Measured in caloric supply per person as a percentage of requirements, the requirements being based on estimates by the Food and Agricultural Organization (FAO). See World Bank (1980, 15).

[4] The "size distribution of income" refers to the distribution by families or individuals.

[5] These proportions and those for manufacturing are based on Inter-American Development Bank data, which differ from SIECA data. The IDB data are used here on the presumption that they are more strictly comparable across all of the countries of Latin America and the Caribbean.

[6] In 1977, the net income (after taxes) of US investment in Central America was less than $100 million.

REFERENCES*

Inter-American Development Bank (IDB). 1981. *Economic and Social Progress in Latin America, 1980-1981.* Washington: IDB.

——— 1983. *Economic and Social Progress in Latin America.* Washington: IDB.

Jain, Shail. 1975. *Size Distribution of Income.* Washington: World Bank.

LaFeber, Walter. 1983. *Inevitable Revolutions: The United States in Central America.* New York: Norton.

*When sources are listed, the name of the relevant organization is given in the same language as the document or report. Thus, IDB and BID refer to the same organization as do ECLA and CEPAL.

Overseas Development Council (ODC). 1977. *Agenda, 1977*. Washington: ODC.

Secretaría Permanente del Tratado General de Integración Económica Centroamericana (SIECA). 1973. *Series Estadísticas Seleccionadas de Centroamerica y Panama*. Guatemala: SIECA.

———— 1980. *Series Estadísticas Seleccionadas de Centroamerica y Panama*. Guatemala: SIECA.

Woodward, Ralph Lee Jr. 1976. *Central America: A Nation Divided*. New York: Oxford University Press.

World Bank. 1976. *World Tables, 1976*. Baltimore: Johns Hopkins University Press.

———— 1979. *Economic Memorandum on El Salvador*. Washington: World Bank.

———— 1980. *World Tables, 1980*. Baltimore: Johns Hopkins University Press.

3

Growth Performance of the Central American Economies

Analytical Framework

In books and articles on Central America one commonly encounters the use of the term "state" to refer to Guatemala, Honduras, El Salvador, Nicaragua, and Costa Rica rather than or along with the term "country."[1] This usage is not accidental or a mere case of synonyms; writers do not in general use the word "state" when referring to Mexico, Peru, and other countries of South America. The usage indicates a judgment on the part of the writer that there is something slightly ambiguous about the country status of the territories in Central America. The governments of the region have shown the same ambiguity by demonstrating little concern for neighbors' borders and nominal sovereignty.

The issue of what term one uses to describe the territories of Central America reflects the fact that "country" is at one level a legal and practical category, and at another level a conceptual category. Theorizing in the social sciences frequently locates itself at the level of countries, and the concept of a country plays a particularly important role in economic theory. The theory applied to the analysis of national economic policy would not in general be relevant to the economic policy of subdivisions of a country nor to grouping of countries.[2] Implicit in the abstract theorizing about monetary and fiscal policy are specific institutional assumptions. Before we can analyze the economies of Central America, we must first consider whether these economies operate within the country category in the sense of economic theory.

The modern theory of economic policy deals with aggregate concepts such as national income, investment, and the money supply. The basic theory relates these aggregate categories in the context of what is called a "closed" economy: that is, the first theoretical approximation of an actual economy abstracts from international trade and capital flows. While no capitalist economy in fact is "closed," the method of macroeconomics is to postulate such a situation, develop theoretical generalizations, then to "open" the abstract model by considering the trade and capital flows as complications which move the abstract model closer to reality.

The abstraction of a closed economy refers to countries as implicitly or explicitly defined by macroeconomic theory. The first characteristic of a country in economic theory is that it have its "own" currency and monetary system, by which we mean a currency controlled by the government. Two geographic areas which have the same monetary system must for purposes of economic theory be considered to form a single country, independently of their legal or diplomatic status, for monetary theory analyzes the relationship between economic variables and the money supply. The state of California, for example, has no money supply independent of the U.S. money supply, and therefore its government cannot pursue any monetary policy of significance. A second characteristic is the immobility of labor: two geographic areas partly qualify as countries in economic theory if they can be treated as two separate labor markets. While theoretically important, this second characteristic will not concern us here.

There is considerable doubt whether the Central American countries should be treated as countries for purposes of economic theory. First, the abstraction of a closed economy is open to challenge. Treating an economy as closed, even as a first approximation to reality, implies that one can conceptually partition the domestic economy from international trade. But foreign trade so dominates the Central American economies that little can be understood by such a conceptual partitioning. These are not national economies which trade part of their production, but economies whose foreign trade penetrates into every aspect of economic life.

Each of the Central American countries has its own currency, but in practice these currencies have not represented monetary systems separate from that of North America. In the case of Guatemala, the *quetzal* was established as the national monetary unit in the 1920s, but for almost sixty years it was exchanged one-to-one with the U.S. dollar. Except for the Costa Rican *colón*, all of the Central American currencies held constant exchange rates with the dollar from the end of World War II until the late 1970s.[3] This exchange rate stability has allowed the U.S. dollar to circulate as an accepted medium of exchange alongside the local currencies throughout Central America.

Since the Central American economies lack the autonomy necessary to apply the closed economy model even when it is expanded to include trade, one must seek an alternative framework. Given the small size and intrinsic openness of these economies, it is useful to view them by analogy to a company or firm in a competitive market.[4] A company, even a large one, does not grow by increasing exchanges within the company, but by sales to other companies and to individuals. By analogy, the management by government of internal aggregate demand has been of little importance in determining growth in the Central American countries. Rather, it has been the level of productivity in each country that has been the central determinant of growth, for the level of productivity determines competitiveness and the ability to export within the region and outside of it. With regard to its export crops, Central America is a small producer on the world market, so expansions and contractions of Central American supply have no significant effect on world prices. As a consequence, the volume of these exports is determined by production costs in the Central American countries compared to costs elsewhere and the margin between world prices and production costs. When export prices have been high and/or production costs falling, the Central American economies have grown rapidly, and vice versa.

Analyzing the economies of Central America by analogy to firms gives this chapter and the ones that follow a particular orientation. The central relationship we consider is that between economic growth and foreign trade both at the aggregate level and the sectoral level. Specifically in this chapter, we do not treat government monetary and fiscal policy, for we consider these policies to have been of marginal importance in the growth process. Our analytical framework does require that we briefly describe a major institutional change of the 1960s, the formation of the Central American Common Market (CACM), since this institution relates directly to the dynamic element in the region's economies, foreign trade. The five Central American governments began negotiations in the 1950s with the object of forming a customs union. The governments of Guatemala, El Salvador, and Nicaragua signed the common market treaty in 1961, followed by Honduras in 1962 and Costa Rica in 1963.

The heart of the agreement involved the complete removal of tariffs on a list of commodities traded within the region, a common tariff level for imports from the rest of the world, and a regional development bank. The list of commodities that would be tariff-free included items to be produced within the region, with the new production facilities to be distributed equitably among the member countries and in part financed by the regional development bank. More ambitious plans for a common monetary policy and steps toward political union never went beyond the proposal stage. The tariff recommendations were adopted by all of the governments, and all five currencies were freely convertible within the common market (and with other countries for the most part). The effect of the common market was to initiate a process of regional import substitutions vis-à-vis the rest of the world, which we consider in Chapters 4 and 6. For present purposes, the consequence of the CACM was to further reduce the autonomy of each economy, thus to make each country of Central America qualify less and less as a country in the sense of economic theory and conform more and more to our analogy with the behavior of a firm or company.

In summary, the territories of Central America are countries in the legal sense, in that their boundaries are accepted in international law and their governments recognized as sovereign within those boundaries. But for purposes of economic analysis they do not fit the qualifications of the abstract concept "country" and must be analyzed in different terms. This last point should not be interpreted as calling into question the relevance of data collected at the level of countries by the legal definition, but rather how one analyzes that data. The national income of, say, Honduras, remains a measure of the production of that country, existing independently of how one interprets it.

Growth of National Product

As argued above, it is not possible to analyze the growth of GNP or sectoral growth without considering regional and extraregional trade; that is, the openness of the economies mentioned above. Therefore, the discussion in this chapter necessarily deals with the subjects of the following three, providing a general survey of growth performance, which will be pursued in greater detail in the chapters which follow. While considering growth performance, we shall try not to beg the question of the real degree of regional integration and the extent to which regional interdependence has had a positive or negative impact upon the development of the five countries.

Although our survey of the economies will deal almost exclusively with the last twenty years, Table 13 presents the growth of national products for three decades. While data before 1960 must be considered of questionable reliability (antedating the regional standardization of national income data by the statistical office of the CACM), it does appear that growth in the 1950s was slower than subsequent growth. The only exception to this is Costa Rica, which enjoyed the fastest growth rate of all the Central American countries when we consider the thirty years from 1950 to 1979, or the twenty years from 1960 to 1979 (slightly exceeding Nicaragua's growth rate even when the war years, 1978 and 1979, are excluded). In Table 13 we have used average annual growth rates rather than the more usual compound rates. That is, we have calculated the growth rate each year, then taken the simple average

TABLE 13
Growth Rates of Gross National Product in Central America, 1950–1979[1]
A. Average Annual Growth Rates by Five-Year Periods

Country	1950–1955	1955–1960	1960–1965	1965–1970	1970–1975	1975–1979
Costa Rica	8.3%	6.0%	5.0%	7.4%	5.2%	7.5%
El Salvador	4.5	4.8	7.4	3.6	5.5	7.4[2]
Guatemala	2.3	5.3	5.5	5.4	5.2	6.3
Honduras	2.7	4.1	4.8	6.3	1.8	9.0
Nicaragua	8.4	2.3	11.1	3.5	5.1(3.4)[3]	5.5[2]
Central America	4.3	4.8	7.9	5.1	4.7	7.1[2]
Panama	4.1	5.7	9.6	8.3	3.1	4.5

B. Average Growth Rates by Decades

Country	1950–1960 Average	1960–1970 Average	1970–1979 Average
Costa Rica	7.2%	6.2%	6.4%
El Salvador	4.7	5.5	6.4
Guatemala	3.8	5.5	5.8
Honduras	3.4	5.6	5.4
Nicaragua	5.4	7.3	5.3[2]
Central America	4.6	6.5	5.9[2]
Panama	4.7	9.0	3.5

[1] For 1950–1960, constant prices of 1960; for 1960–1979, constant prices of 1970.
[2] To 1978.
[3] Figure in parenthesis omits year following the earthquake of 1972.
Source: SIECA 1973 and 1981.

of these rates, rather than calculating the compound rate between two end-years. While both methods of calculation are sensitive to the periods selected in the temporal division, use of annual average rates allows us to analyze the variation in growth rates over time, which proves to be useful below.

By calculating annual rates of growth of national products, we can consider the extent to which the five Central American economies have grown in concert over time. No comparison to Panama is made, since it was not a member of the CACM and thus hardly integrated with the Central America countries. If one takes the five countries two at a time, or each one compared to the other four taken together, there is some evidence of common growth patterns, but it is not great and could be due to chance.[5] This weak evidence does not necessarily indicate that there are not important interrelationships between the five economies, but does suggest that if they exist perhaps they are not mutually reinforcing. In any case, the results show that one cannot presume that the five economies always tend to grow or not grow in concert.

Both parts of Table 13 verify that there was considerable variation in growth rates among the five countries. From 1950 to 1975, in each five-year period the rate for the fastest-growing country was at least twice that for the slowest. The growth rates among countries over the space of a decade varied considerably less, as one would expect. Relative growth performance of the countries since the formation of the CACM has been a sensitive political issue, interpreted by the governments of the region as indicating the distribution of benefits from the customs union. The Honduran government in particular complained from the outset of the CACM that Honduras received less than its share of benefits. This issue and political conflict with El Salvador (culminating in a brief war in 1969 which Honduras lost) prompted the Honduran government to withdraw unilaterally from the CACM in 1970. Inspection of Table 13 suggests that the Honduran economic objections were exaggerated: during the 1960s, the country's growth rate equaled those of El Salvador and Guatemala and changed very little for the 1970s when Honduras was outside of the CACM.

To a greater extent than in most of the other underdeveloped countries of the hemisphere, the countries of Central America are agricultural, and the growth of agriculture has been relatively rapid by hemispheric standards. The rate of growth of real output in agriculture during the 1960s and 1970s in Latin America and the Caribbean was just over 3 percent. In Central America it was a percentage point higher (see Table 14A). In all five countries agricultural output grew faster than population in both decades, with the possible exception of El Salvador in the 1970s. The faster growth of agriculture in Central America than in the rest of Latin America and the Caribbean reflects an adherence to different development policies. Despite the formation of the CACM, the governments of Central America pursued considerably less protectionist policies than other governments in the hemisphere and encouraged the development of agribusiness. The agribusiness character of the region's agricultural strategy has meant that there has been no move toward self-sufficiency in food production, since production for export has been the dynamic element. Agribusiness has also tended toward large-scale production units and reinforced the concentration of land in a few hands. Thus, the openness of the economies is closely related to the problems of land concentration and landlessness, stressed in the introduction.

While the overall rates of agricultural growth for the last twenty

TABLE 14
Growth Rates of Value Added, Selected Sectors, for
Central America, 1960–1979[1]

A. Average Annual Growth Rates of Agriculture

Country	1960–1965	1965–1970	1970–1975	1975–1979	1960–1970	1970–1979
Costa Rica	0.5	5.7	3.3	1.6	3.1	2.5
El Salvador	3.8	3.8	4.5	1.9	3.8	3.2
Guatemala	4.0	4.5	6.0	3.7	4.3	4.9
Honduras	5.2	4.1	−1.4	8.0	4.7	3.3
Nicaragua	11.0	0.6	5.7	3.5[2]	5.8	4.7
Central America	4.6	4.0	4.2	3.8[2]	4.3	4.0[2]
Panama	6.6	4.1	2.7	0.9	5.3	2.0

B. Average Annual Growth Rates of Manufacturing

Country	1960–1965	1965–1970	1970–1975	1975–1979	1960–1970	1970–1979
Costa Rica	8.3	8.9	7.3	8.4[3]	8.6	7.9
El Salvador	10.0	3.3	5.6	6.9[2]	6.7	6.0[2]
Guatemala	6.8	7.9	4.6	8.0	7.4	6.1
Honduras	4.9	6.7	2.8	9.9	5.8	6.0
Nicaragua	15.0	8.9	5.7(4.0)[4]	5.9[2]	12.0	5.8[2]
Central America	8.7	7.1	5.6	7.0[3]	7.9	6.1[2]
Panama	12.4	9.4	2.6	1.6	10.9	2.2

[1] Constant prices of 1970.
[2] To 1977.
[3] To 1978.
[4] Omitting year following earthquake of 1972.
Source: See Table 13.

years have been relatively rapid, each of the countries of the region has experienced periods of slow or negative agricultural growth. Because of geographical proximity and a more-or-less common set of export crops, one would expect the variation in agricultural growth rates to display a similar pattern among the five countries, since the similarities would imply a common set of world prices and similar technologies of production. But such has not been the case, as Table 14A shows. In each five-year period at least one country's agricultural growth was extremely slow (even disastrously so), while one or more of the other countries experienced rapid or spectacular growth. If we pair-off the five countries in turn and look for a correspondence between annual growth rates of agriculture, we find that no pairing results in a close relationship.[6] While all the Central American economies are sensitive to changes in the world economy, each responds to different degrees or even with different directions of change. This, in turn, suggests that the particularities of each country are as important as the commonalities (see Chapter 5).

As in the case of the agricultural sector, manufacturing growth has been quite variable among the countries and overtime (Table 14B). When we divide the two last decades into five-year periods, only Costa Rica shows a relatively steady growth rate. A major goal of the CACM was to foster industrial development in the five countries. Proponents of the CACM argued that because of the small size of each economy individually, some industries could only be developed on the basis of a regional market. The Nicaraguan and Salvadoran manufacturing sectors apparently responded spectacularly to the impetus of the common market during its first five years, but subsequently failed to attain growth rates near those levels. Manufacturing growth was also rapid in Costa Rica and Guatemala throughout the 1960s, with Honduras having the slowest rate of growth both for 1960–1965 and 1965–1970. Withdrawal from the CACM did not coincide with any immediate improvement in the growth of Honduran manufacturing. On the contrary, in the five years after withdrawing, Honduras had the slowest rate of growth in manufacturing for any of the countries during any of the five-year periods. It may be that the rapid growth of manufacturing in the five Central American countries during the 1960s was coincidental with the formation of the CACM rather than caused by it. Panama, which had little trade with the five countries, had a rate of growth of manufacturing faster than four of them. But by hemispheric comparison, manufacturing grew rapidly in all of the Central American countries over the last twenty years.

At the start of this chapter we argued that the nature of the Central American economies makes them analytically analogous to firms, in which the major determinant of growth is productivity or production costs. The pattern of manufacturing tends to confirm this. Costa Rica, the most developed of the five countries of the CACM, with generally the highest output per worker, had both the fastest and the least variable rate of manufacturing growth on an annual basis from 1960 to 1979. Honduras, the least developed of the five and with the lowest productivity level had the slowest rate of growth over the same period and the greatest year-to-year variation in growth. The growth rates indicate that Costa Rica's manufacturing sector was the most competitive in the region and that of Honduras the least, with the latter able to achieve modestly high rates of growth only under favorable regional and world market conditions.

Although there was considerable variation in growth rates of manufacturing over time, in all of the countries but Honduras growth was faster in the 1960s than 1970s. This has led some (the World Bank, for example) to conclude that the initial impetus to manufacturing generated by the formation of the CACM had been exhausted by the 1970s. The argument is that the rapid growth in the early 1960s exhausted the major avenues of regional import substitution. There are a number of reasons to be skeptical about this argument. First, manufacturing is so underdeveloped in Central America that it is difficult to believe that further possibilities for import substitution do not exist (see Chapter 6). Second, in two of the four countries that stayed in the CACM, manufacturing growth during 1975–1979 was as rapid or more rapid than it had been in the 1960s. Third, it is reasonable to assume that intraregional exports were the major stimulus to growth resulting from the creation of the CACM. In the 1970s these grew faster than extraregional exports, suggesting that regional demand was still relatively buoyant. Finally, the view that the regional market had been exhausted is primarily based on the slow rates of growth of manufacturing in the first half of the 1970s. There is an alternative and more empirically verifiable explanation of growth in this period, which we give below.

In the case of agriculture, we found no common pattern of growth rates when we paired the countries off in turn. For manufacturing, however, there is quite strong correspondence. Any two of the countries taken together show a highly significant positive relationship between their rates of manufacturing growth for 1960–1977. That the significant correspondence between growth rates is related to the evolution of the CACM is strongly suggested by the fact that the least correspondence involves Honduras, which left the CACM in 1970. It was, of course, precisely the concerted growth of manufacturing that the CACM was intended to achieve. As we shall see in later chapters, this had a negative as well as a positive consequence, for many of the industries created for the regional market produced commodities that could not compete on the world market. The continued existence of many companies was (and is) dependent upon the governments of the region adhering to the preferential accords of the CACM.

The relatively rapid growth of the Central American economies during the last twenty years was accompanied by a strong growth of exports. With few exceptions, the pattern of exports was as follows: primary products to extraregional trade and manufactures to intraregional trade. The exceptions to this dichotomy have been food exports within the region, which constituted 32 percent of intra-CACM trade in the mid-1970s. This proportion largely involved processed foods based on imported inputs. Exports of manufactures, on the other hand, were less than 5 percent of extraregional trade when one excludes products such as frozen meat and fish and refined sugar.

TABLE 15
Growth Rates of Exports and Imports
for Central America, 1960–1979[1]

A. Average Annual Growth Rates of Exports

Country	1960–1965	1965–1970	1970–1975	1975–1979	1960–1970	1970–1979
Costa Rica	4.8	14.2	7.1	6.6	9.5	6.9
El Salvador	12.5	−0.4	8.6	2.7	6.1	6.0
Guatemala	9.1	7.1	1.2	5.4	8.1	3.0
Honduras	10.3	7.0	1.2	13.1	8.7	6.5
Nicaragua	14.7	2.4	7.6	2.3[2]	8.6	5.6
Central America	10.3	5.9	5.3	5.3[2]	8.1	5.3
Panama	13.8	8.4	0.5	8.6	11.1	4.0

B. Average Annual Growth Rates of Imports

Country	1960–1965	1965–1970	1970–1975	1975–1979	1960–1970	1970–1979
Costa Rica	7.3	8.5	3.0	12.2	7.9	7.1
El Salvador	10.2	1.0	6.4	10.7	5.6	8.3
Guatemala	8.0	3.4	1.2	8.0	5.7	4.2
Honduras	7.0	9.3	1.2	8.0	5.7	4.2
Nicaragua	11.2	3.5	5.4	8.1[2]	7.4	6.2
Central America	9.8	4.4	3.9	12.6[2]	7.1	7.2
Panama	11.4	9.1	1.8	7.2	10.2	4.2

[1] Constant prices of 1970.
[2] To 1978.
Source: See Table 13.

The growth of exports shown in Table 15A includes as its most dynamic element the expansion of manufactured exports within the region. Just as the growth of manufacturing was slower in the 1970s than in the 1960s, so the growth rate of exports declined, giving support to the view that the regional market was "saturated." Indeed, the decline in the rate of growth of exports in the 1970s was more pronounced than for manufacturing. In all five of the countries, manufacturing growth recovered some dynamism in the second half of the 1970s, while in three of the countries export growth was lower during 1975–1979 than for 1970–1975. This conflicting pattern casts some doubt on the "saturation" thesis. If the regional market was saturated in the 1970s, it should have been saturated in each country taken alone. But in fact manufacturing production did recover some dynamism in the second half of the decade, though exports did not. Since manufactured exports in extraregional trade did not increase to any great degree, it must be concluded

TABLE 16
Annual Average Rates of Inflation
in Central America, 1960–1977

Country	1960–1972	1972–1977
Costa Rica	2.4%	13.4%
El Salvador	0.5	12.8
Guatemala	0.7	13.8
Honduras	2.6	9.1
Nicaragua	1.8	12.6
Central America	1.4	12.8
Panama	1.7	7.4

Source: SIECA July 1981.

that the increased rate of growth of manufacturing in Costa Rica, El Salvador, and Guatemala was absorbed by the domestic market in each country. The exception to this last generalization is Honduras, which experienced a dramatic increase in the rate of growth of manufacturing and exports in the second half of the 1970s, and a sharp increase in intraregional exports (from 3.3 percent of its total exports in 1971–1972 to 9 percent for 1974–1979).

We have yet to offer an alternative explanation for the slowdown in growth rates in the Central American countries. Before doing so we must consider a further economic variable which is closely related to our explanation, namely the price level in the five countries. As Table 16 demonstrates, inflation in the Central American countries was extremely low from 1960 to 1972; in fact astonishingly so, with two countries (El Salvador and Guatemala) experiencing annual rates of less than 1 percent, and Nicaragua less than 2 percent. These rates of inflation are all the more astounding when compared to the relatively rapid GNP growth rates and rising exports, and call for some explanation. In Latin America, low rates of inflation usually imply two characteristics: openness to international trade and oppressive dictatorships.[7] It is no accident that El Salvador and Guatemala had the most stable price levels, for they strongly qualify on both characteristics. Unless there is world inflation, a relatively open economy will tend to have a stable price level. When a government pursues a "liberal" policy toward imports, any excess demand generated in the economy will be absorbed by increased imports. If the country's exchange rate is constant (as in Central America during 1960–1972) and if import prices are relatively constant (as during 1960–1972), then the excess demand can be absorbed by imports with no upward pressure on the price level. This is what occurred in the 1960s in Central America. However, such a process cannot usually be sustained for long by an economy of an underdeveloped country, unless the excess demand generated by economic growth is matched by the growth of exports. Otherwise, the inflow of imports will cause deterioration of the balance of payments position and the government will be forced to reduce the rate of growth (thus reducing import demand) or introduce import controls. In general, Latin American governments have chosen the latter alternative in the post-World War II period prior to resorting to the former. The consequence of import controls is to contain the excess demand domestically, which creates inflationary pressures. In El Salvador, Guatemala, and Nicaragua (until 1979), repressive dictatorships faciliated the management of the problem of excess domestic demand. In all three of these countries the incomes of the peasantry and urban workers have not kept pace with per capita growth. This has dampened the growth of consumption demand and, therefore, the excess demand that would draw in imports and put greater pressure on the balance of payments.

After the decade of price stability, inflationary pressures hit all of the Central American countries with a vengence. For all the five countries together inflation had proceeded at the almost minuscule rate of 1.4 percent for 1960–1972. During the next five years it averaged almost 13 percent annually, facilitated by the same liberal import policy that before 1973 had held inflation in check. What had changed was the trend in import prices. From 1960 to 1972, import prices had risen at a rate of slightly less than 2 percent a year; from 1972 to 1977, they rose by 11 percent a year. The increase in import prices was most dramatic for petroleum and petroleum products, as Table 17 shows. From 1965 to 1970, the price index of petroleum imports actually declined, then increased at an annual rate of 30 percent from 1973 to 1979. At the same time, the price of imported chemical products, almost twice as important as petroleum in the region's import bill, also rose rapidly. These two categories together accounted for 30 percent of regional imports in the mid-1970s, and their price increases had a powerful inflationary effect. Due to the openness of the Central American economies to imports, the inflation in world prices passed rapidly through the economies of each country. Even had excess demand been avoided, price stability could have been achieved in each country only by drastically reducing industrial and agricultural production (both of which used petroleum and chemical products as inputs), or by revaluing the national currencies (increasing their dollar value). The latter measure would have been absurd, of course, given the balance of payments pressure resulting from the increase in import prices (extraregional exports would have been made less competitive due to the revaluation).

It was the increase in import prices which reduced the rate of

Table 17
The Regional Price Level and Import Prices
for Central America, 1969–1979[1]

Years	GNP Deflator[2]	General Import Price Index	Petroleum Products	Chemicals
1960	87	83	—	—
1965	92	90	106	92
1970	100	100	100	100
1973	116	127	144	118
1975	155	195	378	216
1977	195	208	456	183
1978	207	224	451	181
1979	224	245	677	267
Proportion of imports, 1975–1977	—	—	11.2%	19.3%

[1]Not including Panama.
[2]Measure of domestic price inflation.
Source: SIECA July 1981.

growth of the Central American economies and the growth of exports in the 1970s, not a "saturation" of the regional market. A disaggregation of regional imports shows that prices rose most for agricultural and manufacturing inputs, somewhat less for machinery and equipment, and least of all for imports of consumer commodities. Again, we can analyze the five economies by analogy to firms. The increased price of imported inputs increased costs of production in agriculture (especially large-scale agriculture) and manufacturing. Capitalists, as a consequence, had to accept lower profit margins, which induced them to reduce output (much in the way the static neoclassical theory of the competitive firm would predict). To an extent profit margins were maintained by raising prices in the domestic and regional markets, where Central American producers enjoyed monopoly power for many products. This, however, made regionally manufactured consumer commodities less competitive with extraregional imports, since prices of imported consumer commodities rose only moderately. The cost pressures were intensified by the increased prices of imported machinery and equipment. Since in no Central American country is there a machinery-producing sector of any importance, no domestic substitutes for these imports were available. As a result, the cost of investment rose and capital expenditures declined. Most adversely affected by the relative price movements were the manufacturing sectors of El Salvador and Nicaragua. As a result of the shock of increased import prices, the inefficiency of production in the five countries asserted itself, with the high-cost producers for each commodity losing market shares.

The growth performance of the Central American countries illustrates our themes of openness and vulnerability of the five economies. Particularly in the 1960s, economic growth was rapid, stimulated by an expanding world economy and the creation of the CACM. Under these favorable conditions, the openness of the economies to regional and world trade seemed to be a strength of the economic strategy being followed. This proved illusory, for the Central American economies benefited much as high cost firms benefit from an expanding market: when demand is rising, there is room in the market for almost everyone. The 1970s brought on a more difficult and unfavorable international environment, and the openness of the economies transmitted the instability of the world economy quickly and severely into each economy of the region. As we shall see in Chapter 8, the economic difficulties reached crisis proportion in all five countries by the end of the decade.

During the 1960s the growth of the countries showed considerable instability, reflecting the small size, the openness, and the vulnerability of the economies. Instability of growth was particularly marked in agriculture, the sector providing most of Central America's foreign exchange. Industrial expansion looked quite impressive for the first decade of the CACM, but the transmission of the shocks occurring in the world economy (e.g., oil prices) to the domestic economies destabilized manufacturing growth.

NOTES

[1] I refer to the literature in English, since the nuances of the equivalent Spanish words, *estado* and *país*, are somewhat different from the English. The use of "state" in place of "country" is particularly prominent in Woodward (1976).

[2] To give one example: in neoclassical economic theory production within a country is determined by "absolute advantage" (the lowest cost producer drives the others from the market); but trade among countries is determined by "comparative advantage" (each producer-country specializes in the commodities it produces *least inefficiently*).

[3] Only the Warsaw Pact countries can claim a similar exchange rate stability among themselves in the postwar ear.

[4] To be explicit, I am applying the neoclassical "theory of the firm in perfect competition" to each economy.

[5] The annual growth rates are tested for correlation by ordinary-least-

squares regression. The results suggest that the growth rates for Guatemala are highly correlated to those of the other four countries taken together, but that there is low correlation between the other four countries taken separately and compared to the rest.

[6] By taking the five countries two at a time, we get ten distinct pairs. In eight of the cases, the probability that the growth rates during 1960–1977 were randomly related is near 50 percent or exceeds 50 percent. In two cases, Costa Rica and Nicaragua, and El Salvador and Honduras, the probability of randomness is low, but the relationship *negative*; e.g., when agricultural growth was rapid in Costa Rica, it was slow in Nicaragua. While such a relationship may be of statistical significance, it makes little sense.

[7] The reverse is not true, however: repressive dictatorships do not necessarily imply low rates of inflation (Argentina and Uruguay).

REFERENCES

Cline, W. R. and E. Delgado, 1978. *Economic Integration in Central America.* Washington: The Brookings Institution.

Delgado, E. 1981. *Evolución del Mercado Común Centroamericano y Desarrollo Equilibrado.* Costa Rica: EDUCA/SIECA.

Economic Commission for Latin America (ECLA). 1979. *Nicaragua: Economic Repercussions of Recent Political Changes.* Santiago, Chile: ECLA.

Inter-American Development Bank (IDB). 1983 (January). *Economic Report: Honduras.* Washington: IDB.

——— 1983 (June). *Economic Report: Guatemala.* Washington: IDB.

——— 1983 (July). *Economic Report: Costa Rica.* Washington: IDB.

——— 1983 (July). *Economic Report: Nicaragua.* Washington: IDB.

——— 1983 (August). *Economic Report: El Salvador.* Washington: IDB.

Secretaría Permanente del Tratado General de Integración Económica Centroamericana (SIECA). 1973. *Series Estadísticas Seleccionadas de Centroamérica y Panamá.* Guatemala: SIECA.

——— 1981 (July). *Estadisticas Macroeconomicas de Centroamerica 1970–1980.* Guatemala: SIECA.

——— 1981. *VII Compendio Estadístico Centroamericano.* Guatemala: SIECA.

Woodward, Ralph Lee, Jr. 1976. *Central America: A Nation Divided.* New York: Oxford University Press.

World Bank. 1978. *Memorandum on Recent Economic Developments and Prospects of Nicaragua.* Washington: World Bank.

——— 1981. *Current Economic Memorandum on Honduras.* Washington: World Bank.

4

The External Sectors of the Central American Economies

All countries are to some degree linked to the world market through trade and the flow of financial and productive capital. The impact of economic relations among countries upon economic development within countries has been an issue of analysis and debate for centuries, an issue which antedates the emergence of economics as a clearly defined social science. The nineteenth century economist David Ricardo was the first person to present a systematic analysis of commodity trade among countries. While the technical details of modern trade theory differ from Ricardo's, what remains the same is the fundamental conclusion that trade among countries is beneficial to all of the trading partners. This conclusion is for the most part rejected by nationalists in Latin America who see in the trading relationship the mechanism by which the Latin American countries are kept in a state of underdevelopment (foreign investment is also seen as culpable in this regard).

The critique of the benefits-of-trade thesis is almost entirely based on arguments about the terms under which trade occurs. This is an old argument, going back at least to the nineteenth century. It was set forward by Raúl Prebisch after World War II with particular reference to Latin America. At the risk of oversimplifying Prebisch's argument, the position can be summarized quite simply: underdeveloped countries tend to export primary products under competitive world market conditions, and capitalist developed countries (centrally planned economies are usually omitted from consideration) tend to export manufactures under monopolistic conditions. As a result, it is argued, over the trade cycle the prices of primary products tend to rise and fall with little upward trend, while the prices of manufactures rise during periods of expanding world demand but do not fall when demand is slack. This analysis implies a secular tendency for the prices of manufactures to rise relatively to prices of primary products—the terms of trade tend to deteriorate for underdeveloped countries. Empirical work in the 1960s tended to cast doubt on the generality of this argument, but it received a strong impulse with the dramatic increase in oil prices in the 1970s. It is open to debate whether the direct effect of the increase in oil prices was greater in developed or underdeveloped countries, but the indirect effect was to raise the costs of all products that used petroleum as an input. Since these are largely manufactures (chemical products being the most obvious), the indirect effect of petroleum price increases seems to verify the Prebisch argument.

However, independently of the increase in petroleum prices, critics of the benefits-from-trade argument tend to identify monopoly as responsible for the deterioration of the terms of trade for underdeveloped countries. It is argued that the increase in oil prices only made an intrinsically unequal relationship more disadvantageous. We have criticized this line of analysis elsewhere,[1] and here only point out that there are theoretical and empirical reasons for being skeptical about the degree and importance of monopoly in international trade.

That the trading relationship is unequal between Central America and the rest of the world, and among the Central American countries themselves, is partially correct. But the disadvantages arise not from monopoly pricing in the developed countries, but the contrary. For example, manufacturing in the Central American countries is relatively inefficient, and cannot compete with manufacturers produced in the developed countries except with tariff protection or at extremely low profit rates. The effect of liberalizing trade with the rest of the world would be a process of deindustrialization of Central America. Unless one is a true believer in the benefits of free trade, such a process could not be viewed as favorable to the successful development of the region.

In the context of the terms of trade critique of the gains from trade, the economies of Central America are a rather special and interesting case. This critique is of the trading relationship between underdeveloped and developed countries, and presumably would not apply to trade among underdeveloped countries, as in the Central American Common Market. This makes our consideration of the CACM of more than regional interest. As we shall see, the governments of the Central American countries began from the outset to complain about the inequality of benefits from trade, and the government of Honduras unilaterally withdrew from the CACM when it was barely a decade old.[2]

Placing emphasis upon the terms of trade is a narrow way of treating the impact of the international economy upon the development of individual countries. This is particularly the case for Central America, whose openness to the world economy has resulted in a particular and debilitating form of semicolonial status. The negative aspects of this relationship go beyond the terms under which trade has occurred, favorable or unfavorable.

Pattern of Trade and Terms of Trade

As we saw in Chapter 1, coffee production integrated Central America into the world market in the mid-nineteenth century and just before World War I still accounted for over 80 percent of the value of exports. Banana exports changed the region from one-crop to two-crop economies, reaching their peak of importance between the world wars. Since the end of the Second World War, there has been further diversification of exports, but almost exclusively into other primary products except for intraregional trade.

In keeping with the high concentration of land in the region, the more recent export commodities—cotton, beef, and sugar—are all based in large-scale units, not peasant production. Indeed, the only peasant export crop from Central America is coffee, and even in this case there is considerable plantation production, most notably in El Salvador. The most successful post-World War II crop has been cotton, which emerged as a major earner of foreign exchange. In most years since 1960, it has been the most important export of Nicaragua, but also significant in El Salvador and Guatemala (particularly in the 1960s, see Table 18). Beef production and its export expanded rapidly in Nicaragua in the 1960s and early 1970s, partly due to the relative abundance of land in that country and the facilitating role of a government willing to overlook legal formalities that might have impeded the creation of large estates. Sugar, like cotton an ancient crop in Central America, has been the least important of the five so far mentioned, but exceeded 10 percent of regional exports in 1975, when sugar prices were phenomenally high (almost $.30 a pound in 1974 and $.20 in 1975). Of these five products, only beef and sugar are consumed domestically to any significant extent.

Timber is another primary product that has been an important export in the last twenty years. In the case of Honduras, timber products oscillated around the level of 10 percent of export earnings before declining to about 5 percent in the late 1970s. In no other country of the region has lumber been more than about 3 percent of total exports. To an extent, this represents the underdevelopment of infrastructure, not lack of forestry resources. Both Guatemala and Nicaragua possess large rain forests on their Atlantic sides, but transport facilities are so poor— virtually nonexistent in the Atlantic coast of Nicaragua—that capitalists (usually foreign) have made only half-hearted efforts to exploit these resources. Over-timbering earlier in this century also explains in part the low current level of exports.

When we consider the six primary products so far mentioned along with the manufactured exports of Central America, it is apparent that the overwhelming proportion of exports are the result of large-scale production. This characteristic both reflects and produces the extreme income inequalities in the region. Except in Costa Rica where smallhold-

TABLE 18
Share of the Five Major Primary Products of Total
Commodity Exports in Central America
A. Central America

Product	1960–1964	1965–1969	1970–1974	1975–1979
Coffee	44%	32%	28%	33%
Cotton	14	14	12	10
Bananas	13	13	13	9
Beef	3	4	7	4
Sugar	3	3	4	6
Total	77%	66%	64%	62%

B. Costa Rica

Product	1960–1964	1965–1969	1970–1974	1975–1979
Coffee	49%	36%	28%	29%
Cotton	—	1	—	—
Bananas	26	25	27	24
Beef	4	6	9	6
Sugar	4	5	5	4
Total	83%	73%	69%	63%

C. El Salvador

Product	1960–1964	1965–1969	1970–1974	1975–1979
Coffee	57%	47%	43%	47%
Cotton	20	12	11	10
Bananas	—	—	—	—
Beef	—	—	1	1
Sugar	2	3	6	6
Total	79%	62%	61%	64%

D. Guatemala

Product	1960–1964	1965–1969	1970–1974	1975–1979
Coffee	58%	39%	33%	30%
Cotton	13	18	11	12
Bananas	8	3	5	2
Beef	2	3	5	2
Sugar	3	3	5	10
Total	84%	66%	59%	56%

E. Honduras

Product	1960–1964	1965–1969	1970–1974	1975–1979
Coffee	16%	13%	15%	28%
Cotton	2	3	1	2
Bananas	45	47	38	24
Beef	3	3	7	6
Sugar	—	—	1	1
Total	66%	66%	62%	61%

F. Nicaragua

Product	1960–1964	1965–1969	1970–1974	1975–1979
Coffee	24%	15%	15%	25%
Cotton	33	38	25	24
Bananas	1	1	1	1
Beef	6	9	14	10
Sugar	5	5	5	6
Total	69%	68%	60%	66%

Sources: SIECA 1973 and 1981.

ers are important in the coffee sector, the growth of exports has not tended to create a prosperous peasantry. On the contrary, export production has tended to dispossess the peasantry and transform large portions of it into a virtually landless rural class.[3] While obviously the gains from the expansion of exports have not been solely limited to capitalists and landlords in Central America, relatively constant real wages over the last two decades and the slower growth of employment than production have tended to make the "trickle down" of benefits a meager trickle indeed.

A brief scrutiny of Table 18 indicates that the export package of the Central American countries has become more diversified over the last twenty years. For all of the five countries the most important export has declined as a share of total exports, and in some cases there has been a change in which product is most important. Further, the five primary products together—coffee, cotton, bananas, sugar, and beef—accounted for a smaller proportion of total exports in the 1970s than in the 1960s. The relative importance of coffee and cotton declined in every country from the 1960s to the 1970s, with the exception of the share for coffee in the total exports of Honduras. These two commodities had accounted for 52 percent of Central American exports in the 1960s and almost two-thirds of the total for Nicaragua, El Salvador, and Guatemala. In the 1970s, their share for Central America fell to 40 percent and was below 50 percent for every country except El Salvador. The importance of bananas fell only very slightly from the 1960s to the 1970s, but in the country most dependent upon banana exports, Honduras, the share fell sharply. The diversification differed by commodity among the countries: for example, increased coffee production represented diversification in Honduras, while Guatemalan exports diversified by coffee becoming less important. What was common to all five countries was the absolute and relative growth of beef and sugar exports (though the level of beef exports remained insignificant in El Salvador). Beef exports from Central America are largely low quality and purchased by North American "fast-food" chains. As a result, Central American beef prices are low and the sales concentrated to a few buyers.

Considering the extreme underdevelopment of the Central American economies and the lack of export diversification for most Caribbean countries and many of South America, the success of the Central American economies in diversifying their exports is impressive. It is worthwhile to consider what has been gained and what has been lost by the particular pattern of diversification. The major gain has been protection against—or at least a hedge against—fluctuations in world demand for primary products. The prices of Central American export commodities have not moved in concert, and diversifying exports is certainly a risk-averting strategy. However, the particular products into which diversification has occurred have two drawbacks. All of the countries except El Salvador have diversified into beef and sugar. Beef, while having the advantage of an elastic income demand, generates very little employment. In particular, the relative shift from cotton and coffee to beef dramatically reduces the employment content of exports. The same point applies to a lesser degree to sugar. While sugar production generates peak demands for field labor, it creates very few permanent jobs per unit of investment. The relationship between exports and employment has also been affected by the decline in the share of the major primary products. The five major primary products accounted for 72 percent of exports in the 1960s and 63 percent in the 1970s for Central America as a whole. Most of the difference—eight percentage points—is manufactured exports (for the CACM). These exports create very little employment indeed compared to coffee or cotton. A case in point is Nicaragua, whose most important manufactured exports in the 1970s were chemical products and construction materials, both characterized by very high output per worker. The same point applies to Guatemala, which also became a regional exporter of chemicals. The diversification of Central American exports over the last twenty years has tended to reduce employment generation, and thereby contributed to the underutilization of labor and a more unequal distribution of income.

The second drawback of the diversification pattern also relates to manufactured exports, which we treat more extensively in Chapter 6. As unstable as world markets for primary products may be, the CACM has proved to be even more unstable, and it is to this market that most of the manufactures went. With the collapse of the CACM in the late 1970s,[4] manufactures for the regional market proved unsellable outside the region for the most part (at least in the short run), and installed capacity in many cases far exceeded domestic demand. The diversification to regional exports has created a major problem requiring the restructuring of manufacturing production in the region.

Despite the rapid growth and diversification of exports, the Central American countries taken together have generally suffered from deficits in their commodity trade over the last twenty years. As Table 19 shows, in only four years out of twenty were commodity exports greater in value than commodity imports and only in one year after 1963 (the balance was virtually zero in 1977). However, this is largely the result of twenty consecutive years of deficits for Costa Rica with the other countries frequently in surplus. Continuous deficits in trade were possible for Costa Rica because of an inflow of private foreign capital. Despite the relatively high wages in this country, its political stability, developed infrastructure, and pro-foreign investment policies have made it the most attractive country in Central America for international capital.

If we consider the years prior to the rapid rise in oil prices (1960–1972), all four of the other countries of Central America exported more than they imported. Setting aside for the moment the years of petroleum price boom, it is interesting to note that the patterns of deficits and surpluses are very different among countries. While there are some common movements (e.g., all commercial balances improved from 1971 to 1972), there is no common pattern. The Costa Rican deficit increased almost continuously; Guatemala had deficits in the early 1960s and surpluses thereafter; Nicaragua ran surpluses and deficits in a pattern opposite to Guatemala; and El Salvador and Honduras show sharp fluctuations around their averages with no trend or pattern.

Beginning in 1973, coincidental with oil price increases, all of the countries ran large commercial deficits. However, the behavior of the countries is not as similar as a first impression might give. The extremely high deficits for Nicaragua during 1973–1975 were more due to the earthquake which destroyed Managua than to oil price increases, as is evidenced by the fact that exports exceeded imports in 1976. Costa Rica,

TABLE 19
Balance in Commodity Trade (Exports-Imports) by Country
(millions of current dollars)

Years	Costa Rica	El Salvador	Guatemala	Honduras	Nicaragua	Central America
1960	−14.6	−8.0	−8.6	−1.1	7.5	−24.8
1	−12.2	20.3	−6.2	7.8	11.2	20.9
2	−9.4	25.5	−4.4	8.7	11.7	32.0
3	−17.8	12.1	−1.9	−3.9	15.7	4.2
4	−11.4	1.1	−15.2	0.5	15.7	−9.3
5	−49.2	5.5	−22.8	15.1	16.4	−35.0
6	−26.5	−12.1	30.1	6.4	−8.7	−10.8
7	−30.3	2.4	−22.6	3.9	−25.0	−71.6
8	−23.6	13.5	−4.2	11.6	−4.2	−6.9
9	−31.9	9.3	21.6	1.2	−0.9	−0.7
1970	−55.8	33.7	27.2	−25.2	0.1	−20.0
1	−91.7	17.8	−3.0	16.5	−3.0	−63.4
2	−58.2	51.9	41.2	33.5	43.6	112.0
3	−67.3	18.6	50.6	24.6	−48.7	−22.2
4	−208.7	−59.5	−49.1	−86.9	−160.6	−564.8
5	−134.3	−17.4	−31.5	−70.0	−107.3	−360.5
6	−103.1	63.6	−198.8	−26.3	56.8	−207.8
7	−97.3	112.5	73.2	−20.3	−68.0	0.1
8	−185.6	−102.2	−191.4	−26.9	92.7	−413.4
9	−315.1	285.8	−173.3	−26.9	227.2	−2.3
Averages						
1960–1972	−33.3	13.3	2.4	5.8	6.2	−5.6
1973–1977	−132.7	2.6	−57.8	−34.3	−39.2	−261.4

Sources: SIECA 1973 and 1981.

Guatemala, and Honduras all ran continuous deficits from 1974 to 1978 (with the exception of Honduras in 1977), but El Salvador alternated between deficits and surpluses.

Inspecting the commercial balances in Table 19 and the different patterns among the countries raises the question of whether one can identify a common external influence on Central American trade, despite the differences. Table 19 does show that for all five countries average surpluses declined or turned to deficits (or the deficit got larger in the case of Costa Rica) after 1972 compared to before. To what extent was this the result of the alleged terms of trade effect discussed earlier? In Table 20 we have calculated the static terms of trade effect on imports and exports by assuming that 1970 prices prevailed throughout the twenty years.[5] The calculation is static or partial because we do not adjust for the possibility that a different set of prices, those of 1970, might have generated a different composition of export commodities. We can presume that the exported quantity of each product was in part in response to the prevailing price, and that different prices would have called forth different quantities. As is common in terms of trade calculations, we ignore this effect. Selection of 1970 prices is arbitrary but dictated by the data base. Another year's prices would produce a different numerical estimate of the terms of trade effect. However, by coincidence the base year prices (1970) are before the petroleum price increases and therefore indicative of the most important price changes of the twenty year period.

In part A of Table 20, we see that if the prices of 1970 had prevailed for the twenty years, the value of Central American exports would have been about $10 billion less, but the value of commodity imports would have been over $11 billion less, implying a foreign exchange loss of $1.3 billion for the twenty years due to relative price changes. Put another way, Central America had a cumulative twenty year trade deficit of $1.7 billion, and had 1970 prices prevailed through the period, the deficit would have been only $350 million, less than a quarter of the actual deficit.

However, the effects for each country are very different. At one extreme is Guatemala, which lost almost $1.2 billion by our measure of the terms of trade effect. At the other extreme is Honduras, which had a net *gain* of almost $300 million. Indeed, for the twenty years as a whole, El Salvador, Honduras, and Nicaragua did better with the actual movement in relative prices than they would have done at the prices of 1970. Selection of another base year for comparison to actual prices would change the figures, as noted above, but would not change the conclusion that the Central American countries have not been similarly affected by relative price changes. This point is shown in Table 21, where

TABLE 20
Calculation of the Static Terms of Trade Effect in Central America
1960–1979
(millions of dollars)
A. Central America

Years	Current Prices			Constant Prices		
	Export	Import	X-M	Export	Import	X-M
1960–64	2689	2667	+ 22	3054	3086	− 32
1965–69	4410	4537	− 127	4829	4860	− 31
1970–74	7466	8038	− 572	6533	6343	+ 190
1975–79	18358	19354	− 996	8457	8932	− 475
Total	32923	34596	− 1673	22873	23221	− 348
Net Effect						− 1325

B. Costa Rica

Years	Current Prices			Constant Prices		
	Export	Import	X-M	Export	Import	X-M
1960–64	474	539	− 65	513	626	− 113
1965–69	751	913	− 162	752	955	− 203
1970–74	1519	2001	− 482	1398	1578	− 180
1975–79	3719	4554	− 835	1950	2241	− 291
Total	6463	8007	− 1544	4613	5400	− 787
Net Effect						− 757

C. El Salvador

Years	Current Prices			Constant Prices		
	Export	Import	X-M	Export	Import	X-M
1960–64	686	635	51	807	652	155
1965–69	1001	983	18	1175	999	176
1970–74	1582	1531	51	1362	1216	146
1975–79	4321	3982	339	1675	1892	− 217
Total	7590	7131	459	5019	4759	260
Net Effect						+ 199

D. Guatemala

Years	Current Prices			Constant Prices		
	Export	Import	X-M	Export	Import	X-M
1960–64	673	710	− 37	812	859	− 47
1965–69	1120	1119	+ 1	1315	1206	+ 109
1970–74	1944	1877	+ 67	1748	1424	+ 324
1975–79	4874	5407	− 533	2348	2077	+ 271
Total	8611	9113	− 502	6223	5566	+ 657
Net Effect						− 1159

E. Honduras

Years	Current Prices			Constant Prices		
	Export	Import	X-M	Export	Import	X-M
1960–64	400	389	+ 11	418	458	− 40
1965–69	780	742	+ 38	771	821	− 50
1970–74	1151	1190	− 39	966	982	− 11
1975–79	2629	2798	− 169	1131	1461	− 330
Total	4960	5119	− 159	3286	3722	− 431
Net Effect						+ 277

F. Nicaragua

Years	Current Prices			Constant Prices		
	Export	Import	X-M	Export	Import	X-M
1960–64	456	394	62	504	491	13
1965–69	758	780	− 22	816	879	− 63
1970–74	1270	1439	− 169	1059	1143	− 84
1975–79	2815	2613	202	1353	1261	92
Total	5299	5226	73	3732	3774	− 42
Net Effect						+ 115

Sources: SIECA 1973 and 1981.

TABLE 21
Summary of the Static Terms of Trade Effect for Central America
1960–1979
(millions of dollars)

Years	Costa Rica	El Salvador	Guatemala	Honduras	Nicaragua	Central America
1960–1964	$+ 48	$− 104	$+ 10	$+ 51	$+ 49	$+ 54
1965–1969	+ 41	− 158	− 108	+ 88	+ 41	− 96
1970–1974	− 302	− 95	− 257	− 23	− 85	− 762
1975–1979	− 544	+ 556	− 804	+ 161	+ 110	− 521
Total	− 757	+ 199	− 1159	+ 277	+ 115	− 1325

Source: Table 20, above.

the calculations in Table 20 are summarized. During the five-year period 1970–1974, all the countries had a negative terms of trade effects (though only barely for Honduras). In the other five-year periods, three of the five countries had positive effects (benefited from world price changes) and two countries had negative effects. The unavoidable conclusion is that one cannot treat Central America as a unit when considering the effect of world prices, for the composition of imports and exports varies too much among the five countries.

Honduras, for example, was the least industrialized of the five countries and therefore least affected by the increase in oil prices; at the same time, the prices of its major exports, coffee and bananas, rose sharply over the twenty years. Guatemala and Costa Rica suffered large negative terms of trade effects, ironically enough due in part to the diversification away from coffee. The average coffee price increase from the late 1960s to the late 1970s was 340 percent, compared to a 230 percent increase in import prices in Costa Rica and 320 percent in Guatemala for the same period. Nicaragua and Honduras show positive terms of trade effects in part as a result of coffee *not* losing importance and because beef exports expanded, the price of the latter commodity rising even more than that of coffee.

On the basis of the Central American experience over the last twenty years we can conclude that the "deteriorating terms of trade for developing countries" thesis remains unconfirmed: two of the countries had net negative effects, but three did not. In this context, it is interesting to do a calculation identical to that in Tables 20 and 21 for the North American economy.[6] When this is done, we discover that from 1960 to 1979 the North American economy suffered a net negative terms of trade effect of over $100 billion, three times the total commodity exports of

Central America for the same period. While this is an insignificant amount compared to total North American GNP for the period, it does suggest caution is required when generalizing about the net gains from world trade by industrialized countries.

Our current discussion of the terms of trade effect might seem to contradict the argument made at the end of Chapter 3. There we attributed the slowdown in Central American growth and industrialization to relative price changes. The two arguments are not inconsistent, however. In this chapter we have considered the effect of relative prices on the value of imports and exports; in Chapter 3, the argument referred to the impact of relative prices on costs and competitiveness. The two effects are different and we pursue this point in Chapter 6.

Direction of Trade

Since the end of the nineteenth century, North America has been the major trading partner of the Central American countries. This has been more the result of a semicolonial status than geography. Central America has primarily traded with North America for the same reason that the trade of Belize, Jamaica, and Barbados has gone to the United Kingdom (geography notwithstanding). However, by the 1960s, the direction of trade had diversified, so that North America no longer claimed a majority of the value of exports or imports.

The most important change in the direction of trade has been to the regional market. However, the CACM has not overtaken North America as the principal market for the Central American countries, as Table 22 shows. For the isthmus as a whole, 36 percent of exports were to North America in the 1960s and 34 percent in the 1970s, and the year-to-year variation makes the difference between the decades insignificant. Only in the case of Costa Rica was there a significant drop in the North American share. Central America's trade remains dominated by the United States, with arrangements such as the US sugar quota being of importance to the region.

Before we consider intraregional trade we should stress that the vast majority of Central America's exports and imports are with developed countries, about 70 percent in the last two decades. After the United States, the Federal Republic of Germany is the region's most important trading partner, absorbing 10 percent of Central American exports. Western Europe as a whole takes about a quarter of all exports, roughly the same proportion as intra-CACM trade. Primary products account for virtually all of these exports to Europe, with coffee the most important. Since the end of World War II, Japan has been a growing

TABLE 22
Proportion of Total Commodity Trade of Central American Countries
with the United States

A. Exports

Years	Costa Rica	El Salvador	Guatemala	Honduras	Nicaragua	Central America
1960–1964	51%	25%	38%	55%	33%	39%
1965–1969	46	23	33	50	28	34
1970–1974	37	24	31	54	30	34
1975–1979	37	30	33	52	26	34

B. Imports

Years	Costa Rica	El Salvador	Guatemala	Honduras	Nicaragua	Central America
1960–1964	47%	34%	46%	48%	48%	44%
1965–1969	38	31	40	47	42	39
1970–1974	34	29	32	42	33	34
1975–1979	34	30	33	43	30	34

Sources: SIECA 1973 and 1981.

market for Central American products, particularly cotton. The pattern for imports is quite similar to that for exports. The United States supplied 36 percent of Central America's imports in the 1960s and 1970s, virtually the same as its share in exports (Table 22). Again, Japan and Germany follow in importance, reflecting the tendency for trade to be reciprocal between partners.

While developed countries accounted for 70 percent of Central America's imports and exports in recent years, this represents a sharp drop from the 1950s, when the proportion was over 90 percent. Almost all of the decrease represents growth of intraregional trade, which was only 5 percent of exports and imports in the years just before the creation of the CACM. As Table 23 shows, the rapid expansion in intraregional trade was in the 1960s, with the peak of 26 percent of total trade reached in 1968 and maintained through the 1970s. It is not correct, however, to view these peak years as a turning point in the dynamism of intraregional trade. The stagnation in the proportion of intraregional trade after 1968 reflects in part the decision of the Honduran government to unilaterally withdraw from the CACM, due to political conflict with El Salvador and a judgment by the Hondurans that the benefits of economic integration were accruing elsewhere.

Whether or not the CACM on balance generated benefits for the region and each country is essentially an unanswerable question, since we cannot know what would have occurred in its absence. That its formation stimulated capitalist development throughout the region cannot be denied, and a small number of foreign and national companies made great profits at least for a decade and a half. It is certainly open to doubt whether the masses of the Central American population enjoyed any tangible gain. This should not be blamed on the policies of regional economic integration, however. Given the anti-democratic character of the governments in four of the five countries during the 1960s and 1970s, it is unlikely that anything but an unequal distribution of the gains from growth was possible.

We can, however, consider the narrow question of how the CACM affected the balance of trade for each country. Table 24 gives the trade balance of each Central American country with respect to all the others.[7] We pointed out in Chapter 2 that Honduras is the least developed of the five countries. In Table 24, we see that it was Honduras which had on average the largest negative commercial balance in intraregional trade for the years from 1960 to 1978. This is despite the fact that Honduras had the least intraregional trade of any of the countries for the period

TABLE 23
Proportion of Total Commodity Exports within the CACM
by Country
(current prices)

Years	Costa Rica	El Salvador	Guatemala	Honduras	Nicaragua	Central America
1963	4.2%	19.7%	11.4%	15.2%	4.5%	11.7%
1964	13.5	20.7	18.0	17.9	5.7	15.6
1965	16.3	24.1	19.1	16.3	8.3	17.4
1966	18.6	31.0	22.5	13.5	11.4	20.3
1967	18.7	38.2	29.3	15.0	12.0	24.0
1968	21.2	40.1	31.2	16.9	15.2	26.0
1969	19.9	37.0	32.8	13.3	20.0	25.7
1970	19.9	32.3	35.3	10.6	25.8	24.9
1971	20.9	35.5	32.5	3.0	25.3	24.6
1972	18.3	33.4	30.1	3.0	22.5	22.9
1973	20.5	31.4	29.8	4.1	21.7	23.0
1974	23.7	32.4	28.5	9.4	24.0	25.2
1975	21.7	27.6	27.0	9.1	24.7	23.3
1976	22.0	24.4	24.9	9.1	21.7	21.6
1977	21.0	21.8	19.2	8.5	21.0	19.1
1978	20.7	37.0	22.9	8.2	22.6	22.4

Sources: SIECA 1973 and 1981.

TABLE 24
Commercial Balance of the Five Central American Countries
in Regional Trade
(millions of current dollars)

Years	Costa Rica	El Salvador	Guatemala	Honduras	Nicaragua
1960	−1.2	−0.8	−0.3	2.1	0.7
1961	−2.1	−0.2	1.4	1.9	−1.1
1962	−1.4	−3.6	2.2	4.9	−2.1
1963	0.6	0.8	1.0	0.7	−3.1
1964	7.5	−4.1	3.6	0.3	−7.4
1965	4.2	3.8	6.8	−3.3	−11.5
1966	2.7	5.4	21.2	−12.6	−16.0
1967	−3.2	20.7	23.6	−17.2	−24.0
1968	−11.2	19.7	28.1	−17.4	−19.2
1969	−15.1	11.6	35.0	−20.0	−11.4
1970	−6.0	12.3	19.1	−31.3	5.9
1971	−7.7	3.4	15.6	−13.5	2.3
1972	−32.2	11.6	19.7	−13.8	14.5
1973	−25.3	−5.0	13.2	−18.3	−15.3
1974	−46.5	−6.4	16.7	−17.8	−39.0
1975	−5.8	−2.1	36.1	−12.8	−15.3
1976	−18.2	−21.2	37.0	−6.5	8.9
1977	−3.5	−48.1	65.5	−14.0	0.1
1978	−33.0	−39.0	75.1	−4.2	1.1
1979	−8.1	−48.3	141.9	21.0	−66.5
1980	17.2	−105.7	274.5	37.3	−223.3

Sources: SIECA 1973 and 1981.

and in most of the years taken separately. If we include 1979 and 1980, its negative balance is exceeded by that of Nicaragua and matched by El Salvador, but this reflects the effects of war in those countries. From 1960 to 1964 Honduras ran modest trade surpluses (the only country to so), but a deficit in 1965, and deficits of continuously growing size through 1970. These deficits were a factor influencing the decision of the Honduran government to abandon the CACM. Leaving the CACM coincided with a fall in the absolute size of the intraregional trade deficit, since Honduras' total trade with the other four countries dropped sharply. The prima facie evidence suggests that abandoning the CACM did contribute to improving the Honduran balance of payments in the short run. In 1970 the Honduran balance on total commodity trade was a negative $25 million (see Table 19), less than its intraregional deficit, which implies a positive balance in extraregional trade for that year. In

1971, the intraregional balance improved by $18 million, and Honduras' total trade balance turned positive and stayed positive for three years. But notwithstanding its break with the CACM, Honduras continued to run intraregional trade deficits until the collapse of the Salvadoran and Nicaraguan economies in 1979.

Nicaragua also was in deficit for most of the years of the CACM's operation (Table 24). This did not, however, prompt the government to withdraw, though it certainly prompted complaints in regional meetings about alleged disadvantages. Perhaps Nicaragua's continued membership can be exampled by support for regional integration from a number of Nicaraguan capitalists who were reaping considerable benefits. While overall Nicaragua was in deficit in intraregional trade, locally produced chemicals (particularly fertilizer, pesticides, and caustic soda), plastics, and construction materials found a rapidly expanding regional market. No comparable export growth on a sectoral level occurred in Honduras.

Since Honduras and Nicaragua were relatively underdeveloped countries in the area, it is not surprising that they tended to run deficits in intraregional trade. What is surprising, however, are the continuous and large surpluses enjoyed by Guatemala. Except for a tiny deficit in the first year of the CACM, Guatemala in every year exported more to its regional trading partners than it imported from them, with the most important commodities being prepared foods, cosmetics, glass containers, and metal products for construction. To a certain extent, this success seems to have been at the expense of trade with the rest of the world. Guatemala's extraregional trade was in growing deficit though the 1960s and 1970s, suggesting a trade-off or conflict between regional and extraregional exports.

When the CACM began there was fear among the governments and capitalists of the other Central American countries that Costa Rica, because of its higher level of development, or El Salvador, because of low wages, would benefit disproportionally from regional trade liberalization. Certainly this has not been the case for Costa Rica as measured by the trade balance. As we showed in Table 7, Costa Rica had about 20 percent of regional GNP in the 1960s and 1970s. Until the mid-1970s its share of regional exports was below this proportion and roughly equal to it from 1973 to 1979. Further, in the 1970s its share of regional imports was above its share of GNP. The case of El Salvador is slightly more complicated. From the outset of the CACM, El Salvador's share of regional exports was well above its share of regional GNP. In the first half of the 1960s, over 40 percent of intraregional exports came from El Salvador, but this proportion fell to about 35 percent in the second half of the 1960s, and was consistently below 30 percent in the 1970s. This decline is suggestive of reduced competitiveness, particularly when we recall that the share of Honduras dropped drastically in the 1970s. If we exclude Honduras, the Salvadoran portion of the exports among the remaining four countries falls even more drastically, from 39 percent during 1965–1969 to 29 percent during 1970–1974, and remaining at that level for the rest of the decade.

The countries that increased their share of intraregional trade most during the brief flowering of the CACM were Nicaragua and Costa Rica, though the latter only to its weight in total regional production. It could be argued that Nicaraguan capital was the real success story of the CACM. In 1960, the Nicaraguan economy had a tiny industrial base which was almost totally without export possibilities. By the 1970s, Nicaragua was an exporter of manufactures and semi-possessed commodities. Products of agroindustry went to North America, Japan, and Europe, and chemicals, synthetic resins, and construction materials were exported within the region (as well as some agroindustrial products such as vegetable soil). In the first half of the 1970s, Nicaragua's share of regional exports was greater than Costa Rica's, despite having a much smaller GNP and being much more underdeveloped. Further, with the exception of Guatemala, Nicaragua had the most diversified intraregional exports of the five Central American countries. Precisely this success would confront Nicaraguan capitalists with disaster when the CACM broke up at the end of the 1970s.[8]

Balance of Payments

During the decade of the 1960s and up until the petroleum price boom in 1973, all of the Central American countries enjoyed trade surpluses except Costa Rica. However, the balance of payments situation was quite different, as Table 25 shows. In this table we give the annual balance on the external current account, which includes not only commodities, but also services ("invisibles"), and purely monetary flows of a short-term nature (tourism, profit remittances, and transfer payments from abroad). The rather loose term "balance of payments" is often used to refer to the concept employed in Table 25. In that table there are five countries and nineteen years, or ninety-five observations. For only seven of the ninety-five observations is the current account balance positive, four years for El Salvador, two for Honduras, and one for Nicaragua. Beginning in 1963, only for four of the remaining eighty observations is the balance positive. By contrast, if we look back to Table 19, we find that for the same nineteen years the trade balance was positive in thirty-eight of the ninety-five cases.

Two factors explain the consistently negative balances on the cur-

TABLE 25
Balance on the External Current Account by Country
(millions of dollars)

Years	Costa Rica	El Salvador	Guatemala	Honduras	Nicaragua	Central America
1960	−19.8	−27.7	−25.9	−3.3	−7.6	−77.5
1961	−13.8	−0.4	−16.2	−2.3	3.3	−31.4
1962	−17.8	2.6	−24.2	−2.4	−9.7	51.5
1963	−25.3	−10.2	−30.6	−17.9	−4.8	−88.0
1964	−22.9	−23.3	−43.4	−11.2	−9.1	−109.9
1965	−67.2	−12.7	−48.7	−7.1	−22.0	−137.7
1966	−44.3	−41.0	−18.7	−19.2	−49.1	−172.3
1967	−50.2	−23.5	−66.4	−28.5	−64.9	−233.5
1968	−42.9	−15.1	−48.9	−24.6	−41.9	−173.4
1969	−51.6	−19.3	−17.3	−30.5	−35.7	−154.4
1970	−73.9	1.0	−11.1	−63.7	−38.3	−186.0
1971	−117.0	−14.2	−45.9	−22.5	−42.8	−239.4
1972	−100.0	12.5	−9.5	−8.9	21.7	−84.2
1973	−111.9	−41.7	11.0	−35.5	−65.1	−243.2
1974	−266.7	−135.5	−99.4	−105.7	−256.7	−863.4
1975	−217.7	−91.8	−62.3	−119.9	−184.1	−675.8
1976	−201.4	23.5	−70.6	−111.7	−38.7	−398.9
1977	−225.6	30.4	−35.4	−128.8	−182.0	−541.4
1978	−363.2	−238.6	−262.2	−155.7	−25.0	−1,077.2

Sources: SIECA 1973 and 1981.

rent accounts of the Central American countries: services and profit remittances. One aspect of the underdevelopment of Central America is that the institutions facilitating international trade are extremely underdeveloped. None of the countries possesses nationally owned shipping fleets worthy of the term, and virtually all the insuring and commercial services necessary for international trade are contracted to overseas companies, and even those for intraregional trade. The consequence is that from 1960 to 1979 only one Central American country in one year had a positive balance on all noncommodity flows (Honduras in 1960), and only in Costa Rica are the financial institutions sufficiently developed for the balance on services alone to be positive.

The major noncommodity item in deficit has been net profit remittances, that is, the balance between profits remitted to Central America from abroad and remittances from Central America to other countries. For the twenty years from 1960 to 1979, almost $3 billion flowed out of Central America in net profit remittances, which equaled 1.6 percent of the regional GNP for the period and 9 percent of merchandise exports.

Quite interesting is the distribution of these, for proportionately to GNP Honduras and Nicaragua had the highest rate of profit remittances, with the Nicaraguan rate twice that for El Salvador. The rate for Nicaragua is influenced by the capital flight in 1978 and 1979 due to war (see Chapter 7) but remains quite high even if these years are excluded.

The short-run outflow of profits should not be viewed in isolation from the inflow of direct foreign investment, though the two flows are not necessarily the result of actions by the same people or corporations. From 1960 to 1978, direct foreign investment flows amounted to $1,683 million, or about $800 million less than net profit remittances. This would seem to suggest that the net monetary flows associated with foreign investment have been negative in Central America. However, the situation is a good bit more complicated than the negative balance between direct investment and profit remittances would imply, as Table 26 demonstrates. For all of Central America, net foreign investment was over 10 percent of private domestic investment, a quite substantial portion of regional fixed capital formation. At the same time, profit remittances equaled 3 percent of the value of the region's exports.

It is striking to note, however, that the countries in which foreign investment flows were proportionally largest were also the countries in which the balance between these flows and profit remittances was most favorable. That is, if it is correct to argue that foreign investment tends to generate profit remittances that cancel capital inflow, then we should expect that countries which proportionally have the greatest investment inflows should proportionally have the greatest profit remittances. The opposite is the case in Central America. In Costa Rica, net foreign investment was 15 percent of total private investment during 1960 to 1978, twice the proportion for El Salvador and Nicaragua and three times the proportion for Honduras.[9] Yet in Costa Rica profit transfers exceeded net foreign investment inflows by a minuscule $44 million over nineteen years, compared to astronomical totals of over $400 million for Nicaragua and Honduras.

In absolute terms, Guatemala had the largest net direct investment flows (almost half of a billion dollars in the 1970s alone). And Guatemala was the only country for which foreign investment exceeded profit remittances. A large portion of the investment flow to Guatemala was a nickel-mining project, whose investment cost reached $224 million by the mid-1970s. The major shareholder in the project (80 percent) is the International Nickel Company of Canada, with the Hanna Mining Company holding the rest of the ownership. The World Bank reported that the initial ratio of income expatriated to gross revenue on nickel sales would be only about 20 percent. In fact, there has been little income

TABLE 26
Measures of the Importance of Foreign Investment and Remitted Profits for Central America

A. Central America

Years	(millions of dollars) Net Profit Transfers	Net direct Investment	NDI-NPT	(Percentages) NDI-NPT Exports	NDI GDI
1960–1964	$153.6	$158.5	$4.9	0.2%	9.9%
1965–1969	450.5	332.8	−117.7	−2.7	13.3%
1970–1974	735.4	422.8	−312.6	−4.3	10.3
1975–1978	1132.6	768.9	−363.7	−2.7	9.9
Total	2472.1	1683.0	−789.1	−2.9	10.5%

B. Costa Rica

Years	(millions of dollars) Net Profit Transfers	Net direct Investment	NDI-NPT	(Percentages) NDI-NPT Exports	NDI GDI
1960–1964	$36.5	$51.4	$14.9	3.2%	12.9%
1965–1969	80.5	70.0	−10.5	−1.4	14.6
1970–1974	139.6	158.0	18.4	1.2	16.2
1975–1978	306.7	239.9	−66.8	−2.4	14.6
Total	563.3	519.3	−44.0	−0.8	14.9

C. El Salvador

Years	(millions of dollars) Net Profit Transfers	Net direct Investment	NDI-NPT	(Percentages) NDI-NPT Exports	NDI GDI
1960–1964	$25.1	$31.4	$6.3	0.9%	9.7%
1965–1969	40.2	42.5	2.3	0.2	9.7
1970–1974	64.1	42.6	−21.5	−1.3	6.2
1975–1978	136.9	112.2	−24.7	−0.8	7.7
Total	266.3	228.7	−37.6	−0.6	7.8

D. Guatemala

| Years | (millions of dollars) | | | (Percentages) | |
	Net Profit Transfers	Net direct Investment	NDI-NPT	NDI-NPT Exports	NDI GDI
1960–1964	$65.8	$54.7	$ − 11.1	− 1.7%	12.0%
1965–1969	151.0	110.4	− 40.6	− 3.1	14.3
1970–1974	232.2	132.8	− 99.4	− 4.2	10.6
1975–1978	168.1	340.6	172.5	3.3	11.8
Total	617.1	638.5	21.4	0.2	11.9

E. Honduras

| Years | (millions of dollars) | | | (Percentages) | |
	Net Profit Transfers	Net direct Investment	NDI-NPT	NDI-NPT Exports	NDI GDI
1960–1964	$9.9	$ − 6.1	$ − 16.0	− 4.1%	− 3.2%
1965–1969	89.2	46.6	− 42.6	− 5.5	12.4
1970–1974	99.2	24.1	− 75.1	− 7.7	4.6
1975–1978	239.1	35.3	− 203.8	− 10.9	4.1
Total	437.4	99.9	− 413.3	− 9.9	5.1

F. Nicaragua

| Years | (millions of dollars) | | | (Percentages) | |
	Net Profit Transfers	Net direct Investment	NDI-NPT	NDI-NPT Exports	NDI GDI
1960–1964	$16.3	$27.1	$10.8	2.4%	4.5%
1965–1969	99.6	63.3	− 36.3	− 4.8	14.1
1970–1974	200.3	65.3	− 135.0	− 10.6	9.8
1975–1978	281.8	40.9	− 240.9	− 11.0	4.4
Total	598.0	196.6	− 401.4	− 8.6	7.4

Key: NDI—Net direct investment
NPI—Net profit transfers
GDI—Gross domestic investment
Sources: SIECA 1973 and 1981.

either to remit or retain in Guatemala. Due to the world recession of the late 1970s, exports of nickel have been below capacity since production began in 1977 and in the early 1980s ceased altogether (see Chapter 8). This large investment which has borne little fruit largely explains why Guatemala has had a positive balance between foreign investment flows and remitted profits.

The outflow of profits is an extremely controversial issue in Latin America, with nationalists arguing that the repatriation of earnings by multinational corporations goes far to negate the benefits of foreign investment. It is incorrect, however, to place blame for profit remittances exclusively on foreign capital, at least in Central America. Nicaragua is the clearest case. During the 1960s and 1970s, the Somoza family alone controlled much more of the Nicaraguan economy than foreign capital, and the high rate of profit transfers abroad from 1965 onwards was primarily the work of Nicaraguans. In the case of Honduras, the culprit behind the net capital outflows may have been foreign capital. During the late 1960s and 1970s the banana companies were quite profitable, but made relatively few new investments. However, in light of the Nicaraguan experience, one cannot argue that profit remittances would have been any less had the banana companies been Honduran-owned. It is not the purpose of this study to defend the role of foreign capital in Central America, but rather to indicate that judgments about this role should not be made superficially. The fact that profits flow out does not necessarily mean that it is foreigners who bank them abroad.

Our analysis of the trade and balance payments of the Central American countries provides us with at least one important conclusion. Despite rapid growth in the volume of exports, relatively favorable terms of trade in the last decade, and some export diversification, the Central American economies have not been able to achieve stability in their balance of payments. All of the countries have tended to import more commodities than they exported, even under favorable world market conditions. This, combined with large deficits in "invisibles" and substantial profit remittances, has forced the governments of the region to rely on concessionary and commercial loans to balance their external accounts. The semicolonial status of Central America during the last twenty years has meant that concessionary financing of the balance of payments was particularly forthcoming from North America. In the 1970s multilateral agencies—the World Bank, Inter-American Development Bank, and the International Monetary Fund—became more active in the region, but considerable debt was also contracted from private banks. By the late 1970s this debt would prove to be a massive obstacle to achieving external equilibrium.

The Special Case of Panama

The economy of Panama has evolved in a manner which has made it one of a kind in the hemisphere. Until the last two decades Panama's economy, like its political life, was dominated by the canal. No geological barrier ever divided a country so effectively as the man-made waterway from Colón on the Caribbean to Panama City on the Pacific. Virtually the entire economic life of Panama lies to the west of the canal[10]—that which is not within the Zone itself. The uniqueness of Panama's economy is manifested in a quite astounding statistic: during the 1960s, less than 40 percent of foreign exchange earnings were from the export of commodities; and in the late 1970s this had dropped to below 20 percent. By comparison, for the five Central American countries, commodity exports were about 85 percent of foreign exchange earnings during both decades. Thus, for the most part, Panama does not obtain foreign exchange through production. While in the case of the five Central American countries one can refer to a "export economy" or "export sector" in each which is the motor of growth in those countries, in Panama exports as such are relatively unimportant. From 1975 to 1979, "exports of goods and services" in the current account of the balance of payments equaled 46 percent of Panama's national income, but exports of agricultural, manufacturing, and mining products (including petroleum) were a bare 10 percent.

Table 27 shows the distribution of current account foreign exchange inflows for the 1960s and 1970s. The importance of commodity exports increased in the early 1960s, but contributed well less than half of these inflows. Until the mid-1970s, the majority of foreign exchange came from "invisibles," such as insurance, transport earnings, and commer-

TABLE 27
Composition of Panama's Current Account
Foreign Exchange Inflow

Years	Current Account Foreign Exchange Inflow*	Commodities	"Invisibles" Total	"Invisibles" Capital Flows	"Invisibles" Other
1960–1964	$ 170	34%	66%	2%	64%
1965–1969	296	38	62	2	60
1970–1974	534	30	70	8	62
1975–1980	1836	18	82	45	37

*Millions of US dollars, annual average.
Sources: SIECA 1973 and 1981.

cial fees and services (the "other" category). In recent years, these items have taken second place to short-term capital flows, reflecting the boom in multinational banking. Panama's extremely liberal banking laws have made it attractive for financial institutions to hold money in Panama where no questions are asked and depositors can escape taxation, exchange controls, and other restrictions normal to both developed and underdeveloped countries. The unique character of Panama's external sector gives the country two paradoxical distinctions in Latin America: it is the country with the largest ratio of foreign exchange inflow to national income and also the country that exports the smallest proportion of its national production.

The consequence of this unlikely combination is that the Panamanian economy derives fewer benefits from its external sector than any economy in the region, perhaps in the hemisphere. In the rest of the region increased foreign exchange earnings derive from increased production, which requires more employment and investment in export production, and also stimulates activities linked to exports through the demand for local inputs. While Central America's exports have become less employment-generating over time, the increased production of cotton, for example, does require more laborers, clearing of land, fertilizers, and so on. Such is not the case for over 80 percent of Panama's foreign exchange inflow. The service activities may require more employment when they expand, but have few linkages to the rest of the economy. The employment itself is largely white-collar, so it has little impact on the problem of unemployment among unskilled workers, a major social malady in urban Panama. And the inflow of short-term capital has virtually no impact whatsoever on employment or investment. Once the buildings are constructed for the banks and the office equipment put in place, a given number of employees can move a virtually limitless amount of money, since little more than ledger entries are involved.

Simultaneous with the growth of externally oriented services and capital inflow, commodity exports have done poorly. From 1960 to 1971, banana exports in tons grew at 9 percent a year, and subsequently achieved the 1971 level in only one year, 1978. Exports of shrimp also stagnated in the 1970s, averaging the level of the previous decade despite a buoyant world demand that caused prices to triple from the late 1960s to the late 1970s. Among Panama's primary product exports only sugar increased substantially. Panama was the only country in the region which actually exported less tonnage of products in the 1970s than in the 1960s, though rising prices increased the money value of commodity exports.

Perhaps more important than the economic effects of the nature of Panama's unique external sector are the political effects. Success in providing services to foreign firms and attracting short-term capital depends upon maintaining what is usually called a "favorable investment climate." Maintaining an agreeable climate for money capital is quite restrictive for host governments. As a rule, productive investors cannot afford to be as fickle as purely financial investors. A factory or plantation is an illiquid asset, not easily converted to money and expatriated. However, the slightest hint of regulation or restricting the privileges of capital could prompt a massive flight of short-term capital from Panama to more compliant countries, such as the Cayman Islands. It may be that the growth of multinational banking in Panama has created constraints on political sovereignty as limiting as those when the country was a virtual protectorate of North America.

Summary

We have argued that production for export has been the dynamic factor in the economies of Central America. Not only are these economies small and open, but their extraterritorial trade has determined their pattern of development. One can go beyond this and conclude that within total trade that part which is extraregional has determined the tempo of growth. Despite the rapid expansion of CACM trade in manufactures, five primary products accounted for over 60 percent of Central America's export earnings in the 1970s. Country-by-country some diversification in primary products has occurred in the last twenty years, so each is less dependent on one or two commodities. However, for the region as a whole, the importance of coffee, cotton, bananas, beef, and sugar has declined very little in extraregional trade. These products constituted about 85 percent of that trade in the 1960s and 82 percent in the 1970s. Going along with this is the continued concentration of Central American exports with one trading partner. The share of total exports to the United States has remained at about a third even with the growth of the CACM. And the growth of production for the regional market is fraught with problems, problems even more serious than those associated with production for the world market (see Chapters 6 and 8).

The exports of the Central American countries have expanded rapidly, particularly in the 1960s, but the region as a whole has imported more than it exported in most years, and all of the countries except El Salvador had trade deficits for the 1970s.[11] The deficits for the 1970s result in part from the rise in petroleum prices, but have increased in the 1980s (see Chapter 8).

For Central America as a whole, changes in export and import prices have had a negative effect on the regional balance of payments. Over the last twenty years most of this terms of trade effect has been visited upon Costa Rica and Guatemala, with the other three countries actually gaining from relative price movements. Much more serious for the balance of payments than price effects has been the impact of what are called "invisibles." It has been a rare year in which any one of the Central American countries has enjoyed a positive balance on its external current account. This is in great part because the Central American countries have been capital exporters, with a net profit remittance of almost $3 billion for 1960–1979. Net direct investment flows into the region have not come close to balancing the outflow.

NOTES

[1] See Dore and Weeks.

[2] A detailed presentation of the negotiations leading up to the formation of the CACM and the disputes that resulted in its collapse is found in Delgado (1981).

[3] Insightful on this point is Wheelock (1975). Jaime Wheelock Román has been the cabinet minister responsible for the agricultural sector after the fall of Somoza.

[4] The collapse of the CACM is considered in Chapter 8.

[5] That is, commodity exports have been divided by the index of export prices and commodity imports by the index of import prices.

[6] Also using 1970 import and export prices.

[7] Since one country's intraregional exports are the intraregional imports of another, for any year the trade balances should sum to zero. For reasons which are unclear, this is not always the case with the SIECA data for the 1960s, used in Table 24.

[8] The problems of Central America's manufactured exports are considered in Chapter 6 and the decline of the CACM in Chaper 8.

[9] One must keep in mind that the data for gross investment may not be very accurate, so the differences in the percentages may be more apparent than real.

[10] The canal runs from the Caribbean to the Pacific in a southeasterly direction, not east-to-west as one might expect.

[11] Nicaragua ran a small surplus for the decade only because of a massive surplus in 1979 as a result of the war there. See Chapter 7.

REFERENCES

Cline, W. R. and E. Delgado. 1978. *Economic Integration in Central America*. Washington: The Brookings Institution.

Delgado, E. 1981. *Evolución del Mercado Común Centroamericano y Desarrollo Equilibrado*. Costa Rica: EDUCA/SIECA.

Lizano, E. and L. N. Willmore. 1975. "La Integración Económica de Centroamerica y el Informe de Rosenthal." *El Trimestre Economico* 42:164. Mexico.

Secretaría Permanente del Tratado General de Integración Económica Centroamericana (SIECA). 1973. *Series Estadísticas Seleccionadas de Centroamérica y Panamá*. Guatemala: SIECA.

———— 1980. *Series Estadísticas Seleccionadas de Centroamérica y Panamá*. Guatemala: SIECA.

———— 1981. *VII Compendio Estadístico Centroamericano*. Guatemala: SIECA.

Siri, G. and L. R. Domínguez. 1981. "Central American Accommodation to External Disruptions," in *World Inflation and the Developing Countries*, edited by W. R. Cline, et al. Washington: The Brookings Institution.

Villagran Kramer, Francisco. 1967. *Integración Económica Centroamericana*. Guatemala: Universidad San Carlos de Guatemala.

Weeks, John and Elizabeth Dore. 1979. "International Exchange and the Causes of Backwardness." *Latin American Perspectives* 6:2 (Spring).

Wheelock Román, Jaime. 1975. *Imperialismo y Dictadura: Crísis de una Formación Social*. Mexico: Siglo Ventiuno.

Woodward, Ralph Lee, Jr. 1976. *Central America: A Nation Divided*. New York: Oxford University Press.

World Bank. 1978. *Memorandum on Recent Economic Developments and Prospects of Nicaragua*. Washington: World Bank.

5

Development of Agriculture in Central America

Pattern of Agricultural Production

Despite the relatively small size of the Central American region, the nature of the terrain and climate varies considerably, though this does not allow for the great variety of cultivation as in, say, Peru or Bolivia. All of the countries except El Salvador have both an intensively settled Pacific region which is alternatively inundated by heavy rains and bleached by a long dry season, and an extensive, sparsely populated Atlantic side of swampy rain forest. El Salvador and Nicaragua are stereotypically tropical, with mountain regions of modest altitude and with no high valleys or plateaus conducive to temperate-climate agriculture. In Honduras, Costa Rica, and Guatemala, the mountains rise higher or there are broad highlands (as around San José) which allow for a diversification of agriculture not possible in El Salvador and Nicaragua. As a result of the high valleys and plateaus, it is possible to grow products such as apples and strawberries, which are exotic in the tropics.

Central America is a region of extensive unutilized land. Two-thirds of Central America was not under cultivation in the late 1960s, but there was considerable variation among countries. As to be expected, agricultural utilization of land was greatest in El Salvador, 75 percent. None of the other four countries approach this degree of land use, and Costa Rica is the only other country in which at least half of the surface area was in agriculture. The population density of the countries is not a guide to intensity of land use, except in the extreme case of El Salvador. Nicaragua is the least densely populated country in the region, with less than a third the density of Guatemala, yet the intensity of land use was almost the same in both countries. This reflects large landholdings in Nicaragua devoted to export crops requiring largely seasonal labor. The same pattern holds for Costa Rica, which has a population density two-

TABLE 28
Area in Food Crops, Export Crops, Grazing, and Fallow in
Central America, 1970[1]
(Percentages)

Land use	Costa Rica	El Salvador	Guatemala	Honduras	Nicaragua	Central America
Food Crops[2]	12.3%	16.3%	25.3%	16.5%	10.1%	16.2%
Export Crops[3]	5.9	19.4	10.9	9.7	7.8	9.9
Grazing	43.0	42.5	29.8	50.4	51.8	43.2
Idle	38.1	19.6	32.9	21.9	29.6	29.6
Other	0.7	2.2	1.1	1.5	0.7	1.1
Total Land in Farms (hectares, 000's)	2742	1646	3752	2462	3939	14542

[1]The table uses the average harvested area for food crops and export crops for 1969–1971.
[2]Corn, beans, rice, potatoes, wheat, yuca, tomatoes, onions, plantain and citrus fruits.
[3]Coffee, cotton, sugar, bananas, and sorghum.
Source: SIECA 1972 and 1981.

thirds of Guatemala's but a much higher degree of land use. The population of Costa Rica is concentrated on the coffee-growing plateau around San José, but large cattle ranches elsewhere result in a high degree of land use while generating very little permanent employment.

In few areas of the world is such a large proportion of agricultural land devoted to products which the local population does not consume or consumes only to a limited degree. In the early 1970s a detailed study of the agricultural sector in Central America was carried out by the Food and Agricultural Organization (FAO) of the United Nations (SIECA 1972). The study found that 39 percent of the cultivated land was in use for export production in this period, with El Salvador and Nicaragua having the highest proportions.[1] If one adds idle arable land and grazing land to cultivated areas, the share of food crops drops considerably, as Table 28 shows. For Central America, only 16 percent of total land held by agricultural production units was used for food crops in 1970, and this regional average was exceeded only in Guatemala. Compared to this, over 50 percent of land was applied to export crops or grazing. Quite striking is the case of El Salvador. This tiny country has the greatest population density in the region, but also the highest proportion of land in export crops and grazing, 62 percent, higher even than sparsely populated Honduras and Nicaragua. The extreme land-hunger of the Salvadoran peasantry is eloquently explained by the fact that the use of land for cattle raising is proportionally the same in El Salvador and Costa Rica, though population density is almost six times greater in the former country.[2] Table 28 sustains our earlier assertion that in Central America land is used for export production to an extraordinary degree.

It is instructive to consider trends in land use, which we do in Table 29. Here land use for the five major export crops is compared to that for the three staple food crops—corn, rice, and beans. The data in Table 29, based on annual surveys, shows a substantial decline in the area planted in basic food crops compared to export crops, from 60 percent of the total in the second half of the 1960s to 52 percent in the second half of the 1970s. For Central America as a whole and for three of the five countries, the absolute area reported in food crops declined from the first period to the last. Increases in harvested area for food crops occurred in El Salvador and Honduras, though small in both cases, 10 percent and 5 percent, respectively over the period of a decade. This indicates that the major thrust of agricultural development in all of the countries of Central America in recent years has been in export crops, not basic food crops. For the most part, this has implied the development of large-scale agriculture at the expense of peasant agriculture, since the two most important basic food crops, beans and corn, are almost exclusively peasant-produced. The growth of export crops has been at the expense of food crops in several ways. First, state resources to open new land for cultivation have been spent for export crops. Along with this, there is evidence that peasants have been expelled from their lands during the last 20 years and food crops replaced by export crops, particularly in Nicaragua (FIDA 1980).

Land use is shown in another way in Table 30. Here the annual average production of eight crops is measured for the 1960s and 1970s, and the percentage increase calculated.[3] At the bottom of the table are given inter-decade rates of population growth. The increases for the two staples of the Central American diet—beans and corn—were less than the rate of population growth for the region as a whole. The production of beans and corn increased less than the population in four of the five countries, with El Salvador the exception for both products. The basic food crop that increased more than population was rice, which throughout the region is a plantation product. On the other hand, the production of all export crops (and sorghum, primarily for animal feed) increased considerably faster than population. We can conclude that over the last twenty years the Central American economies have become less self-sufficient in basic foods and have favored large-scale over peasant agriculture.

Given the information in Table 30, it comes as no surprise that imports of corn and beans into the region have increased over the last decade. In Table 31 we measure net imports as a portion of total consumption,[4] with a positive percentage indicating net imports and a negative number net exports. The percentages for each country include exports and imports with the other countries of the region, but the percentages for Central America refer to net commerce with the rest of

TABLE 29
Harvested Area of Basic Food Crops and Major Export Crops in Central America
(areas in 000s of hectares)

Country	1965–1970			1970–1975			1975–1979		
	Total Area	Basic Foods	Export Crops	Total Area	Basic Foods	Export Crops	Total Area	Basic Foods	Export Crops
Costa Rica	338	56.8%	43.2%	285	47.4%	52.6%	320	48.4%	51.6%
El Salvador	568	43.7	56.3	630	41.3	58.7	670	39.7	60.3
Guatemala[1]	1242	67.3	32.7	1123	61.9	38.1	1156	57.6	42.4
Honduras	573	63.9	36.1	585	65.5	34.5	627	61.1	38.9
Nicaragua	646	52.8	47.2	597	49.1	50.9	669	48.9	51.1
Central America	3367	59.7	40.3	3220	54.8	45.2	3442	52.2	47.8

Basic foods: corn, rice, and beans.
Export crops: coffee, cotton, sugar, bananas, and sorghum.
[1] Last period 1975–1977
Sources: SIECA, 1972, 1977, and 1981.

TABLE 30
Percentage Change in Production of Major
Food and Export Crops, Annual Averages
1960s to 1970s
(1960–1969 compared to 1970–1979)

Basic Foods	Costa Rica	El Salvador	Guatemala[1]	Honduras	Nicaragua[2]	Central America
Corn	1.0%	77.8%	24.8%	14.5%	17.4%	28.9%
Beans	−31.3	105.6	16.0	10.6	−2.7	14.9
Rice	90.2	32.0	60.6	108.4	60.6	72.3
Export Crops						
Sorghum	152.1	53.4	97.0	17.6	14.5	47.1
Sugar	64.2	105.6	105.8	78.3	93.8	91.9
Cotton	−59.4	27.6	66.7	−33.8	60.9	48.9
Bananas	142.3	—[3]	98.4	44.5	822.1	84.9
Coffee	27.4	19.8	38.0	155.0	54.1	38.0
Population Growth	25%	30%	32%	35%	34%	31%

[1] Through crop year 1977/1978.
[2] Last crop year of decade omitted because of effects of war.
[3] El Salvador has negligible banana production.
Source: SIECA 1972 and 1981.

the world. In the second half of the 1960s, Central America as a whole was almost self-sufficient in both corn and beans, but became a net importer of both between 1970 and 1974. The case of Honduras is particularly striking. In the first period in Table 31, Honduras had net exports of corn equal to 12 percent of domestic consumption. Between 1970 and 1974, this fell to 2 percent, then changed to net imports of 4 percent between 1975 and 1977. The only country to import smaller amounts of corn and beans throughout the 1970s compared to 1965 to 1969 was El Salvador, as one would expect from Table 30. The region did achieve self-sufficiency in rice, switching from being a net importer to a net exporter, though only marginally.

Despite the increase in imports of beans and corn in the 1970s, estimated consumption of these products has risen considerably slower than population growth. In part A of Table 32 we give the change in apparent consumption from the 1960s to the 1970s, and in part B we adjust these for population growth. The base of our index is the average for the 1960s (= 100). Despite the fact that income per capita rose in all of the Central American countries from the 1960s to the 1970s, consumption per capita of beans and corn fell in four of the five countries, and increased at miniscule rates in the fifth (El Salvador). Costa Rica's situation differs from the others, for rice is the most important of the three products there, and its consumption rose per capita by 35 percent, about the same as per capita income. But in the other four countries beans and corn are the staples and apparently the masses of the population ate less of them in Guatemala, Honduras, and Nicaragua in the 1970s than in the 1960s.

It is possible that the per capita declines in the consumption of corn and beans reflect what economists call "inferior goods"; i.e., that rising incomes of the masses prompted a switch to more preferred (and more expensive) alternatives, such as rice. This argument could not be made in the case of Nicaragua (per capita rice consumption fell by 25 percent),

TABLE 31
Net Imports of Basic Foods as a Percentage
of Total Consumption

A. Corn

	Costa Rica	El Salvador	Guatemala	Honduras	Nicaragua	Central America
1965–1969	8.8%	12.9%	1.4%	−12.2%	1.4%	1.2%
1970–1974	32.4	−0.2	3.7	−2.0	7.8	3.7
1975–1977	4.8	3.8	3.9	3.9	4.2	3.9

B. Beans

	Costa Rica	El Salvador	Guatemala	Honduras	Nicaragua	Central America
1965–1969	31.9%	40.1%	1.9%	−50.4%	−5.6%	0.1%
1970–1974	65.8	8.5	1.6	−19.1	−8.3	7.9
1975–1977	2.2	10.4	6.6	−5.1	−2.3	2.4

C. Rice

	Costa Rica	El Salvador	Guatemala	Honduras	Nicaragua	Central America
1965–1969	3.9%	−34.7%	1.3%	22.3%	11.1%	3.5%
1970–1974	2.2	4.1	5.4	11.7	−11.4	−0.8
1975–1977	−9.8	3.9	15.7	16.3	−3.5	−1.8

Source: SIECA 1981.

TABLE 32
Indicators of the Change in Consumption of Basic Foods, 1960s and 1970s
A. Percentage Change in Consumption, 1960s to 1970s[1]

Product	Costa Rica	El Salvador	Guatemala	Honduras	Nicaragua	Central America
Corn	1.8%	44.4%	1.8%	21.6%	2.7%	14.3%
Beans	−24.7	37.5	4.6	13.3	−3.5	5.5
Rice	68.9	39.9	42.3	57.8	2.7	41.1

B. Indices of Per Capita Consumption for 1970s[1] (1960s = 100)

Product	Costa Rica	El Salvador	Guatemala	Honduras	Nicaragua	Central America
Corn	81	111	77	90	77	87
Beans	60	105	79	84	72	81
Rice	135	107	108	117	75	108
Weighted by calories[2]	111	107	80	95	76	89

[1] The average for 1964–66 is compared to the average for 1974–76.
[2] The indices are combined by using the unit caloric content of each and the weight of each in apparent consumption in each country.
Source: SIECA 1972, 1977, and 1981.

but consumption of rice did rise in Guatemala and Honduras. Precisely because rice is a relative luxury, it is not valid to assume that its increased consumption was equal among classes. In Guatemala, for example, one can assume that for the poor, corn consumption fell per capita by a bit less than 23 percent and rice consumption rose by less than 8 percent. But even assuming the increases were the same for the entire population, rice consumption did not counterbalance the decline in beans and corn. In the last row of Table 32B we have aggregated the three foods on the basis of their caloric content and relative importance in consumption in each country. This aggregation shows that the per capita calories obtained from the three products together declined in Nicaragua, Guatemala, and Honduras and experienced small increases in El Salvador and Costa Rica (about 1 percent per year for both countries).

It is possible that the declines in the consumption of corn, rice, and beans shown in the table were offset by increases in other foods not included in the table. This is not very probable, however. In Honduras, for example, a type of sorghum is a food staple, but its production grew slower than the population from the 1960s to the 1970s. Limited production data on potatoes, wheat (grown in Guatemala), yuca, and plantain do not indicate rates of increase sufficient to offset the decline in caloric consumption in Table 32B. The production of beef increased dramatically between the decades, but data show that the expansion was for export, not the domestic markets in Central America. Until other data are forthcoming, it appears that the real consumption of the poor was no greater in the 1970s than the 1960s in three of the five countries of Central America and probably lower; in the other two countries consumption of the poor probably rose slightly.

The orientation of agricultural development in Central America since the end of the Second World War has been toward large-scale agribusiness, which has meant production for export. Any successful development strategy for the countries of the region would have to have this emphasis to a degree, regardless of the political and ideological motivations of the governments involved. For the foreseeable future, the demand for manufactures in Central America must be met in part by imports, particularly the demand for capital equipment. These imports must be paid for by exports, and there is little prospect for significant manufactured exports (see Chapter 6). Thus, agroexports will necessarily play a vital role in any rational development strategy. However, the emphasis upon large-scale production for export has not been implemented rationally, but in a way such that production for export has been at the expense of and perhaps caused the absolute decline of the peasant sector. The consequence of this has been declining self-sufficiency in food production, stagnation in the level of mass consumption of basic staples, and increased population pressure on the land.

Productivity and Land Use

As we noted earlier, the growth of agriculture in Central America, while not impressive, has been faster than population growth. However, this growth has been uneven with regard to specific products. The production of the major food staples, corn and beans, has grown slower than the population, requiring increased net imports. Meanwhile, the production of export crops has grown considerably faster than the population. The increase in production of any crop is by definition the result of an increase in yields per unit of land (for whatever reason) and/or an increase in area planted. In Table 33 we consider changes in the former, from the 1960s to the 1970s.

TABLE 33
Percentage Change in Physical Output per Hectare
of Major Crops, 1965/67 to 1975/77

Crop	Costa Rica	El Salvador	Guatemala	Honduras	Nicaragua	Central America
Basic Foods[1]	68.4%	40.8%	32.5%	−3.0%	−0.6%	19.7%
Corn	63.8	43.9	36.3	−3.4	3.5	21.5
Beans	108.0	9.4	20.6	−1.4	−25.8	9.7
Rice	49.0	69.4	−30.8	−2.8	14.1	26.6
Export Crops[1]	30.8	19.1	33.0	29.6	29.5	24.0
Sorghum	4.5	22.0	108.1	8.3	28.9	33.1
Sugar	58.8	54.9	9.6	25.9	19.3	31.4
Cotton	−60.1	22.3	37.3	−5.1	−6.8	10.9
Bananas	12.7	—	40.0	120.0	187.1	66.9
Coffee	29.1	7.6	19.7	23.1	87.9	21.3

[1]Weighted by area planted.
Sources: SIECA 1981.

Over this ten year period, the yields for export crops generally rose faster than for food crops for Central America as a whole. With the exception of cotton, all of the export crops experienced increases in yields greater than or equal to the increases for corn and beans. To provide a summary measure for the two types of crops, export and food, we have weighted the yield increases by the average area planted for each crop from 1965 to 1977. This measure can be interpreted as the yield increase for a composite hectare of export crops or food crops. The composite yield increase for export crops in the region was 24 percent (2.2 percent per year compounded), and was virtually the same for all of the countries except El Salvador, whose composite yield is drawn down by the virtual stagnation of coffee output per hectare. Only for bananas was the increase in the productivity of land impressive, with all other export yields increasing at below 3 percent a year. A comparison of Tables 30 and 33 shows that production increased considerably faster than yields, verifying that more land was used for export crops.

While the yield increases for export crops are quite similar among the countries, there is tremendous variation for food crops. In part this may reflect the greater accuracy of the data for the former, but the pattern of the variation by country suggests that the data are roughly indicative of trends. In Costa Rica—the land of the most educated and prosperous peasantry—yields for food crops rose fastest, twice the rate at which population grew, and we know that apparent per capita consumption of rice, at least, increased from the 1960s to the 1970s. Composite yields for food crops also appear to have increased at or above the rate of population growth in Guatemala and El Salvador. However, in Honduras and Nicaragua, composite yields seem actually to have declined. This, again, is consistent with the pattern of agricultural development in these two countries, with credit and technical assistance directed to large-scale agriculture. This is not to say that in El Salvador or Guatemala the peasantry enjoyed government encouragement during the 1960s and 1970s. However, the *minifundista* character of landholding in these two countries presented (and presents) obstacles to the rapid development of large-scale agriculture. The stagnation of food crop yields in Honduras and Nicaragua is consistent with a peasantry in the process of being dispossessed from the land. This interpretation is supported by the fact that the only one of the three food crops with significantly increased yields in Honduras or Nicaragua was rice, in the latter country, where it is produced primarily on large plantations.

The productivity of land in Central America, as elsewhere, is closely related to the social relations by which the working of land is organized, and this, in turn, is related to the size of holding. For the underdeveloped world, it is common to make the generalization that output per unit of land tends to be higher on small peasant plots and output per worker higher on large plots. The basis for this generalization is the presumption that the small holder works his land more intensively, while on large holdings more machinery and modern inputs are used, so that output per unit of land and output per unit of labor-time are inversely related. However, such is not the case in Central America. The FAO study conducted in 1970 found that output per hectare on farms larger than thirty-five hectares was more than double the yield for farms from four to thirty-five hectares, and over three times the yield for farms of less than four hectares. The FAO study covered eight crops grown on all three size categories of holdings, and except for coffee, output per unit of land was lowest for farms of less than four hectares and highest for the largest holdings. Since large holdings tend to be less labor-using than peasant plots, it is not surprising that output per man-year was highest on the former, except for coffee. For coffee, yields on all three categories of holdings were quite similar, though highest on the intermediate-sized farms.

We can account for the low yields on small plots in two ways. First, except in Costa Rica, the technique of production on *minifundia* is quite primitive in Central America. The small size of plots precludes use of machinery even if the peasant families could afford it. Further, the 1970 FAO study reveals no significant use of modern fertilizers or other production-enhancing inputs on small plots. Total purchased inputs accounted for only 2 percent of the value of output on the smallest size category of farms compared to 20 percent on the largest. In part, this reflects government policy throughout the region of directing technical extension work to large holdings and to a lesser extent to medium-sized ones. The much-publicized INVIERNO project of the U.S. Agency for International Development (USAID) in Nicaragua, for example, was consciously directed to medium-sized farmers. Second, it is probably the case that over the last thirty years, the *minifundista* has been pushed off the more fertile land onto marginal land, though governments are not inclined to collect the information to document this, nor to encourage others to do so. The expansion of cotton and sugar, particularly in Nicaragua, El Salvador, and Honduras, probably had this effect as well as increasing the amount of idle land. Given these two factors, it is not surprising that the FAO study estimated net income per hectare (value added) on the largest estates to be four times what was generated on plots of less than four hectares.

The only agricultural activity for which small-scale farms show a productivity advantage is grazing. In this case, output per hectare and per man-year decline with increased farm size. This is partly explained by the difference between dairy farming and cattle ranching. The former tends to be smaller scale and more land-intensive and labor-using than the latter. However, the small *ganadero* is relatively unimportant in terms of the total number of *minifundistas* in Central America.

Land Tenure and Concentration

The countries of Central America are complex societies, with both pre-capitalist and capitalist social relations characterizing production. Notwithstanding the industrialization and urbanization processes of the last two decades, the Central American countries are not predominantly wage-labor societies. The proportion of permanent wage earners with no links to the land is small in all of the countries, and "the land question" is of tremendous social and political importance. The struggle for land by the Central American peasantry has a long history, and following independence from Spain this struggle played a key note in the break-up of the Central American Federation.[5] The commercial development of agriculture has tended to generate a differentiation among the peasantry, between the landless and those with land, and between the holdings based on family labor and those based on hired labor. The latter differentiation is in part made possible by the process of dispossession which creates the landless peasant, who must work for the wealthier peasants or migrate to the cities.

The extent of this differentiation among the countries of Central

America varies, but Table 34 shows that in each country the process was well advanced by 1970. For Central America as a whole, over one-quarter of rural families were landless in 1970, a quite high proportion even by Latin American standards. In the development literature and particularly the reports of multilateral agencies, the problems of landlessness and *minifundia* are often attributed to population pressure.[6] The statistics in Table 34 indicate that landlessness in Central America is not

TABLE 34
Distribution of Rural Families and Agricultural Land by Size of Holding, 1970

A. Percentage Distribution of Rural Families

Size of Holding	Costa Rica	El Salvador	Guatemala	Honduras	Nicaragua	Central America
(Hectares)						
Landless	26.3%	26.1%	26.6%	31.4%	33.8%	28.1%
Less than .7	32.2	24.4	15.0	10.3	1.5	16.8
0.7–4	13.1	36.2	42.3	24.1	24.2	32.6
4–7	4.8	6.2	6.9	11.9	7.9	7.4
7–35	14.6	4.9	7.4	18.1	18.1	10.7
35–350	8.3	2.0	1.4	3.9	13.5	4.0
more than 350	0.7	0.2	0.4	0.3	1.0	0.4
Total	100%	100%	100%	100%	100%	100%
Landless or insufficient land	—	86.7	83.9	65.8	59.5	—

B. Percentage Distribution of Agricultural Land

Size of Holding	Costa Rica	El Salvador	Guatemala	Honduras	Nicaragua	Central America
(Hectares)						
Less than .7	0.3%	1.3%	1.0%	0.8%	—	0.6%
0.7–4	1.5	12.3	11.3	5.5	1.6	6.0
4–7	1.5	5.2	6.3	6.1	1.8	4.0
7–35	14.3	16.7	15.1	27.4	11.3	16.2
35–350	41.1	33.6	23.9	32.7	44.1	35.2
more than 350	41.3	30.9	42.4	27.5	41.2	38.0
	100%	100%	100%	100%	100%	100%
Con. Index	.79	.85	.81	.79	.69	.85

Note: — indicates less than 0.1%.
Source: INTAL 1973; and SIECA 1981.

explained by population pressure. The proportion of families without land is highest in the two least densely populated countries of the region, Nicaragua and Honduras. Indeed, it is the most sparsely populated country, Nicaragua, which has the highest proportion of landless families, 34 percent. Thus, the phenomenon of landlessness is greatest where land stretches most abundant.

The relatively high proportion of landlessness in Nicaragua and Honduras reflects the development of large-scale, commercial agriculture in the 1950s and 1960s. In the case of Nicaragua, the expansion was in cotton and cattle (and to a lesser extent sugar). From the late 1950s to the late 1960s, the land cultivated in cotton rose by over 100 percent in Nicaragua, and the area planted per producer also rose as production became more concentrated. Over the same period the land in sugar cane also doubled, though the total area involved was only a fifth that of cotton. Although there are no data on total grazing area over time, land devoted to this use must have increased dramatically from the 1950s to 1970, for the estimated number of cattle slaughtered in Nicaragua in 1960 was 133,400 and 310,000 in 1970. In Honduras, the expansion of grazing and plantation agriculture was not so dramatic, but still quite rapid. In the 1960s the production of beef doubled and the harvested areas of bananas increased by 50 percent (though it declined in the 1970s).

The growth of large-scale grazing and plantation agriculture goes far to explain the high proportion of landless families in Honduras and Nicaragua. And the other side of this coin is the relative lack of *minifundia* in these two countries. For Central America as a whole, approximately 17 percent of the families had some land but less than .7 hectares, and almost 50 percent of families had four hectares or less.[7] The corresponding proportions for Honduras and Nicaragua are much lower. We can characterize Nicaragua and Honduras as countries of impoverished landless laborerers, on the one hand, while El Salvador and Guatemala are countries of impoverished peasants. In both of the latter countries landlessness is of major importance, but the great majority of rural families fall into the *minifundia* range, cultivating less than four hectares of land: 61 percent for El Salvador and 57 percent for Guatemala. What is striking in both of these countries is the virtual absence of the "middle peasant"; i.e., the peasant with enough land to be self-sufficient.

The size ranges in Table 34 can be interpreted as analytical categories as well as numerical ones. For example, the "landless" category implies that a family must engage in wage labor. For families with land, ideal analytical categories would be a division of landholding families into four groups: (1) families whose landholding is insufficient to satisfy the basic necessities of life, implying at least part-time wage labor for some family members (the non-self-sufficient peasant); (2) families with sufficient land to satisfy the basic necessities using family labor alone (the self-sufficient peasant); (3) families with landholdings which require wage labor in addition to family labor (the "middle" or "yeoman" peasant); and (4) capitalist, large-scale production units (capitalist farm). These analytical categories correspond to the process of commercial differentiation of agriculture mentioned above.

The size categories in Table 34 do not precisely correspond to the analytical categories, because they are arbitrary and because differences in the fertility and use of land affect the income which can be received from working a given area and the labor necessary to work it. For example, several hectares of land in high grade coffee can support a family in Central America at an adequate standard of living. Further, the labor requirement for coffee production is quite high (exceeded only by tobacco), so a small coffee *finca* might require hired labor (particularly at harvest time), while the same land applied to sorghum would be inadequate to occupy all family members (and even less adequate if the land is pastoral).[8]

With this qualification in mind, we can roughly match our analytical categories with the size of holdings in Table 34. Certainly the first size range is insufficient to provide either adequate income or employment for a family. Families in this category are part-time wage laborers. The same is probably true of the .7–4 hectares range, particularly in Nicaragua where land use is not intensive. On the plateau around San José, Costa Rica, a landholding approaching four hectares may be adequate to sustain a peasant family, since the coffee yield per hectare in that area is the highest in the region. This would, however, presume maximum yields, a rather strong assumption. One can reasonably define farms with less than four hectares as too small for self-sufficiency, and the families occupying such plots must seek wage labor to supplement their incomes. Leaving Costa Rica aside, this definition implies that for the four other Central American countries, from 87 percent (El Salvador) to 60 percent (Nicaragua) of the agricultural families have insufficient land to sustain themselves (landless or *minifundistas*). This insufficiency may take two forms. If there are opportunities, members of these families supplement farm income with wage employment. This wage employment may involve migration within a country or the region. Over the last twenty years, examples of the latter have been the immigration of Salvadorans and Hondurans to Nicaragua for the cotton harvests, and Nicaraguans to the banana plantations of Costa Rica (though this has been a longer-term migration). On the other hand, there is no reason to assume that wage employment has been sufficient historically, and many of the land-hungry families obviously must accept the wretched poverty to which their small holdings condemn them.

The Central American equivalent of the self-sufficient "middle" peasant would include those families working from four to thirty-five hectares. Depending upon the land use, this size range can require wage labor, primarily at harvest time. In El Salvador and Guatemala there is a striking absence of farms in this size range, only 11 percent and 14 percent of family holdings, respectively. These two countries are land-lord-dominated societies, with relatively little development of a "yeoman" peasantry. If we combine parts A and B of Table 34, we see that in El Salvador and Guatemala approximately 2 percent of agricultural families hold about 65 percent of the land in farms, striking evidence of the power base of the landed aristocracy.

In Honduras and Nicaragua the proportion of families working from 4 to 35 hectares is quite high, but this may be misleading. In both countries agricultural production is land-extensive compared to the rest of Central America, so the size of holding which is sufficient to support a family is correspondingly larger. This is particularly the case for small-scale grazing, a peasant activity quite important in both countries. The proportion of peasant families in Honduras and Nicaragua with self-sufficient on-farm income is probably less than the portion working holdings from 4 to 35 hectares. However, during the last twenty years a class of medium-sized capitalist farmers and ranchers developed in Nicaragua, a class virtually absent elsewhere in Central America except for Costa Rica. The range of 35 to 350 hectares is indicative of the importance of this class. In Nicaragua this group developed into a strong source of opposition to the Somoza dynasty. The Somoza family virtually monopolized the slaughtering of beef for export and relegated the medium-sized ranchers to the less profitable domestic market. The marketing system for the other export crops also favored large landholders (namely the Somoza family itself), and the medium-sized agricultural producer generally welcomed the fall of the dictator in 1979.

The second part of Table 34 shows a concentration of landholding that would probably be unique in the hemisphere if one could get strictly comparable data.[9] The country with the greatest land hunger is probably El Salvador, where 87 percent of the rural families have only 19 percent of the land, though Guatemala is not far behind with 84 percent and 19 percent, respectively. On the other hand, in these two countries (and in Costa Rica) at least 74 percent of the families had *some* land to work, while less than 70 percent had land in Honduras and Nicaragua. Because of the nature of the data in Table 34, it is not possible to attribute a percentage of the land to the wealthiest 5 percent or 1 percent of landowners. But if we could, the dubious distinction for highest concentration by such a measure would probably go to El Salvador.

Available evidence for Honduras and Guatemala indicates that the

TABLE 35
Distribution of Families by Size of Holding in Honduras, 1952 and 1974

Size of Holding (Hectares)	Distribution of Families 1952	1974
Less than 1	9.9%	17.3%
1–10	65.1	61.1
11–20	11.9	9.8
21–50	8.8	7.8
51–100	2.5	2.3
101–1000	1.7	1.6
more than 1000	0.1	0.1
	100%	100%

Source: CEPAL 1981a.

TABLE 36
Distribution of Families by Size of Holding in Guatemala, 1950, 1964, and 1979

Size of Holding (Manzanas)	Distribution of Families 1950	1964	1979
Less than 1	21.3%	20.4%	41.1%
1–2	26.3	23.6	19.4
2–5	28.6	30.9	20.8
5–10	12.2	12.5	8.4
10–32	7.7	8.9	6.6
32–64	1.8	1.6	1.5
64 and more	2.1	2.1	2.2
Total	100%	100%	100%
Index of Average Size			
Less than 1	100	100	63
Less than 2	100	94	63
Less than 5	100	101	71
All	100	78	65

Source: CEPAL 1981b.

Note: The rather odd last three size categories result from the use in the surveys of the archaic measure *cabelleria*, which in Guatemala is about 64 *manzanas* or 43 hectares (which differs from the unit of measure of the same name in Cuba and Puerto Rico).

concentration of land ownership was considerably greater in the 1970s than the 1950s. Table 35 gives the distribution of families by size of farm for Honduras in 1952 and 1974 and shows a process of marginalization of the peasantry.[10] In 1952, 10 percent of families with land worked less than one hectare, and by 1974 this had risen to 17 percent. Since one hectare is insufficient to support a family, the increase implies a growth in the proportion of families which would find it necessary to seek off-farm employment during the year. Further, the average size of holding for the less-than-one hectare category declined by over 5 percent, and if we consider all families with holdings up to ten hectares (the first two categories together), average farm size declined by 17 percent. The number of families holding land increased at about 1.5 percent a year between the two surveys, while the rural population was increasing at about 2.5 percent. This necessarily meant either more people per farm family (increased pressure on the land) or increased landlessness from the 1950s to the 1970s.

The process of marginalization of the peasantry which we observe in Honduras has been even more rapid in Guatemala. In its 1978 country study of Guatemala, the World Bank mission team commented that the majority of the peasantry lived on plots of land too small to satisfy their basic needs, and Table 36 shows that this problem dramatically intensified in the 1970s. The distribution of land by size of holding was more or less constant from 1950 to 1964, with even a slight reduction in the proportion of families on the smallest plots. In 1950, 48 percent of the families had holdings of less than two *manzanas*, while this percentage fell to 44 percent in 1964. The last four rows of the table show that the average size of holdings smaller than five *manzanas* remained constant from 1950 to 1964, though the average for all holdings fell by 22 percent; i.e., the distribution of land became less concentrated. The slight improvement in land distribution can be attributed to the moderate land reform of the early 1950s, all of which was not reversed by the right-wing dictatorships which followed Arbenz. However, since 1964, a process of the marginalization of the peasantry has occurred which goes far to explain the seething rebellion in the Guatemalan countryside. In 1964, 20 percent of agricultural families had less than one *manzana* (.7 hectares) of land, and in 1979, this proportion had risen to 41 percent. In part, of course, this can be explained by population growth, but the rural population was also growing from 1950 to 1964, when the proportion of families with less than one *manzana* declined slightly. In the second half of the 1960s and the 1970s, Guatemala experienced a government-fostered process of marginalization of the peasantry to a degree perhaps unique in Latin America in such a short period of time. This process was integral to the further development of large-scale agricul-

TABLE 37
Distribution of Families by Size of Holding in Costa Rica, 1963 and 1973

Size of Holding (hectares)	Distribution of Families[1]	
	1963	1973
1–10	49.3%	47.8%
10–199	46.9	47.8
200 and more	3.8	4.4
	100.0	100.0

[1]In the census of 1963 families working less than one hectare were not included. In 1973 this group was enumerated, accounting for 21 percernt of all families with land.
Source: BID 1977b, 13.

ture, concentrating land in large estates and increasing the size of the rural labor force to work those estates.[11]

The more extensive data for Honduras and Guatemala demonstrate a process of capitalist transformation of land tenure and land use, and, correspondingly, of the absolute and relative impoverishment of the peasantry. Further, the evidence demonstrates that the changes in land tenure and land distribution cannot be explained by population growth, but reflect changes in the social relations in agriculture, changes frequently affected by threat or use of violence.

In contrast to trends in Guatemala and Honduras, it appears that the concentration of land in Costa Rica has not increased in recent years and perhaps has declined slightly. Table 37 gives data from the agricultural censuses of 1963 and 1973, but in much less detail than the data for Guatemala and Honduras: the size categories are fewer and those families working less than a hectare are not included.[12] With this qualification in mind, we see that the proportion of families in the smallest size category declined slightly. After careful study of the Costa Rica data, an international mission to the country in the mid-1970s concluded that land ownership was "highly concentrated" and that the proportion of families with insufficient land to support themselves had increased since the mid-1960s.[13] Even if this is correct, the problem of families with insufficient land has worsened very little in Costa Rica compared to Honduras and Guatemala.

Most would consider Costa Rica the only democracy in Central America (and one of the few in Latin America), and it provides the most extensive social services perhaps of any country south of the Rio Grande. Therefore, it is common for observers to assume that it is also a relatively egalitarian society. This is largely myth, as the distribution of land shows.[14] The combination in Costa Rica of high land concentration on the one hand and economic modernization and political democracy on the other would seem to undermine the stress we have placed upon landed property as a barrier to progress in Central America. If Costa Rican society managed to develop into one of the most prosperous and humane in Latin America without reforming the ownership of land, how can one argue that land reform is central to economic and political development elsewhere in the region?

The answer to the question lies in the distinction between the pattern of land ownership and the system of land tenure. In Costa Rica ownership has been and is as highly concentrated as in the other countries of the region. But the high concentration of ownership in Costa Rica emerged later than in the other countries and with an entirely different set of land-tenure relations. The commercialization of agriculture in the other four countries occurred in the context of a coercive system of labor relations inherited from colonial times. As we saw in Chapter 1, the commercialization, first via coffee, resulted in the reinforcement of servile labor systems, and coercive legislation forcing peasants to work in virtual indentured servitude continued well after World War II. Thus, more important than the concentration of land in the other four countries have been the social relations between peasant and landlord and between landless laborer and landlord. These social relations excluded the landless and small holder from political participation as well as maintaining them in poverty.

But in Costa Rica land concentration arose differently and had different consequences. At the time of independence, the central mesa around San José was occupied by small-scale, independent peasants. The export boom of the mid-nineteenth century commercialized this area, which proved to be the most fertile for coffee-growing. The transformation of rural society into an exchange economy resulted in a rapid economic differentiation of the peasantry, and by the 1860s half of the rural families on the mesa were landless or part-time wage earners on larger coffee farms (Seligson 1980, 23). But this dispossession of the small holder from his land occurred almost entirely by economic means. The profitability of coffee resulted in a twenty-fold increase in land prices from 1820 to 1850, inducing small peasants to sell their farms. Once landless, these peasants enjoyed relatively high wages as coffee pickers due to the scarcity of agricultural labor. All land sales did not reflect free choice on the part of small holders, however. Fluctuations in world coffee prices generated mortgage foreclosures, further contributing to the growth of landlessness (Seligson 1980, 23 ff.).

Though the commercialization of peasant production led to concentration of land ownership in Costa Rica, it did not generate the cohesive labor control systems characteristic of the other countries of the region. Once landless, rural workers still had alternatives to working as coffee laborers. As mentioned in Chapter 1, Costa Rica had considerable unclaimed and arable land until quite recently. When coffee wages proved unattractive or working conditions too harsh, farm laborers could migrate to the Pacific lowlands, which they did in large numbers in this century. The concentration of land ownership generated a coffee elite which monopolized Costa Rican politics,[15] but because of the free wage labor system, the scarcity of rural labor, and the abundance of land, this coffee elite could not employ repressive labor control systems which made peasants elsewhere in the region virtual serfs.

El Salvador's rural relations of production represent the polar opposite of Costa Rica's and have yet to fully emerge from their pre-capitalist mold. To this day semi-feudal land tenure arrangements continue to characterize parts of the countryside. Table 38 gives an indication of the importance of these arrangements. The last two columns of the table show the proportion of farm families paying rent in money form. This proportion was only 19 percent in 1961, then rose to 28 percent in 1971, while the proportion of all renters, paying in cash or kind, remained the same.[16] The increase in families paying monetary rents reflects a decline in the category in the agricultural surveys called *en colonia*. This is a pre-

TABLE 38
Distribution of Families by Size of Holding
and Percentage Renting Land in El Salvador
1961 and 1971

Size of Holding (Hectares)	Distribution of Families		Percentage Renting	
	1961	1971	1961	1971
less than 1	47.2%	48.9%	22.8%	38.2%
1–2	21.4	21.8	25.2	31.1
2–5	16.6	16.0	15.0	14.2
5–10	6.2	5.8	4.7	3.6
10–19	3.7	3.4	2.4	2.4
20–50	3.0	2.6	1.8	2.5
50–100	1.0	0.8	2.7	2.2
100–1000	0.8	0.7	3.6	4.4
more than 1000	0.1	0.02	—	—
	100%	100.1%	19.2%	28.2%

Source: El Salvador 1978.

capitalist form of land tenure, in which the producer delivers a portion of the harvest as rent and may also be required to perform labor services for the landlord.[17] From 1961 to 1971, families in this category of tenancy fell from 25 percent of all families with land to just over 6 percent. The decline signals the long-delayed modernization of Salvadoran land tenure. The shift from rent-in-kind to monetary rent is basic to the capitalist development of agriculture, since it forces the peasant family to sell at least part of its production. This, in turn, makes the peasant subject to the fluctuations in prices, creating the possibility of indebtedness and loss of land through forced sale to creditors. But compared to Costa Rica, this is a relatively recent process in El Salvador. Further, it is within a semi-feudal context which never existed in Costa Rica.

In the last few years land tenure and land reform have become the most important issues in El Salvador for all political groups. In March 1980, the military government issued a land reform decree, which on the face of it appeared astoundingly radical in the Salvadoran context. Since 1980, the land reform program has generated bitter conflict among the legal Salvadoran political parties, as well as becoming a basic cornerstone of Washington's counterinsurgency program in the country. Many observers argue that successful implementation of the land reform is a necessary condition to prevent a military victory by the left.

Because the reform program is so politically sensitive, objective assessment of its potential impact, much less its actual impact, is difficult to obtain.[18] When announced, the land reform was to have three phases. The first phase involved the takeover of all properties over 500 hectares, which the government announced would include 376 estates or 15 percent of agricultural land. Phase II was to extend the reform to estates between 100 and 500 hectares, another 23 percent of agricultural land. The final phase involved no further land distribution, but would allow peasants who rent to purchase title to their land (the "land to the tiller" program). Soon after the announcement of the decree, *The New York Times* reported that the Salvadoran government had expropriated 60 percent of the country's best farm land, and that nearly one million peasants would benefit, or 36 percent of the rural population. (*The New York Times*, March 7, 1980 and September 28, 1980).

This estimate has proved to be grossly exaggerated. The Salvadoran government postponed, then canceled Phase II of the program, leaving only Phase I land for redistribution, which affected about 15 percent of the total farm land, not 60 percent. Further, this 15 percent of the country's agricultural land is not the most productive by any measure. Almost 70 percent of the land nationalized was in cattle grazing, low-productivity land requiring considerable investment to convert to cultivation. The most productive land in El Salvador is that applied to coffee, and only 9 percent of this land falls under the agrarian reform without Phase II. Whatever the quality of the land available for distribution, relatively few peasants seem to have received any. By official estimate, about 35,000 families had received land two years after the announcement of the reform, and an independent research center at the national university estimated the number considerably less.[19] Nor has the "land to the tiller" program been a great success. Effective opposition mounted by landowners has caused Phase III to be implemented at a snail's pace. After the elections of 1982, the ministry in charge of land reform passed into control of the far-right, and titles have actually been taken back in some cases. Leaders of peasant cooperatives have been executed by the army and para-military groups, and it has proved a dangerous venture for a peasant to apply for title to land (Wheaton 1982).

The Salvadoran experience with land reform demonstrates the difficulty of resolving the land problem in Central America. Important sectors of the Salvadoran elite, such as parts of the business community, have supported land reform. Since the late 1970s the US Embassy has lobbied and pressured for it, even at times made implementation a condition for economic aid from Washington.[20] Yet the landed aristocracy has proved extremely effective in blocking its advance. This has caused many in the region to doubt the possibility of a peaceful solution to the land question in Central America.

Agriculture in Panama

Panama is the most tropical of the countries north of Colombia. It has no highlands and receives the heaviest annual rainfall on the isthmus. The western Pacific lowlands are the most important agricultural area, though the central savanna—with its large haciendas—was more important in colonial times. Despite its small size, Panama has been characterized by unutilized areas, and it has been common practice for peasants to migrate to new lands. In the 1880s commercial banana cultivation began on previously unoccupied lands, as in the countries to the north. Along with the Canal Zone, bananas provided most of Panama's foreign exchange until the late 1960s. In the last decade, sugar has become a significant export, actually exceeding the value of bananas in 1980. Coffee exports are insignificant, so in Panama even more than in Central America, agricultural exports are produced on large-scale plantations.

Plantation agriculture along with the large cattle estates gave Panama an extremely unequal distribution of land. But unlike that of

Central America, land tenure has been reformed in Panama. While quite mild by comparison to the Peruvian land reform, for example, the results are certainly dramatic by Central American standards. In the early 1970s, Panama had about two million hectares in agricultural use. Between 1972 and 1977, the state purchased about seven hundred estates, which accounted for 25 percent of this two million. These purchases resulted in 10,000 new peasant holdings and the legalization of the squatting rights on another 11,000 farms. Together, the 21,000 new titles represented about 23 percent of all farms. It remains, however, that only 108 properties account for 16 percent of the land, and the 3.3 percent of properties over one hundred hectares encompass almost 50 percent of agricultural land (Inforpress 1982). High as this concentration is, it is modest compared to El Salvador and Guatemala, where 1 percent of agricultural families hold well over half of the land.

The land reform has not achieved a reduction in the number of landless families, which rose from 34,000 in the early 1970s to 55,000 at the end of the decade. Nor has it arrested the long-term decline of Panamanian agriculture. As Table 39 shows, the land planted in food crops fell by 22 percent from the 1960s to the 1970s, and of the export crops only sugar increased its area. The decline in area for corn and beans indicates an absolute decline in peasant production, since yields have not risen to compensate. Rice yields have risen, but slower than population growth. As in the case of the Central American countries, evidence indicates a decline in the per capita consumption of basic staples. In Panama rice is the major food in the mass diet, followed by corn

TABLE 39
Area Cultivated in Most Important Crops in Panama,
1960s and 1970s
(thousands of hectares)

		1965–1970	1975–1980	Percentage Change
Food Crops:	Corn	106	76	−28.3
	Beans	20	14	−27.6
	Rice	130	109	−16.2
Total		256	199	−22.3
Export Crops:	Coffee	26	25	−3.8
	Sugar	22	42	90.9
	Bananas	15	14	−6.7
Total		63	81	30.2

Source: SIECA 1981.

TABLE 40
Apparent Domestic Consumption of Major Food Crops
in Panama, 1960s and 1970s
(thousands of metric tons)

Product	1965–1970	1975–1980	Percentage Change
Corn	86	67	−22.1
Beans	8	7	−19.3[1]
Rice	154	167	8.4
Population Index	100	130	30.0

[1] Percentage calculated prior to rounding-off.
Source: SIECA 1981.

and beans. In Table 40, the "apparent consumption" of these is given (domestic production and imports, minus exports). In the case of beans and corn, total apparent consumption fell by large proportions. The apparent consumption of rice rose, but at a third of the rate of population growth.

The only agricultural activity—other than sugar production—to show a substantial increase from the 1960s to the 1970s was cattle grazing. In the second half of the 1960s, just over one million head of cattle were grazed, and this rose to 1.4 million ten years later. There are no data for area in grazing, but it can be presumed that this 40 percent increase in the size of herds required at least some increase in land use.

In Panama, as in the Central American countries, the expansion which has occurred in agriculture has been of a large-scale capitalist type (sugar and ranching), which generates a relatively low demand for labor compared to peasant agriculture. Its land reform notwithstanding, Panama fits the Central American pattern of declining self-sufficiency in food production and peasant production retreating before expanding agribusiness. Agribusiness has not boomed in Panama to the degree it has in Central America, however.

Agricultural Progress in Central America

The livelihoods of a majority of the Central American population derive from agriculture, and this is likely to remain the case for the foreseeable future. In consequence, reduction of poverty requires substantial and sustained progress in peasant agriculture. However, the prospects for a pattern of development which will improve the lot of the rural masses are not bright. Most observers, including the international agencies, conclude that major improvements in the quality of peasant life in Central America are dependent upon a redistribution of land, but such a measure would directly contradict the concentration of land implied by agribusiness.

Until the Nicaraguan revolution, little redistribution of land or challenge to landlord power occurred in Central America, notwithstanding the existence of government institutions nominally empowered to do so. The problem of landlessness and peasant demands for land has been a source of considerable political instability for the ruling elites of the region, and has not gone unnoticed by even the most reactionary governments. In place of land redistribution (or even rational use of idle land), the regimes have sought the safety-valve of colonialization schemes on vacant lands, though this was not possible in El Salvador. In Nicaragua the Somoza regime attempted to induce peasants onto the Atlantic side of the mountains, and in Guatemala schemes were started in the Petén and Franja Transversal del Norte areas. As elsewhere in the hemisphere (for example, Peru and Bolivia), colonization has been a failure. It is not without reason that vacant lands remain vacant. Little infrastructure has been provided in the new areas, and without considerable investments the lands on the Atlantic side of Central America are of low quality for peasant agriculture. The only "colonization" scheme of any importance and success (of a type) has been the informal migration of Salvadorans into Honduras, which sparked war in 1969.

Without fundamental reform of land tenure in Central America, the future for small and medium-scale agriculture is bleak. With the exception now of Nicaragua, the trend is agribusiness on a large scale and the transformation of the small holder into a landless laborer. The prospects for further success in this strategy vary among the countries, for the process requires the reduction of peasant agriculture in order to free land and labor for large-scale use. The dispossessing of the peasantry depends upon the strength of peasant institutions, and in no country has it been achieved without violence. In Nicaragua the Somoza dynasty made considerable progress in land concentration until its fall, a fall not unrelated to the opposition generated in the peasantry by the development of capitalist agriculture.

Further agricultural progress is particularly problematical in El Salvador and Guatemala. In both countries capitalist agriculture confronts a large peasantry and tiny, fragmented land holdings. During the 1970s, agribusiness expanded relatively rapidly in Guatemala, but as the 1978 World Bank country report points out, most of the land suitable for export crops was in use by the late 1970s. Further expansion of large-scale farming and ranching will have to be on less productive land (cattle in the lower Petén, for example) or by dispossessing the peasantry. The current peasant uprising in Guatemala is in great part the result of actual and threatened land seizures. A similar situation exists in El Salvador, but to a greater degree, for the country lacks the alternative of expansion onto marginal land. In both countries a reform of precapitalist land tenure would probably serve the cause of capitalist agriculture, just as taxation of large estates in England several centuries ago resulted in more rational use of land. However, in the context of Central America—particularly the Northern Triangle of El Salvador, Guatemala, and Honduras—the landed classes are so powerful that 300-year-old European reforms appear revolutionary; which, in a sense, they are.

A probable scenario for agriculture in El Salvador and Guatemala is further stagnation of food crop production and jerky expansion of export production. Given that in neither country is a peasant-oriented agricultural policy likely without radical political change, a continued forced dispossession of the peasantry from the land is necessary for further development of large-scale agriculture. Squeezing the peasant will undermine food crop production, with growth for these products slower even than in the 1970s. At the same time, the dispossession of the peasantry is a slow and uneven process and could intensify the already strong armed peasant movement in the countryside. In El Salvador food production grew faster than export production from the 1960s to the 1970s, but this is unlikely to continue. The civil war in that country will not end soon, and its effects on the agricultural sector are disastrous.

For the region as a whole, except for Nicaragua, one can anticipate a pattern common to capitalist development in the hemisphere, in which countries that are net food exporters become net food importers. As we noted, Central America as a whole was virtually self-sufficient in staples—corn and beans—in the 1960s, but net imports of both were about 4 percent of apparent consumption in the 1970s. This rise in net imports should increase with the push for large-scale agriculture, whether successful or unsuccessful.

For reasons of efficient land use, reduction of poverty, and basic human rights, agrarian reform which will reduce the concentration of land is fundamental in Central America. This conclusion is generally accepted and appears repeatedly in reports of multilateral institutions such as the World Bank, Inter-American Development Bank, and the agencies of the United Nations, none of which can be accused of radical perspectives. Also generally accepted is the conclusion that except in Nicaragua, none of the present regimes in Central America is likely to consider serious land reform of any variety.[21]

NOTES

[1] Except in Honduras, sorghum is not primarily consumed by humans, but used as animal feed. As a result, it has been included as an export crop, since it is an input to beef production.

[2] "Land is a scarce resource [in El Salvador] only for the small holders." Quoted by LaFeber (1983, 243), from Durham (1979).

[3] Annual averages are used instead of total production for the decades because there are no data for Guatemala for the last two crop years of the 1970s, and the 1979/80 crop in Nicaragua was disastrously low for most products due to the war there.

[4] The percentages are imports minus exports, divided by imports minus exports plus domestic production, or

$$\frac{M - X}{(M - X) + P}$$

The denominator is referred to as "apparent consumption."

[5] See Woodward (1975) and Chapter 1.

[6] This explanation is particularly popular in the case of densely populated El Salvador.

[7] The rather strange number, .7 hectares, is used as a benchmark because it corresponds to a *manzana*, the measure commonly used in Central America.

[8] For labor requirements by crop, see INTAL (1973, vol. 5).

[9] The last line of Table 34 provides an index on concentration which varies from zero (complete equality of land distribution) to unity (complete monopoly by one producer or family). The index, the Gini coefficient, has a specific and arbitrary weighting system, and which country has the most concentrated land-holding pattern is largely a matter of judgment.

[10] This table and the next two, for Guatemala and Honduras, are not strictly comparable to Table 34, because the size ranges vary, and two of the tables exclude those without land.

[11] From 1950 to 1964, the proportion of land in estates larger than sixty-four *manzanas* fell from 72 percent to 62 percent. In 1979 it had risen to 65 percent.

[12] See footnote to Table 37.

[13] Joint Inter-American Development Bank, World Bank, and US Agency for International Development mission. BID (1977b, 11–13).

[14] Nor is the distribution of income particularly equal. Chenery, *et. al.* in their path-breaking study of income distribution, characterized the Costa Rican distribution as "highly unequal" among developing countries. Chenery, *et. al.* (1974).

[15] Seligson notes that thirty-three of the forty-four presidents from 1821 to 1970 descended from only three families. Seligson (1980, 36).

[16] At 40 percent, so 50 percent of all renters paid in money in 1961 and 70 percent in 1971.

[17] For complete definition, see El Salvador (1978).

[18] A clear summary of the law is found in BID (1983). The assessment of actual impact given in this source is based on Salvadoran government figures.

[19]Inforpress, 1982. For other estimates of beneficiaries under Phases I and III, see the review of available evidence in Thome, 1984.

[20]The US Congress in 1983 made a portion of foreign aid to El Salvador dependent upon progress in the implementation of the land reform.

[21]See above for analysis of the Salvadoran attempt at land reform.

REFERENCES

Aria Penate, Salvador. 1980. "Las perpectivas del desarrrollo agropecuario en relación a la tendencia de la tierra," *Estudios Centroamericanos* (El Salvador) 35.

Banco Interamericano de Desarrollo (BID). 1977a. *Informe General Sobre el Desarrollo Agropecuario y Rural de Guatemala.* Washington: BID.

———. 1977b. *Informe General Sobre el Desarrollo Agropecuario y Rural de Costa Rica.* Washington: BID

———. 1983. *Informe Económico: El Salvador.* Washington: BID.

Centro Interamericano de Desarrollo Agrícola. 1965. *Tendencia de la Tierra y Desarrollo Socioeconómico del Sector Agrícola: Guatemala.* Washington.

Chenery, Hollis B., *et al.* 1974. *Redistribution with Growth.* New York: Oxford University Press.

Comisión Económica para América Latina (CEPAL). 1981a. *Honduras: Estudio de las Condiciones Ocupacionales,* Seminário sobre Pobreza y Grado de Satisfacción de las Necesidades Básicas en el Istmo Centroamericano, Documento Informativo no. 5.

———. 1981b. *Naturaleza y Alcance de la Pobreza en Guatemala,* Seminario sobre Pobreza y Grado de Satisfacción de las Necesidades Básicas en el Istmo Centroamericano, México, D.F., March 31 to April 2, 1981.

Consejo Superior Universitário Centroamericano. 1978. *Estructura Agrária, Dinámica de Población y Desarollo en Centroamericana.* San Jose: EDUCA.

Durham, Willliam H. 1979. *Scarcity and Survival in Central America.* Palo Alto: Stanford University Press.

El Salvador, Government of. 1978. *Anuario Estadística, 1977.* San Salvador.

Food and Agricultural Organization, Grupo de estudio en tendencia de la tierra y desarrollo rural. 1971. *Tendencia de la Tierra y Desarrollo Rural en Centroamérica.* FAO/CEPAL/OIT/CIDA/IICA/SIECA/1971.

Inforpress. 1982. *Centro America 1982.* Guatemala: Inforpress Centroamerica.

Instituto para la Integración de América Latina (INTAL). 1973 *El Desarrollo Integrado de Centroamérica en la Presente Decada.* Vol. 5. Buenos Aires: BID.

Manger-Cats, S.G. 1966. *Land Tenure and Economic Development in Guatemala.* Ithaca: Cornell University Press.

Secretaría Permanente de Tratado General de Integración Económica Centroamericana (SIECA). 1972. *Estadísticas sobre Alimentación y la Agricultura en Centroamérica.* Guatemala: SIECA.

———. 1977. *Situación y Perspectivas de los Granos Básicos en Centroamérica.* Guatemala: Colección Manuel Noriga Morales.

————. 1981. VII *Compendio Estadístico Centroamericano.* Guatemala: SIECA.

Seligson, Mitchell A. 1980. *Peasants of Costa Rica and the Development of Agrarian Capitalism.* Madison: University of Wisconsin Press.

Thome, Joseph R. 1984. "Agrarian Reform in El Salvador," paper presented to conference on "Alternative Strategies for Central America," Overseas Development Council and the School of Advanced International Studies, Washington, May 15–16, 1984.

Wheaton, Philip. 1982. *Agrarian Reform in El Salvador: A Program of Rural Pacification.* Washington: EPICA Task Force.

World Bank. 1978. (Nicaragua).

————. 1978. *Guatemala: Economics and Social Position and Prospects.* Washington: World Bank.

————. 1979. *Economic Memorandum on El Salvador.* Washington: World Bank.

Woodward, Ralph Lee, Jr. 1976. *Central America: A Nation Divided.* New York Oxford University Press.

6
Development of Manufacturing in Central America

In 1960, gross manufacturing output of the five Central American countries was about $550 million, less than the total sales of many North American manufacturing companies in the same year. Imports of manufactures from outside the region were slightly less, making for a total manufacturing demand in the region of considerably less than a billion dollars.[1] Taken together the Central American countries constituted a small market for modern industry, though domestic production has grown relatively rapidly over the last twenty years. And if the regional market was small, the markets of the individual countries were tiny, so miniscule that for many products the technically feasible minimum plant size far exceeded domestic demand.

The problem of market size was a major argument for the creation of the Central American Common Market (CACM). Supporters of the CACM argued that a regional free trade zone would make economic lines of production which would not be viable if limited to the tiny national markets. While this is certainly true, many observers remained dubious as to the benefits to be reaped. Neoclassical economists generally view common markets (or "customs unions") with considerable suspicion, since a priori reasoning suggests they are more likely to be "trade diverting" than "trade creating." In other words, it is predicted that the negative effect of high-cost suppliers replacing low-cost suppliers will outweigh the positive effect of stimulating intra-common market trade based on "comparative advantage."

The Central American left has also been extremely critical of the CACM, but for other reasons. It argues that the CACM was the creation of the multinational corporations, as a vehicle to penetrate and dominate the economies of the region, and to facilitate investments by integrating the national markets. This same line of argument goes on to conclude that the industrialization fostered by the CACM has been distorted and dependent. This is a variation on the thesis of "dependent capitalist development," which is commonly argued throughout Latin America. This concept, so central to what is called "dependency theory," suffers from serious ambiguities of definition. It is based upon an implicit opposite, "independent" (or perhaps, "non-dependent") capitalist development, which is presumably free of the distortions that plague most underdeveloped countries. Attempts to clarify dependence and non-dependence invariably succumb to tautologies. The existence of highly developed capitalist countries necessarily means that presently underdeveloped countries must pass through a period in which they are relatively weak economically. National capitalists will find themselves continuously at a competitive disadvantage in many, if not most, product lines, whether for export or the domestic market. As a consequence, a country's underdeveloped nature will tend to manifest itself in foreign penetration of the domestic market and in governments solicitous of that foreign penetration. This relationship in which foreign capital plays the major role in the economy can be called "dependent development" with a certain definitional accuracy. However, it is the consequence of underdevelopment, not its cause.

Whatever term is used to identify the development process in Central America over the last twenty years, it is difficult to sustain the argument that the CACM was the foster child of the multinationals. Prior to the formation of the CACM, all of the economies of Central America were firmly under the domination of international corporations, and no new vehicle such as the CACM was necessary to affect their control and dominance. Indeed, in the cases of Guatemala and Honduras, it is hard to imagine conditions of greater foreign economic domination than that of the United Fruit Company.

Further, the commerce in manufactures to Central America was overwhelmingly controlled by North American companies, and it is not at all clear what advantage the CACM presented to the multinationals, since markets could hardly have been more monopolized than they already were. The North American multinationals in particular were in a favored position before the formation of the CACM, enjoying governments from the strongly favorable (Costa Rica) to the slavishly fawning (Guatemala). The effect on multinationals of the CACM was to induce these companies to stop exporting certain manufactures to Central America and to produce these within the region. It is open to question whether this represented a gain to the multinationals. It would have been if production costs were lower in the Central American region and the creation of the common market allowed multinationals to construct local plants which had not been feasible when the five countries were insulated by trade restrictions. There is no evidence that this was the case, however. On the contrary, all evidence suggests that for most of the new products costs were higher in Central America than in North America or Europe. Given the underdeveloped infrastructure in Central America it is unlikely that the higher production costs were offset by lower transport costs. With the myriad problems of irregular supply of electricity and water, skilled labor shortages, import bottlenecks for inputs and transport, it was (and is) probably more profitable to produce in North America and ship to Central America than to produce locally.

Nevertheless, the CACM might have benefited the multinationals if its creation granted them more monopolized market positions, allowing them to raise prices to more than compensate for higher unit costs. Again, the opposite seems to have occurred. Prior to the creation of the CACM, North American multinationals were overwhelmingly dominant in the import trade. After 1960, capital flowed in from other countries, particularly Japan and Germany, significantly reducing the monopolistic position of U.S. capital. This tendency was considerably weaker than in other parts of Latin America, but still warrants the conclusion that the creation of the CACM did not strengthen the economic control of North American capital over Central America, though that control remained strong.

A more plausible hypothesis is that the CACM was fostered by the local capitalists of the region, with the intention of obtaining a larger share of the benefits from industrialization. Certainly domestic capital blossomed during the first decade of the CACM, though always as a junior partner to foreign capital. A virtual absence of a class of large domestic capitalists—excluding agriculturally based industry, such as sugar refining—characterized Central America in the 1980s.[2] In consequence, the industrialization of Central America initiated during the 1960s did not involve the denationalization of ownership as elsewhere in Latin America. The export of industrial capital from North America to South America after World War II generated a competitive struggle between foreign and national capital in which the latter was marginalized. In Central America there was little national capital in manufacturing, so the inflow of foreign capital tended on balance to benefit the aspiring local capitalists by creating new areas of investment.

During the years since 1960 the countries of Central America have experienced considerable industrial development, with the main beneficiaries being the local capitalists. Whether the same would have occurred had there been no CACM is the type of counter-factual question which is difficult to answer. The secretariat of the CACM concluded that during the 1960s the rate of economic growth in Central America was one-third higher than it would have been in the absence of the common market (6.5 percent per annum compared to 4.9 percent), and the greatest net benefits were attributed to Nicaragua, with the least to

Honduras and Costa Rica. (INTAL 1973 1:18). It would be useful to have the judgment of a more neutral source, for the superficial evidence is less than conclusive. Obviously in certain product lines great success was achieved in substituting for imports from outside of the region. It is not obvious that success in import substitution for specific products had any broader effects within the industries involved.

Structure of Manufacturing Production

While the CACM still formally existed in the early 1980s, all the governments of the region had ceased to observe the basic provisions of the common market in the late 1970s.[3] During the brief life of regional free trade, it was the Costa Rican manufacturing sector which grew most rapidly. In 1965, Costa Rica, El Salvador, and Guatemala had manufacturing sectors of roughly equal size, each country accounting for just over a fifth of regional manufacturing production, and Nicaragua close behind at slightly less than a fifth. A decade later, the Costa Rican share had risen to 28 percent with the other three countries just mentioned all at 20 percent (Table 41).

It does not appear that Costa Rica's faster growth rate can be explained by the expansion in intraregional trade. Throughout the active life of the CACM, the Costa Rican manufacturing sector exported proportionally less of its output with the CACM than any other except that of Honduras, as Table 42 shows. This indicates that the country with the fastest growth rate achieved that distinction on the basis of an expansion of its domestic market, not a conclusion consistent with the view that

TABLE 41
Distribution of Manufacturing Gross Output
In Central America 1965 and 1975

| Country | Percentage Distribution[1] | | Value[2] |
	1965	1975	1975
Costa Rica	22.9%	28.1%	1204
El Salvador	22.2	19.8	846
Guatemala	21.4	20.5	878
Honduras	14.0	12.0	512
Nicaragua	19.5	19.6	838
Central America	100.0%	100.0%	4278

[1] At 1975 Prices.
[2] Millions of dollars or Central American *pesos* (one *peso* equals a US dollar).
Source: SIECA 1981.

TABLE 42
Percentage of Manufacturing Gross Output Exported
to the CACM and the "Rest of the World"
1970 and 1978

	1970		1978	
	CACM	Rest of the World	CACM	Rest of the World
Costa Rica	8.3%	7.6%	8.5%	8.7%
El Salvador	17.5	5.0	18.0	5.9
Guatemala	13.5	6.0	21.3	15.1
Honduras	6.1	20.7	5.3	18.6
Nicaragua	11.0	15.6	12.6	12.9
Average[1]	11.6%	9.7%	12.9%	11.3%

[1]Weighted average.
Source: SIECA 1981.

regional economic integration provided the major stimulus to industrialization in the 1960s and 1970s.

The central role of the CACM to manufacturing in Central America also seems to be called into question by the fact that in Costa Rica, Honduras, and Nicaragua extraregional exports were more important than, or of equal importance with intraregional exports. However, comparing the shares of CACM and "rest of the world" exports by country is a bit misleading. As noted in Chapter 4, the products exported to the two markets from each country are quite different, and there is little possibility in the short run of switching products from one market to the other. The extraregional manufacturing exports have been largely agriculturally based, such as refined sugar, and sold in competitive markets. These products could not for the most part be sold in Central America because they represent excess supply over a saturated domestic demand (sugar, for example), or are semi-processed raw materials for which the domestic demand (e.g., ginned cotton) is tiny. The intraregional exports on the other hand are largely based on imported materials and components, and are not competitive on world markets due to their high costs of production. The two types of manufacturing production are almost totally separate from each other in all five countries, with few common inputs. As a consequence, the expansion of one does not directly stimulate the other to any great degree.

This partitioning of the five manufacturing sectors between production for extraregional trade and intraregional trade implies that one should not conclude, for example, that Honduran manufacturing was more internationally competitive than Salvadoran manufacturing. In 1978 Honduras could export almost 20 percent of its output to the world market and El Salvador only 6 percent, but this reflects the composition of output in each country, not competitiveness. In this specific case, the high Honduran proportion of extraregional sales results from the importance of sugar exports, a product of little importance in Salvadoran trade.

Economic development is characterized by absolute and relative growth of the manufacturing sector. However, the relationship between the share of manufacturing output in GNP and per capita income is not a perfect fit, and certainly less so in Central America than one would expect. As Table 43 shows, Honduras, the country with the lowest per capita income, has proportionately the smallest manufacturing sector.[4] However, for the other four countries the relationship is a bit perverse. Nicaragua, with a per capita income far below Costa Rica's and probably below that of Guatemala, had the largest manufacturing sector in the region in relative terms after the early 1970s, and Costa Rica was third in the ranking in 1965 and 1970, despite its high income per person.

While Table 43 gives data for 1979, the earlier year, 1975, is probably more indicative of relative industrialization in the late 1970s. In the last years of the decade El Salvador was embroiled in a civil war that resulted in a decline of the manufacturing sector relative to agriculture; in Nicaragua, the war to overthrow the Somoza dictatorship resulted in the reverse pattern. Notwithstanding these specific influences, no change seems to have occurred in the share of manufacturing in the total product of the region during the 1970s. The share of manufacturing in GDP changed hardly at all after 1970 except in Costa Rica, and only marginally in El Salvador and Guatemala after 1965. By far the greatest relative

TABLE 43
Share of Manufacturing Value Added in
Gross Domestic Product, Current Prices
1960–1979

Country	1960	1965	1970	1975	1979
Costa Rica	17.1%	16.9%	18.3%	20.4%	18.6%
El Salvador	14.6	17.7	18.9	18.6	15.7
Guatemala	11.7	14.6	16.0	15.4	16.6
Honduras	11.6	11.4	12.6	14.2	15.0
Nicaragua	12.1	17.6	20.5	22.1	25.4
Central America	13.6%	15.6%	17.1%	17.9%	17.2%

Source: SIECA 1973 and 1981.

TABLE 44
Distribution of Gross Output by UN Two-Digit Sectors
in Central America

| | Percentage Distribution* | | | | |
	1960	1965	1970	1975	1978
31 food	64.6%	52.5%	49.9%	47.0%	49.4%
32 textiles	14.9	19.7	17.0	13.9	13.2
33 wood	6.3	4.6	4.6	4.4	4.3
34 paper	2.4	3.8	3.9	3.9	3.6
35 chemicals	5.5	9.0	10.0	16.2	14.6
36 minerals	2.6	3.5	2.9	3.2	3.3
37 basic metals	0.1	0.2	0.4	0.7	0.6
38 metal products	2.8	5.0	8.2	7.2	7.4
39 miscellaneous	0.8	1.7	3.2	3.5	3.6
	100%	100%	100%	100%	100%

*In the UN system, all non-mining primary production activities are identified with the initial number "1", all mining by "2", manufacturing by "3", etc. Greater disaggregation is achieved by moving to 2-digits (as in this table), then to 3-digits, etc.

growth was in Nicaragua, where the manufacturing share almost doubled from 1960 to 1975, and for the same period the smallest increase was in Honduras.

Table 44 shows the distribution of manufacturing output by industrial category during the 1960s and 1970s. In the early 1960s, the Central American countries had a structure of manufacturing production characteristic of the early stage of industrialization. Food products, beverages, and tobacco (United Nations 2-digit sector 31) accounted for over 60 percent of gross output in all of the countries except Guatemala, and this sector plus textiles and clothing (32) contributed about 85 percent of the total in each case. At the two-digit level of disaggregation, the sectors which grew most in importance were chemicals (35) and metal products (37), with the latter including consumer durables and machinery.

The most impressive increase was in the chemical sector whose proportion in total manufacturing output in the region rose from 6 percent in 1960 to 16 percent in 1975 (Table 44). In all of the five countries this sector was strongly oriented to the regional market, even in Honduras, which left the CACM in 1970. More than any other, the chemical sector was the beneficiary of the regional market. Potentially a diversified chemical industry is important to the development of manufacturing, since virtually all of the other sectors require chemical inputs in their production processes. Industrial chemicals are particularly important for successful import substitution of domestic raw materials for imported raw materials.

The chemical sector in Central America, however, has not developed primarily as a supplier to agriculture and manufacturing but rather as a sector to satisfy consumer demand. In 1960, chemical products were 6 percent of regional manufacturing output and 16 percent in 1975, an increase of ten percentage points (Table 45). Six percentage points of the increase—over half—was the result of local refining of petroleum products. The output of this subsector is virtually all for combustibles and lubricants, with little use in the transformation of products. For the region as a whole, the production of industrial chemicals rose slightly over the two decades, but remained less than 4 percent of total output in the late 1970s. Indeed, industrial chemicals were virtually insignificant proportions in Guatemala and Honduras, and they represented the largest part of chemical production only in Nicaragua.

The growth of the chemical sector epitomizes the industrialization fostered within the tariff-confines of the CACM. First, the commodities produced are largely for consumers, not as inputs to other sectors. Second, well over 50 percent of the inputs for the production of these commodities are imported, even if petroleum refining is excluded. Third, the installed capacity in most cases is far in excess of the demand in the country in which each plant is located. This third point is demonstrated in Table 46, which gives the results of surveys conducted by the secretariat of the CACM. The table provides capacity utilization[5] for five sectors and only in the textile sector was utilization above 50 percent, and this sector declined in relative importance in Central America during the 1960s and 1970s. In the case of drugs and cosmetics, capacity utilization was a meager 24 percent and less than 20 percent in Nicaragua and Honduras. By comparison, capacity utilization of 75 percent in a developed country is considered low for these industries.

The low rate of capacity utilization in large part generated a further

TABLE 45
Distribution of Gross Output in the Chemical Sector
as a Percentage of Total Manufacturing Production

	Industrial Chemicals	Consumer Chemicals	Petroleum Refining	Rubber Products	TOTAL
1960	1.5%	3.5%	—	0.5%	5.5%
1965	2.1	4.6	1.6	0.7	9.0
1970	2.2	4.5	2.3	1.0	10.0
1975	3.6	5.2	6.3	1.1	16.2
1978	3.9	4.3	5.3	1.1	14.6

Source: SIECA 1981; and World Bank industrial statistics data file.

Table 46
Capacity Utilization in Selected Sectors,
1966–1968 and 1972

	Costa Rica	El Salvador	Guatemala	Honduras	Nicaragua	Central America	Year
Vegetable oils	56%	36%	54%	50%	48%	50%	1967
Metal Products	34	37	37	27	31	35	1967
Wood Products	29	44	35	35	42	36	1966
Drugs & Cosmetics	26	29	26	16	17	24	1968
Textiles	56	72	63	—	62	65	1972

Source: INTAL 1973, vol. 4.

characteristic of the products of regional import substitution: their prices were substantially above the prices of competing products from outside the region. Another survey by the secretariat of the CACM, conducted in 1972, showed that on average, the fifty-five products covered in the survey sold at prices 18 percent above competing imports,[6] and utilized capacity was on average less than 50 percent. Even more problematical was the finding that installed capacity was 50 percent more than total demand for many of these fifty-five products. That is, had imports of all substitutes been cut off and had buyers used domestic products in their place, average capacity utilization would have risen only to 67 percent.[7]

These characteristics of Central American manufacturing—an output composition oriented to personal consumption, high import-intensity, and relatively high production costs—apply to manufacturing generally in underdeveloped countries; they are the essence of industrial underdevelopment. However, it does appear that at least with regard to the structure of production, the Central American countries are more underdeveloped industrially than one would expect from their levels of per capita income. One way of judging the development maturity of the manufacturing sector of a country is by the structure of its output with regard to broad categories of product use—consumer products, intermediate products, and machinery. The more developed a country, the smaller is the share of consumer commodities in total production and the larger the share of intermediate commodities and machinery. This indicates that as economies develop, their capacity to supply the means by which commodities are produced also develops.

In order to divide manufacturing production into these three categories, the disaggregation of production in Table 45 is inadequate, since each of the 2-digit UN categories includes at least two of the three types of commodities by broad end-use. There are disaggregated data for Central America for the 1970s, and these are used to construct Table 47. In 1975 over 70 percent of manufacturing production in Central America was of consumer commodities and only a tiny 2 percent could be attributed to the production of machinery and equipment, and almost half of the latter took place in Costa Rica. This in and of itself is striking, but becomes even more so when we compare Central America to selected countries of the hemisphere (Table 47B). Despite the fact that per capita income in Central America was higher than in Colombia or Ecuador, consumption commodities accounted for a smaller proportion of the

TABLE 47
Distribution of Gross Output by End-Use Categories in Central America and Selected Countries
A. Countries of Central America, 1975

Product Type	Costa Rica	El Salvador	Guatemala	Honduras	Nicaragua	Central America
1. Consumer	75.5%	69.3%	71.4%	69.2%	73.7%	72.2%
Non-durables	70.1	65.9	69.2	66.8	73.1	69.8
Durables	5.4	3.4	2.2	2.4	0.6	2.4
2. Intermediate	21.6	28.6	27.1	30.3	25.9	26.0
3. Machinery	2.9	2.1	1.5	0.5	0.4	1.8
Total	100%	100%	100%	100%	100%	100%

B. Central America and Selected Countries

Product Type	Central America 1975	Colombia 1973	Ecuador 1973	Mexico 1975	Peru 1973	USA 1972
1. Consumer	72.2%	69.9%	67.8%	58.5%	60.0%	49.0%
Non-durables	69.8	64.3	63.9	42.6	50.5	30.7
Durables	2.4	5.6	3.9	15.9	9.5	18.3
2. Intermediate	26.0	28.7	29.9	36.9	33.4	33.0
3. Machinery	1.8	1.4	2.3	4.6	6.6	18.0
Total	100%	100%	100%	100%	100%	100%
GNP per capita (CA = 100)	100	84	75	150	136	—

Source: World Bank industrial statistics data files.

total in both these countries. Particularly small in Central America was the share contributed by consumer durables (e.g., radios, refrigerators), only 2.4 percent, compared to 5.6 percent in Colombia and 3.9 percent in Ecuador. Since total national income in both of these countries was less than in Central America, the difference cannot be explained by market size. Looking across the table, we see that there is a continuous rise in the share of consumer durables in total production as per capita income rises, with the single exception of Central America. In the case of machinery, the percentage for Central America is not so out of line as in the case of consumer durables, but one would still expect a proportion greater than in Ecuador and closer to that for Peru.

The underdeveloped structure of manufacturing production in Central America reflects the general economic underdevelopment of the area, but also the relative weakness of the indigenous capital and the semicolonial status of the region, a status recognized by observers of varying political viewpoints. Since the end of World War II, the governments of Central America have not pursued the type of nationalist economic policies which have resulted in considerable import substitution in other Latin American countries. Except for the Arévalo and Arbenz presidencies in Guatemala, Central America has not generated nationalist regimes like that of Perón in Argentina or Velasco in Peru. As a consequence, the structure of manufacturing has evolved in a way determined by market forces. The CACM was in part an attempt by the classes that rule in Central America to foster a modern manufacturing sector, but began later than similar processes elsewhere in Latin America and has been implemented in a considerably less protectionist way (lower tariff levels, for example). It is a matter of conjecture whether these policies have helped to avoid the problems of import substitution strategies elsewhere.[8] In any case it has given the region a structure of manufacturing output rather underdeveloped for its level of per capita income and combined market size.

Manufacturing Strategy of the CACM

The manufacturing development fostered within the confines of the CACM has proved to be quite fragile, as we shall see in Chapter 8, which treats the Central American economic crisis of the late 1970s and early 1980s. This fragility was the result of the problems associated with import substitution strategies generally, plus ones particular to the environment of the CACM. Considering the region as a whole, CACM manufacturing development followed an import substitution strategy; from the viewpoint of each country, it was an export promotion strategy.

Manufacturing development has suffered from the drawbacks of both types of strategies while enjoying the benefits of neither to any great extent.

The advantages of an import substitution strategy arise from the insulation of the domestic manufacturing sector from the world market. Protection of domestic industry allows the production of commodities at relatively high cost, and the hope is that over time production costs will fall as scale of production rises and the quality of the labor force improves. Further, since the production is oriented to the domestic market, fluctuations in world demand make their influence felt only indirectly, through the balance of payments which affects aggregate demand, not directly affecting the demand for each commodity. The drawbacks of the strategy are integrally related to the advantages. Protection, by permitting high cost production by world market standards, means consumers of the domestically produced products must pay higher prices than in the absence of protection. However, since consumers as a group are not strong in Central America, this is not a consideration which assumes much practical policy importance. The protection of domestic industry also is frequently associated with low rates of capacity utilization, particularly in countries with small internal markets, though this underutilization of fixed capital may be the result of the monopolistic position of firms allowed by protectionism. Perhaps most serious from a practical standpoint is that the protected industries are in general highly import-using; indeed, this is one of the reasons they are high cost and require protection. This import-intensity implies that the expansion of manufacturing places a strain on the balance of payments, so that growth repeatedly brings the economy to the brink of a foreign exchange crisis unless exports are growing rapidly. The experience of Latin American countries following the import substitution strategy over the last thirty years has been one of recurring balance of payments crises.

The export promotion strategy seeks to eliminate the foregoing problems by fostering manufacturing production which is competitive internationally. The alleged advantages are several. The commodities which can be produced at low cost in underdeveloped countries tend to be those linked to primary products. If the cost advantage of production is based on use of domestic raw materials, this obviously reduces the import-intensity of production and may stimulate production in related sectors. However, if the cost advantages are purely in terms of "cheap labor," export promotion may result in manufacturing which is equally or more import-using than under an import substitution strategy. The result may be what are derisively called "screwdriver industries," in which the component parts of a product are imported, processed slightly, then re-exported. The major drawback to the export promotion strategy is that production is by design dependent upon world market conditions. As long as demand is buoyant and trade restrictions few, rapid growth of production can result. However, a decline in world demand can result in unutilized capacity even more serious than in the case of import substitution industries.

This last problem is made worse by the tendency for export-oriented manufactures from underdeveloped countries to be inappropriate for domestic markets. In as far as consumer commodities such as shoes, clothing, and consumer durables are designed for developed country markets, they will tend to be luxury products in the context of the domestic market even though they enter the developed countries as cheap substitutes. As a consequence, they are not only produced for export, but must be exported to be sold. Therefore, when external demand declines, the industries in question prove inflexible and only with difficulty able to reorient their production to the internal market. It would be an advantage if "a shoe were a shoe were a shoe," so that the shoe industry could export when world market conditions were favorable and sell at home when they were not. But such is not the case, particularly in Central America where the luxury consumer market is quite small. This inflexibility manifested itself in dramatic form in Nicaragua after the fall of Somoza. A number of consumer commodity factories lost their foreign markets: for example, a company that supplied blue jeans to a large North American retail chain. The machinery proved unadaptable to producing low quality clothing for mass consumption, resulting in the irony that the plant was shut down at the same time that imports of clothing increased. Export promotion generates its own particular rigidities which may be as serious and uneconomic as those inherent in an import substitution strategy.

Whatever may be the relative advantages of each strategy, the countries of Central America have enjoyed the disadvantages of both over the last twenty years. For the most part, the industries stimulated by the CACM have been highly import-using, a drawback associated with import substitution industries. Table 48 shows the most important sectors in terms of exports over the last twenty years, divided between the CACM and extraregional trade. For the five countries the most important sector in regional trade was either textiles or chemicals, both highly import-using, because regional textile production relies heavily on synthetic fibers. Two of the other three sectors important in regional trade, paper products and glass products, are also quite import-intensive. Even the intraregionally traded manufactured food products include many which are based upon imported raw materials.

While in general the manufactured exports of underdeveloped countries use fewer imports than the manufacturing sectors as a whole,

TABLE 48
Most Important Manufactured Exports
by Market and Country[1]
1960s and 1970s

Market	Costa Rica	El Salvador	Guatemala	Honduras	Nicaragua
CACM	textiles	textiles	consumer chemicals	consumer chemicals	basic chemicals
	food	consumer chemicals	textiles	food	food
	basic chemicals	paper products	food		textiles
	consumer chemicals	food	glass products		
Extra-regional	food	food	food	food	food
	basic chemicals			wood products	

[1] A sector's exports must be $10 million in at least one year to be included. Petroleum sector excluded.

in the case of Central America, intraregional exports in each country have been considerably more import-using than manufacturing as a whole. This is the worst of both worlds. The high import content of intraregional exports meant that the products could not be reoriented to the domestic markets of the countries even if domestic demand was sufficient. As long as a substantial proportion of manufacturing output in each country was exported, the high import content of production was compensated by export earnings. But when the CACM began to collapse in the late 1970s, the manufacturing sectors of each country suffered large negative foreign exchange balances. Hardest hit were probably Guatemala and Nicaragua. In the heyday of the CACM, the manufacturing sectors of these two countries more or less broke even between imported inputs and export earnings (though the data is lacking to make precise calculations). But with the collapse of the CACM, both manufacturing sectors, forced back upon domestic demand, created net drains on the balance of payments in each country. The collapse of the CACM eliminated the export promotion aspect of the industrial strategy and transformed the industrial sectors to import substitution. Each economy had evolved on the basis of a CACM-oriented manufacturing sector which would come close to carrying its own weight in terms of foreign exchange, making the sudden change in status of the CACM a severe economic shock. This point is developed further in Chapter 8.

In addition to high import-intensity, production oriented to the CACM had the other typical drawbacks of import substitution industries. The ratio of employment to output tends to be relatively low in these sectors. For all the countries, sectors oriented to the CACM are chemicals, basic metals and metal products, and textiles. In addition, for Costa Rica, El Salvador, and Guatemala, the machinery sectors were heavily dependent upon the regional market, along with rubber and paper products for Guatemala, and again, paper products for El Salvador. With the exception of textiles, all of these are high-productivity sectors, generating relatively little employment per unit of output.

Industry in Central America has the import substitution characteristic of being extremely concentrated, with a few firms controlling virtually the entire market in most sectors. Detailed data for the 1970s are available for El Salvador, and these indicate that concentration of production is quite high and has increased over time in many sectors. The Salvadoran market is quite small, so one would expect high levels of concentration for industries whose sales are primarily domestic. But the concentration of output is also very high for sectors integrated into regional trade, such as chemicals and consumer durables. Data for Costa Rica suggest that its levels of output concentration are even higher than for El Salvador. Limited comparative data indicate that the Central American countries have the highest degree of industrial concentration in Latin America.[9]

It does not appear that either intraregional trade or extraregional trade has any tendency to reduce the concentration of production. In the case of sectors oriented to the CACM, tariff protection has reduced external competition, and excess capacity in most of the sectors has blocked the entry of new firms. For extraregional trade, overseas competition reduces domestic production to only the most efficient. Again, this results in the worst of both industrialization strategies. Production for the regional market is concentrated because of protectionism and the small size of that market; production for extraregional trade is concentrated because competition eliminates the high cost producers. Just as the agricultural sector is dominated by a tiny class of landlords, so the manufacturing sector is dominated by a few powerful firms, foreign and national. This concentration of economic power helps to explain the weakness of nationalism and liberalism in Central America, which thrive among the middle classes and small to medium-sized capitalists.

Only in Costa Rica is middle-class reformism a strong tradition, and it is in Costa Rica that one finds the only significant rural and urban middle-class movement.[10]

Manufacturing in Panama

Since Panama was never a part of the CACM, the development of its manufacturing sector has not been closely linked to those of the Central American countries and is properly considered separately. Panama does trade with the countries of Central America, but to no great degree. Panamanian exports to Central America were less than 1 percent of the region's total import bill during the 1970s and equal to 3 percent of the intraregional trade of the CACM. Further, the trade between Panama and Central America was quite specialized. Of the $140 million in exports from 1970 to 1979, 35 percent represented petroleum and related products. Until refining capacity expanded in Central America, the refinery in Panama served Nicaragua and Costa Rica. Trade has been based on proximity as much as anything else. During the 1970s 80 percent of Panama's exports to Central America went to Costa Rica and Nicaragua, its closest neighbors, and Costa Rica's share was double Nicaragua's. The pattern is similar on the import side. Of the $311 million Panama imported from the CACM from 1970 to 1979, almost 60 percent was from its next door neighbor, Costa Rica.

Thus, the dynamic of manufacturing in Panama has been largely unrelated to developments in the CACM. In the 1960s, without benefit of a regional market, manufacturing in Panama grew at 10 percent a year, and only one of the countries of the CACM, Nicaragua, did better. Growth deteriorated dramatically in the 1970s, falling to 2 percent per year, one-third of the rate for the countries of the CACM taken together. The 1970s saw a decline in growth rates throughout the world, so it is not surprising that manufacturing grew slowly in Panama. However, a manufacturing growth rate for a decade of 2 percent is surprising, since it means that industrial output per capita in Panama was falling.[11] By most standards such a decline would be indicative of economic regress, not progress.

As shown earlier, about half of the manufacturing output in Central America was in the food, beverage, and tobacco sectors in the 1970s. These products constituted a considerably smaller percentage in Panama, only 32 percent in 1975 (Table 49). This proportiton should not be taken as indicative of a diversification of Panama's industry away from traditional consumer commodities, however. Over 40 percent of manufacturing output arises in the chemical sector, and most of this is

TABLE 49
Distribution of Manufacturing Gross Output
by Sector, Panama
1965, 1970, and 1975

Sector	1965	1970	1975
31 food & beverages	46.6%	44.1%	31.9%
32 textiles & clothing	8.5	7.3	3.6
33 wood products	4.6	5.6	3.1
34 printing & paper	4.6	4.9	2.9
35 chemicals	26.7	28.2	42.2
36 non-metallic minerals	5.7	6.3	3.6
37 basic metals	2.8	3.4	2.5
38 metal products	0.0	0.0	10.0
39 other	0.5	0.2	0.2
TOTAL	100%	100%	100%
manuf VA/GDP[1]	15.9%	17.2%	15.4%

[1] Manufacturing value added as percentage of gross domestic product.
Source: SIECA 1973 and 1981.

the refining of petroleum. While petroleum is important to any economy, it is not a product which generates much employment, nor in the context of Panama does it have any linkages to the rest of the economy, except as a fuel. The crude oil is imported, so not even any drilling or exploration is stimulated by the industry's expansion. The industry is essentially an enclave, physically and economically isolated from the rest of manufacturing in Panama. If the petroleum sector is excluded for 1975, the proportion of food, beverages, and tobacco in total manufacturing rises to 53 percent, higher in the same year than for all of the countries of the CACM except Nicaragua. This proportion is indicative of a very undiversified and underdeveloped manufacturing sector, particularly since Panama's per capita income in 1975 was double that of the average for the Central American countries.

The characteristics of the manufacturing sector of Panama seem to be the consequence of the government's liberal trade policies of the last two decades. Compared to the Central American countries, Panama has pursued a low-tariff policy, as well as allowing virtually free capital flow in and out of the country. Further, the state has played a small role in directly financing or subsidizing industry. The positive consequence of this has been that manufacturing in Panama is considerably more competitive than manufacturing in Central America. Output per worker is higher in Panama than in any of the CACM countries, since the low tariffs have not permitted high-cost producers. Even if the petroleum sector is excluded (which exported 30 percent of its output), from 1975 to 1979 Panama exported 17 percent of its manufactures. The relevant comparison would be to the extraregional exports for the Central American countries, since their regional trade is protected. By this comparison, Panama exports a larger proportion of its manufactures than all CACM countries but Honduras. In the case of Honduras, these manufactures sold outside the region were almost all agricultural, while Panama's include clothing, shoes, paper products, chemicals, and metal products.

This competitiveness has been bought at considerable cost. As noted, the manufacturing sector is undiversified, with output concentrated in consumer commodities (almost 75 percent of output excluding petroleum). Considerably more serious is the extremely low rate of growth of manufacturing. According to Inter-American Development Bank data, only three underdeveloped countries in the hemisphere had manufacturing rates of growth slower than Panama's in the 1970s (IDB 1981, 405). While Panama's manufacturing sector may have avoided the extreme inefficiencies associated with an import substitution strategy, its experience is hardly an encouraging model for Central America: the slowest growth rate in the region, declining employment, and lack of diversification.

Relative Decline of Manufacturing in the 1970s

In all of the countries of Central America except Costa Rica, the rate of growth of manufacturing output after the late 1960s was hardly different from the overall rate of economic growth, with the result that four of the five countries arrived at the late 1970s with the relative importance of manufacturing about what it had been a decade before. While the CACM created a regional market for certain products, it is not clear that the production of these products had any spill-over effects that contributed to a more generalized dynamism. In other words, it is not possible to reject with confidence the hypothesis that sectors strongly associated with intraregional exports would have grown just as fast had there been no CACM. Such counter-factual hypotheses are not easy to prove, but we can take a simple and obvious test. If the CACM was the dynamic element in manufacturing development, then one might expect that the sectors most integrated into regional trade would have been the fastest growing, faster than those oriented to extraregional exports or the domestic markets of each country. We can test this expectation for Guatemala and Nicaragua, the two countries for which we have data on output in constant prices at the sectoral level. It would not be valid to test on the basis of growth in current prices, since a positive relationship between growth and regional exports might merely reflect that regional prices rose faster than prices of extraregional exports. In fact, there is empirical evidence and a priori logic to suggest precisely that this occurred.

In the case of Guatemala, the results indicate no significant correlation between sectoral growth rates and the share of exports to the CACM. There is a weak relationship between sector growth rates and the share of exports in extraregional trade for the same time period (1963–1978). The results for Nicaragua are similar: no apparent relationship between sectoral growth rates and the share of exports to the CACM. In economic relationships as complex as that which we are considering, one cannot jump to conclusions, but it can be said that if the CACM generated a general dynamism to the manufacturing sectors of Central America, the proof has yet to be convincingly presented.

In the late 1960s relative price changes began to undermine manufacturing development and particularly the sectors oriented to intraregional trade. The 1970s brought forth a general inflation in world market prices, the most spectacular for petroleum. With the increase in petroleum prices, prices of products based on petrochemicals also rose. Many of the products made in Central America and oriented to the CACM, as well as products directed to domestic markets, were heavily dependent upon petrochemical inputs. The regionally traded products based on petrochemicals were textiles (synthetic fibers), shoes (synthetic rubber soles or totally of plastic), industrial and consumer chemicals, rubber products, construction materials (plastic pipes and paneling), plastic containers, and fertilizers. The investments in the plants processing these products had been made in the 1960s, when petrochemical synthetics were relatively cheap: for example, when synthetic fibers were favorably priced to cotton. With the sudden and rapid price increase in petrochemicals, unit costs increased dramatically for manufacturing in Central America. In some cases, the reversal of relative costs was quite ironic. In Nicaragua, the textile industry was heavily dependent upon synthetic fibers. There was no domestic spinning of cotton into thread, perhaps precisely because synthetic fibers had been so cheap in the 1960s. As a result, it was not possible for the domestic textile industry to take advantage of the country's cotton as an alternative when the price of synthetic fibers rose.

The extent of the cost pressure is indicated in Table 50. The price index for imported inputs to manufacturing rose by over 11 percent yearly in Central America from 1970 to 1978 (and considerably faster in the mid-1970s). This does not imply that total costs rose by this amount, since imports represented less than half of labor and materials costs.

TABLE 50
Annual Compound Rates of Change of Domestic Manufacturing
and Imported Input Prices
1970–1978

| | Prices | |
Country	Domestic Manufacturing	Imported Inputs
Costa Rica	8.1%	12.1%
El Salvador	7.1	11.5
Guatemala	9.1	9.3
Honduras	8.8	14.2
Nicaragua	8.4	11.6
Central America	8.4%	11.4%

Source: SIECA 1981.

However, in key sectors such as chemicals and plastics, imported materials were considerably more than 50 percent of total costs. The increase in costs, in turn, generated upward pressure on manufacturing prices, which rose at over 8 percent per year during the 1970s. The rise in regional manufacturing prices then made imported manufactures cheaper in relative terms. In 1963, a third of the regional market for manufactures was supplied by extraregional imports, and this fell to 29 percent in 1969, reflecting a successful regional import substitution process. But by 1977, the share had risen to 35 percent and was higher in every country than it had been in 1963 except for Costa Rica.

Detailed analysis of the Nicaraguan situation reveals an extremely unfavorable change in relative prices during the 1970s which may characterize the experience of the region. Domestic manufacturing prices rose slower than the prices of imported inputs, resulting in a reduction of profit margins. At the same time, the prices of imported capital equipment also rose sharply, reducing investment and slowing the rate of growth of productivity. To make matters worse for the manufacturing sector, the prices of manufactured consumer imports rose slower than prices of domestic substitutes, inducing consumers to switch to imports.[12] The overall impact was a decline in the rate of growth of manufacturing, an increase in consumer imports, and a decline in the growth of manufactured exports.

The relative price changes also had debilitating effects on large-scale agriculture in Central America, which is a heavy user of petrochemical fertilizers and insecticides. Prices of both imported and domestically processed fertilizers rose sharply in the 1970s, increasing costs, particularly for cotton. However, it appears that extraregional exports suffered less than intraregional exports during the 1970s.

Prospects for Manufacturing Development

In the early 1970s, the secretariat of the CACM (SIECA) made an assessment of manufacturing development within the CACM for the 1960s. The study concluded that despite considerable problems, such as the exit of Honduras, one could be optimistic for the 1970s. In the event, the 1970s proved an unmitigated disaster for the CACM and only a slightly mitigated one for the manufacturing sector. As the mid-1980s approach, the industries fostered within the CACM are in crisis; many of the plants have closed and others are operating at extremely limited capacity.

In retrospect it is difficult to account for the optimism of the 1960s with regard to industrialization on the basis of regional integration. The strategy followed was one of import substitution, with all the drawbacks and inefficiencies of that strategy. Further, the strategy lacked even the major benefit of an import substitution strategy—a guaranteed domestic market. The "domestic" market existed only at the sufferance of the five governments of Central America, and as the 1970s proceeded the enthusiasm for economic integration declined. The complete breakup of the CACM was in the wind before the fall of Somoza, and the hostility of the other four governments to the new Nicaraguan regime only accelerated the demise. As balance of payments pressure increased in Central America in the late 1970s, it appears that all of the governments made the decision to seek separate solutions to the economic crisis that confronted them, rather than a collective one which would have allowed for further economic integration.[13]

This decision or decisions meant catastrophe for much of the manufacturing fostered in Central America during the last twenty years. Many of the plants constructed in the 1960s were much too large for the regional market, much less the domestic market of any one of the countries. The import substitution character of these industries ruled out extraregional exports except with heavy subsidies. With the world market excluded by high costs of production, the regional market disintegrating, and the domestic markets much too small for the CACM industries, the early 1980s brought on a wave of factory closings in all five Central American countries, even in Honduras which had been the least integrated into the common market.

In retrospect, the flowering of the CACM and the manufacturing associated with it was brief indeed. Production, investment, and intraregional exports boomed in the 1960s, then in the 1970s stagnated, declined, and collapsed. At present, it is difficult to imagine normal diplomatic relations among the five countries, much less the coordination of economic policy necessary to breathe new life into the CACM. In consequence, the silent factories of the dormant CACM are unlikely again to clatter and vibrate with activity. This then presents the question, on what basis will industrialization proceed in Central America? For the 1980s there will probably be very little indeed. An import substitution strategy for each country individually or the development of new internationally competitive manufactures would require an inflow of considerable foreign investment. None of the countries possess the technology or expertise to pursue these alternatives on the basis of local capital. While a large inflow of investment is not impossible, it is unlikely given the political tensions in the region: civil war in El Salvador, insurrection in Guatemala, and the potential of a Honduran-Nicaraguan conflict. Most probable is the further growth of agribusiness for the markets of industrial countries. Except for agribusiness, the present installed capacity in the manufacturing sectors of the Central American countries does not seem to provide the basis for viable industrialization in the present decade.[14] These factories, based to a great extent on imported inputs and designed for a protected market, are now largely relics of Central America's past with little relevance for the future.

NOTES

[1] We say "considerably less," because a part of the manufacturing imports were inputs to domestic manufacturing production, so the net demand was less than the sum of imports and regional production.

[2] In the early 1960s there were probably less than 400 manufacturing establishments in the region hiring more than 100 workers.

[3] See Chapter 8.

[4] Throughout this chapter manufacturing statistics will refer to data from establishments engaging five employees or more.

[5] This is measured as actual output divided by a maximum obtainable output under normal conditions. The number of shifts worked under "normal conditions" varies by industry, depending upon the time machinery must be kept idle for repairs and other factors.

[6] The difference between the prices of regionally-produced products and imports probably increased after 1972, due to the sharp rise in petrochemical inputs.

[7] This is the inverse of the ratio of installed capacity to total demand, domestic production plus imports of similar products. See INTAL (1973, vol. 4).

[8] See next section for discussion of this point.

[9] This conclusion is based on data from industrial surveys from various Latin American countries, brought together in the World Bank industrial data files.

[10] See discussion of the Costa Rican peasantry in previous chapter.

[11] Per capita agricultural output also fell. See Chapter 8 for further treatment.

[12] These relative price changes are incorporated into an explanatory model in Weeks (1982).

[13] This is not to suggest that collective action would have been the basis for a solution to the crisis.

[14] Costa Rica, whose industry was least oriented to the CACM among the four full members, is a possible exception. See final chapter.

REFERENCES

Frank, Charles R., Max A. Soto, and Carlos A. Sevilla. 1978. "The Demand for Labor in Manufacturing Industry in Central America." In *Economic Integration in Central America*, edited by William R. Cline and Enrique Delgado. Washington: The Brookings Institution.

Inter-American Development Bank (IDB). 1981. *Economic and Social Progress in Latin America 1980–1981*. Washington: IDB.

———— 1983 (January). *Economic Report: Honduras*. Washington: IDB.

———— 1983 (June). *Economic Report: Guatemala*. Washington: IDB.

———— 1983 (July). *Economic Report: Costa Rica*. Washington: IDB.

———— 1983 (July). *Economic Report: Nicaragua*. Washington: IDB.

———— 1983 (August). *Economic Report: El Salvador*. Washington: IDB.

Instituto para la Integración de America Latina (INTAL). 1973. *El Desarrollo Integrado de Centroamérica en la Presente Decada* vol. 1. Buenos Aires: BID.

———— 1974. *El Desarrollo Integrado de Centroamérica en la Presente Decada: Desarrollo Industrial Integrado* vol. 4. Buenos Aires: BID.

Secretaría Permanente del Tratado General de Integración Económica Centroamericana (SIECA). 1973. *Series Estadísticas Seleccionadas de Centroamérica y Panamá*. Guatemala: SIECA.

———— 1981. *VII Compendio Estadístico Centroamericano*. Guatemala: SIECA.

Weeks, John. 1982. "Impact of Changes in Import and Export Prices on Nicaraguan Manufacturing, 1960–1977". Washington.

World Bank. 1978. *Memorandum on Recent Economic Developments and Prospects of Nicaragua*. Washington: World Bank.

———— 1979. *Economic Memorandum on El Salvador*. Washington: World Bank.

———— 1981. *Economic Memorandum on Honduras*. Washington: World Bank.

7

Social and Economic Transformation in Nicaragua

The Fall of Somoza

The Somoza dictatorship, which had ruled Nicaragua for over four decades, fell in July 1979. Certainly this was the most important political event in the history of that country, and the most important in Latin America since the Cuban Revolution. The fall of Somoza and the social and economic changes which followed are, to say the least, controversial. They are even more so as this book is written, with war raging in the northern departments of Nicaragua, as the ex-National Guardsmen and others fight to re-establish some variation of the old order. In order to comprehend the nature of the developments since the triumph,[1] particularly the changes in economic institutions, one must first place the Somoza dictatorship and its fall in historical context.

It is unfortunate that nationalists and leftists have tended to use terms such as "neo-colonial," "semicolonial," and "satellite" so loosely and to apply the term "puppet ruler" with such frequency. It is unfortunate because extensive circulation of these terms has debased their value, so when one encounters a country to which they apply with great accuracy, they seem mere polemics and name-calling. But when the objective observer tries to characterize the status of the Nicaraguan governments in this century, the terms "semicolonial" and "puppet" present themselves as the most precise. For twenty years (1912–1933, except for one year, 1926), Nicaragua was a militarily occupied territory. The nature of the anti-Somoza movement is closely related to the fact that Nicaragua is the only country in Latin America other than Cuba and the Dominican Republic that has been under the direct rule of North America.

The first direct military intervention in Nicaragua from North America occurred in the 1850s, led by William Walker. Walker gained a dubious place in the history of filibustering by briefly establishing himself dictator of Nicaragua and proclaiming the legalization of slavery. The extent to which Walker had official North American support is open to question, although it is to be noted that the Pierce administration granted Walker diplomatic recognition. Active discouragement from Washington would have prevented Walker from achieving his footnote in hemispheric history, and this point is not lost upon Nicaraguan nationalists. The depth of feeling about this rather sordid episode is shown by the fact that each year the battle in which Walker was defeated by a regional army is celebrated throughout Central America.

The Walker affair was minor indeed compared to North American interference in Nicaragua in the twentieth century. After the collapse of the dictatorship of José Santos Zelaya in 1909,[2] Nicaragua became a de facto North American protectorate and so remained for twenty years, and some would say for seventy. A special North American envoy, Thomas Dawson, oversaw the organization of the post-Zelaya government, and the subsequent agreement even bore his name, the Dawson Agreement. The accord not only allocated political power, but also re-established a number of economic and political concessions for US business interests which Zelaya had interrupted. In 1911, a new president, Adolfo Díaz, made his name in infamy among Nicaraguan nationalists by accepting protectorate status. This ceding of country status stimulated considerable opposition, and Díaz had to request troops from Washington to maintain the presidency. Their arrival and occupation of the country made the protectorate status of Nicaragua virtually colonial. For the better part of twenty years, the US Marines occupied Nicaragua and North Americans commanded the Nicaraguan Army, collected the customs duties, managed the railroads, and directed the national banking system. So blatant was this colonization of Nicaragua that the other governments of Central America—hardly radical—protested, and even won a judgment in the Central American Court against the US-Nicaraguan Treaty of 1916 (Bryan-Chamorro Treaty). The judgment was ignored by the defendants, and the treaty proved more robust than the court, which disintegrated.

In 1925, the Marines were withdrawn, but returned a year later. The second tour of duty proved considerably more turbulent than the first. Again, Washington directly intervened to negotiate political succession, bringing back the faithful Díaz in an agreement forged by Henry Stimson. Part of the agreement included the creation by North American advisers of a national guard (which replaced the ill-trained army), to serve as a permanent and professional pacification force. The new agreement proved too much for many Nicaraguans, including a young mining engineer named Augusto César Sandino. From 1928 to 1933, Sandino led a spectacularly successful nationalist war against the oc-

cupying army. The efforts of Sandino and his gue
the withdrawal of the occupation forces, and Sar
vited by the government to participate in negotiati
the conflict. The negotiations, however, proved
murdered in 1934 after having dined with the pre:
The murder apparently came at the personal ordei _ _ _____ _ __ ___ ___
García, whom the North American government had chosen to lead the
newly-created National Guard. Sandino's peasant army was then ruth-
lessly destroyed. Sandino and his movement, however, would provide
the inspiration for all subsequent Nicaraguan nationalists.[3]

Shortly after the defeat of the first Sandinista movement, Somoza
García became the most powerful person in Nicaragua and formally
assumed the presidency in 1937. The founder of the dynasty ruled until
his assassination in 1956, and was followed by his older son, Luís
Somoza Debayle, who died in office of a heart attack in 1967. Luís
Somoza was followed in turn by Anastasio ("Tachito") Somoza Debayle,
the younger son, who held the throne until fleeing before the advancing
army of the *Frente Sandinista para la Liberación Nacional* (FSLN). The manner by which the Somoza family achieved power determined the nature
of its rule. Fostered by a foreign power, the Somozas always considered
the North American government their most important constituency, and
judged that their rule would continue as long as that constituency was
content. The Somozas ruled as if they sought only the acquiescence of
the Nicaraguan population, not its active support. This, in turn, gave
the economic development of the country its particular character. In
effect, the economy of Nicaragua was managed by the Somozas, who
along with a few loyal associates, received the major benefits.[4] To a
greater extent than any other Latin American dictatorship, with the
possible exception of Trujillo in the Dominican Republic (also an heir of
North American military occupation), the Somoza family ran Nicaragua
as its personal economic fiefdom.

As a result, even the wealthy families of Nicaragua had little enthusiasm for Somocista rule. The attempt at economic monopolization
by the Somoza family and its court of associates took on a qualitative
change with the earthquake of December 1972, which totally devastated
Managua. Bilateral and multilateral aid for reconstruction flowed in
great quantities and was treated as personal revenue by the Somozas. It
is generally agreed that the virtual monopolization by the Somoza group
of the profits from reconstruction pushed the other wealthy families of
Nicaragua from dissatisfaction with the regime to active opposition.
Certainly the corruption of the post-earthquake years remains legendary
in Nicaragua.

The wealthy opposition to Somoza lobbied the North American

ernment to end its support of the dictatorship, but was repeatedly
ebuffed. However, in the late 1970s an alternative manner of ending the
dictatorship gathered strength—armed insurrection by a number of
groups from which emerged the FSLN.[5] As the armed struggle grew in
intensity, the non-Sandinista opposition to Somoza began to coalesce
around a group called "The Twelve" *(Los Doce)*, representing businessmen, professionals, and intellectuals. In September 1978 this group
would ally with the Sandinistas and form a provisional government in
Costa Rica.

By 1978 the Somoza regime faced the opposition of virtually all
Nicaraguan classes: businessmen, landowners, labor, the peasantry, and
the middle class. The armed struggle which brought on the collapse of
the dynasty was carried out by the FSLN and other more radical groups.
But the business opposition also made its presence felt by closing factories and shops on two occasions in protest against the regime. Thus,
the movement which overthrew Somoza was extraordinarily broad-
based; but the acknowledged leadership of this movement was the nine
commanders of the *Frente Sandinista.*

War Destruction and the Emergency Program

The first element necessary for understanding the social and economic
transformation of Nicaragua is the history of North American domination. The second is the extent of the destruction brought by the war that
overthrew Somoza. It is common for North American politicians to compare the Cuban and Nicaraguan Revolutions. Considerable caution
should be exercised when doing so. By comparison to Nicaragua, the
revolutionary seizure of power in Cuba was bloodless. Our main concern here is in the economic destruction caused by the war, but we can
note that the United Nations estimates that 35,000 people died in the
struggle, another 10,000 were seriously injured, and 50,000 children
were orphaned. A quick calculation shows that over 1.5 percent of the
population died and an equal percentage was maimed or disabled
(ECLA 1979, 17–18). Proportionally, these human losses exceeded those
of most of the combatant countries in World War II, and ranks the
Nicaraguan revolution as a human catastrophe.

The losses due to the war, almost all during 1978–1979, devastated
the economy. Gross domestic product had zero growth in real terms
from 1977 to 1978, then in 1979 fell by 30 percent. The World Bank
estimated that the loss of production alone during 1978–1980 (excluding
losses to the stock of productive assets, housing, etc.) amounted to $2
billion or $800 per capita (World Bank 1981, ii). The fall in production in

those three years equaled a year's total output. Table 51 gives sectoral output in 1980 prices for 1971 to 1980, and even with the 10 percent recovery of the GDP in 1980, output barely exceeded its total ten years earlier. Per capita income in 1980 remained far below the peak reached in 1974 (32 percent below), roughly at the level of the early 1960s. Before considering the economic cost of the war in detail, we can note that recovery from economic devastation of this magnitude is the work of decades, perhaps a generation. Many Nicaraguans, and not just Sandinistas, feel that the greater part of these catastrophic human and economic losses were unnecessary; that had the North American government abandoned its support of Somoza earlier and followed the lead of the governments of Mexico, Venezuela, and others, the fighting would have ended much sooner. This in part explains why the new government of Nicaragua felt it was not incumbent upon it to express profuse gratitude for the loans received from the United States immediately after the triumph.

As Table 51 shows, manufacturing and construction activities fell catastrophically in 1979; indeed, construction activity virtually ceased. Since most of the fighting was in urban areas in 1979, agricultural output was affected less, falling by only 6 percent in 1979. However, it fell by another 8 percent the next year, since the 1980 harvest reflected the planting done—or not done—in 1979. Actually, the figures greatly understate the long-term impact on agricultural production. Exports of

TABLE 51
Sectoral Value Added at Constant 1980 Prices
Nicaragua, 1971–1980
(1977 = 100)

	GDP				
Years	Per capita	Total	Agriculture	Manufacturing	Construction
1971	93	76	77	68	48
1972	93	78	77	72	52
1973	94	82	82	74	60
1974	103	92	89	84	91[1]
1975	102	94	95	87	89
1976	103	99	96	91	102
1977	100	100	100	100	100
1978	90	93	109	102	60
1979	65	70	94	71	16
1980	70	76	86	83	30

[1] Large increase due to the earthquake which destroyed Managua.
Source: World Bank 1981.

TABLE 52
Estimate of War Damage to Infrastructure and Productive Capacity
(millions of dollars)

Sector	Plant and Equipment	Other[1]	Total
Infrastructure	77	1	78
Agriculture	28	0	28
Industry	50	100	150
Commerce	40	180	220
Other	4	1	5
Total	199	282	481

[1]Majority represents inventory loss.
Source: ECLA 1981, 36.

beef increased in 1978 and again in 1979, cushioning the fall in agricultural output. These increases reflected massive decapitalization by ranchers, particularly by the Somoza family itself. In the last months before the triumph herds were decimated as the dictator sought to convert his wealth to liquid and exportable form. The estimates of international missions are that three-quarters of a million head of cattle were slaughtered in 1979 (20 percent of the herds), including valuable breeding stock. Considerable investment and perhaps a decade would be required to return Nicaragua to the status of a significant beef exporter. The extensive slaughtering of dairy cattle was particularly costly, transforming Nicaragua from an exporter to an importer of processed milk products.

In terms of destruction of productive capacity, the Nicaraguan economy suffered extensively. In Table 52, we provide the estimate of damage compiled by an ECLA mission, which set total material destruction at $481 million, $200 million of which was to physical plant and equipment. To put this in perspective, the $50 million loss for plant and equipment in the industrial sector represented 22 percent of the net fixed assets of the manufacturing sector as measured by the 1976 industrial survey (Banco Central de Nicaragua 1979). Ironically, the material destruction proved less serious in the short term than the purely financial and monetary losses. In the final months before the fall of Somoza, the economy was bled white by massive outflows of foreign exchange. On commodity exports and imports, Nicaragua ran a large surplus in 1979, over $200 million, the largest in the country's history (see Table 19). However, it is quite probable that a large portion of export earnings never entered the Nicaraguan financial system, as businessmen, ranchers, and cotton and coffee planters exported all they could, even re-exporting intermediate inputs and raw materials in order to expatriate as much hard currency as possible. It is generally agreed that the Somoza family was impressively successful at this. For example, $15 million in stand-by credits from the IMF, granted in March 1979 to the Nicaraguan government, never seems to have reached the Central Bank. Obviously, the perpetrators of this massive capital flight were not inclined to publicize their activities, so one can only guess at the total. However, the 1979 estimate for short-run private capital movements is a negative $315 million, and some estimate the total at 40 percent of GDP. Whatever the total outflow, foreign exchange reserves fell by perhaps $750 million in 1979, compared to a decline of $200 million the year before and a mere $60 million in 1977. Thus, the new government would come to power with foreign exchange holdings far below the level of accumulated past obligations (e.g., imports already delivered), much less with reserves for new imports.

While capital flight was destroying Nicaragua's foreign purchasing power, the fiscal system had totally collapsed. As the rule of the dictator disintegrated, the state bureaucracy became less and less concerned with collecting taxes. At the same time, the tax-paying population felt less and less incentive to meet its tax obligations, because the regime was losing its legitimacy, and because it appeared that the government would not continue long enough to prosecute any tax defaulters should it be motivated to do so. Thus after growing continuously up to 1977, tax revenue remained constant in 1978 and 1979, falling sharply in real terms. The deficit on the current account rose spectacularly: after a 250 million *córdoba* surplus in 1977 ($35 million), the current account passed into deficit in 1978 to the amount of 375 million *córdobas* and almost 900 million for 1979 ($54 and $90 million, respectively). The latter deficit represented over 6 percent of GDP.

Not amenable to precise measurements is the cost of the social disruption caused by the war. This had a profoundly negative impact upon the capacity to reactivate production. One aspect of this social disruption was the confiscation of property by the new government. The first post-triumph government was a coalition of extremely diverse groups. While this government may have agreed upon little (and did not last long with its original members), it did agree on confiscating the property of the Somoza family and its close associates. On the face of it, this measure would seem to have aided the government in war reconstruction, since the state had direct ownership of a significant portion of the productive structure. In practice, this was not the case. It emerged that Somoza and his followers owned considerably less of the economy than had been suspected (pre-confiscation guesses ran as high as 50 percent of production). For the two major commodity-producing sectors, agriculture and manufacturing, only 15 and 27 percent, respectively, of production came into government hands. When one excluded general government expenditures and public utilities, the state portion of GDP was only 25 percent, less than in a number of other Latin American countries.

But even for this 25 percent, the gap between ownership and control was profound. As one foreign expert said, "the government owns a quarter of the economy and controls none of it." While obviously the state had formal control over the enterprises it had confiscated, the real control this afforded was limited. While Somoza's business empire may have been rational for purposes of personal profitability, it could not and does not provide a basis for the economic planning or direction of the economy. In the case of the three major exports, the state assumed ownership of a bare 15 percent of production in the case of cotton, 12 percent for coffee, and 8 percent for cattle raising. The only agricultural product for which the state was the majority producer was tobacco for cigars, representing less than 2 percent of total value of all crops and 1 percent of all agricultural production. Therefore, reactivating the agricultural sector required a major effort to stimulate private production, including large-scale private production. The Nicaraguan land reform set no upper limit on land holdings, so large estates were (and remain) largely unaffected unless they happened to be owned by the Somoza group. In agriculture, as in manufacturing, confiscation was applied as a punitive measure against criminal behavior, much as in other countries tax-offenders might have their property seized. As a consequence, state land holdings were scattered geographically and in no way integrated.

If the state ownership in the agricultural sector lacked rhyme or reason, the situation in manufacturing was chaotic. Of the approximately four hundred firms in the manufacturing sector hiring more than twenty workers (according to the 1976 manufacturing survey), approximately eighty were confiscated at least up to 51 percent of the ownership, and perhaps in another twenty-five the state assumed minority ownership. The state enterprises, brought under an organization called *Corporación Industrial del Pueblo* (COIP), were scattered randomly through the manufacturing sector. And "scattered" is the appropriate term, as Table 53 shows, based upon information provided publicly by COIP and the Nicaraguan Chamber of Commerce (which is private). The only sector in which there are a large number of state enterprises is food, which includes 30 percent of the state enterprises and approximately 50 percent of state production. The typical situation is one in which state enterprises are but one or two competitors among several in a product line.

This dispersion makes centralized organization, much less plan-

TABLE 53
State Participation in the Manufacturing Sector, 1980

UN Code	Product Type	Establish-ments (1976)	Majority State (1980)*	Approximate Share of Output (1980)*
311/312	Food	119	25	35%
313	Beverages	8	2	33
314	Tobacco	4	2	23
321	Textiles	25	8	11
322	Clothing	44	5	5
323	Leather	28	1	12
324	Shoes	22	1	5
331	Wood	21	4	60
332	Furniture	30	1	14
341	Paper	6	1	24
342	Publishing	20	3	7
351	Basic Chemicals	13	1	10
352	Consumer Chemicals	17	2	11
353	Petroleum	1	0	0
355	Rubber	6	0	0
356	Plastic	9	6	14
361	Clay	3	2	75
362	Glass	3	0	0
369	Cement	27	7	67
37/381	Basic Metals	23	6	44
382/383	Electrical & Non-electrical Machinery	9	4	25
390**	Other	6	1	14
		444	82	27%

*For establishments in which the state holds majority ownership.
**Includes transport and professional equipment.
Source: See text.

ning, of state enterprises extremely difficult. This problem is characteristic of economies in which there is a mix of state and private enterprise. But in most of Latin America, in Brazil, Peru, and Venezuela, for example, state ownership has evolved with at least a rough plan in mind for the state to control certain "key" activities, such as heavy industry. The new Nicaraguan government enjoyed no such rational structure of ownership. In some cases, the confiscated enterprises were not even technically efficient, having been built on the basis of corrupt dealings between members of the old regime and equipment suppliers of dubious reputations. Even where this was not the case, the lack of linkages among the state enterprises made central administration difficult. Because all state enterprises competed and compete in some degree with private enterprise, a centralized price policy, for example, could not be implemented. In effect, it was necessary to let price policy devolve to the enterprise level in order to accommodate the particularities of competition in each product line. This, in turn, implied that profits were maximized or losses minimized in a decentralized fashion, not within the context of the state productive sector as a whole. The drawbacks of such decentralization were recognized early on, particularly in the Ministry of Industry. Initially, however, the task of merely ensuring the continued operation of state enterprises overwhelmed all others. Frequently, the account books and other records had been destroyed by the old owners and inventories of inputs sold off in a frantic effort to take liquidity abroad.

As noted above, manufacturing output fell by 30 percent in real terms from 1978 to 1979, and construction in 1979 was less than a sixth of its real value in 1976 (its peak). As a consequence, urban unemployment—a cost of the war we have not yet considered—rose to staggering levels in mid-1979. The concept of unemployment is problematical in

TABLE 54
Unemployment in Urban Nicaragua
1965–1980[1]

Year	Managua	Other Cities
1965	14.4%	8.9%
1966	15.7	9.7
1967	11.3	8.4
1968	11.3	6.9
1969	9.5	7.3
1970	7.3	4.4
1971	6.9	4.1
1972	10.9	6.7
1973	16.3	9.8
1974	8.0	5.1
1975	11.1	6.6
1976	9.8	6.7
1977	—	—
1978	—	—
1979	28.0	—
1980	17.0	—

[1]Unemployment calculated as percentage of the economically active (working or looking for work) of age 10 years or older.
Sources: Republic of Nicaragua 1974 and 1977; and Weeks, 1981.

any underdeveloped country, since only a large portion of the urban labor force is not in wage employment. However, if we take the statistics at face value (Table 54), we see that unemployment in Managua averaged about 10 percent for the five years, 1972–1976, with a sharp upward fluctuation after the December 1972 earthquake, and a sharp subsequent drop associated with the construction boom. In 1979, the rate of unemployment rose to almost three times the level of the mid-1970s. Much of this increase resulted from the fall in manufacturing production and collapse of construction. It is unlikely that the drop in the number of wage jobs was to any significant extent compensated by self-employment in what some call the "informal" urban sector. The devastation caused by the war disrupted and depressed economic activity across the board, and the large increase in unemployment is probably a good indicator of the material suffering in urban areas. As the table shows, reactivation of the economy in 1980 brought unemployment down considerably, and probably by more in 1981. We consider the reactivation in the next section.

In summary, the war which ended the rule of the Somoza family was destructive to an appalling degree. The primary task of the new government was to alleviate the extensive suffering of the war-ravaged population, particularly in urban areas, such as Masaya and Estelí where the fiercest fighting had occurred. This priority, involving what was essentially relief work, outweighed even economic reconstruction in importance.

Limits to Recovery

Despite the catastrophic destruction of the war, there seemed to be some cause for optimism with regard to postwar economic recovery. Though much damage had been caused to productive assets, the drop in national output had been considerably greater, which left extensive excess capacity in agriculture and industry. This idle capacity could of course be put to use only with complementary foreign exchange for imported inputs. Immediately after the fall of Somoza it appeared that the foreign exchange problem, at least in the short run, would be alleviated by foreign loans. Particularly the multilateral agencies—the World Bank and Inter-American Development Bank—responded with astounding rapidity given their normal bureaucratic procedures for granting and allocating loans. Furthermore, export earnings in 1979 had been quite high, the highest in history except for 1977 and 1978. It was not outrageous to presume that the 1979 level of export earnings could at least be duplicated in 1980. Less tangibly, but quite important psychologically,

TABLE 55
Foreign Loan Commitments to the Nicaraguan
Government, July 1979 to July 1981

Agency	Amount	Percentage
Inter-American Development Bank	$ 193	17%
World Bank	91	8
BCIE[1]	36	3
Multilateral Total	320	28
Latin American Governments[2]	258	23
Eastern European Governments	132	11
OPEC Governments	120	10
Western European Governments	97	9
USAID	73	6
Official bilateral total	680	59
Private Banks	150	13
Total	$1,150	100%

[1]Central American Bank for Economic Integration.
[2]Does not include concessionary oil sales.
Sources: World Bank 1981; *Barricada* (official newspaper of the FSLN) various issues.

many in the new government fervently believed that the fall of the dictatorship would have a liberating effect on the productive initiative of the population. There was particular reason to assume this in the case of the small peasant, starved of credit and technical assistance during the old regime. The first development plan reflected these optimistic factors and anticipated an impressively rapid recovery, in which the war-associated economic losses would be recouped in record time (MIPLAN 1980).

Some of this optimism was justified. Certainly the initial inflow of foreign grants and loans (largely the latter) exceeded expectations. Table 55 gives the foreign loans received by the Nicaraguan government in the first two years after the victory. Since the difference between the external debt at the end of 1981 and July 1979 is quite close to the total of $1,150 million in the table, it is unlikely that the table has any major omissions. It is to be noted that just over 28 percent of the loans were from multilateral agencies, with the Inter-American Development Bank (IDB) being the most important. By 1981, the North American government had begun blocking IDB loans to Nicaragua, virtually ending that source of capital aid. However, in the first year after the triumph, the IDB was extremely important, granting an agricultural and industrial reconstruction loan of $61 million in September 1979. At the end of 1979, the World Bank made available two lines of credit totaling $52 million, which were followed by others, the last being a $30 million industrial development loan in July 1981. Particularly important for the repair of damage to infrastructure were the loans from the Central American Bank for Economic Integration (BCIE, centered in Tegucigalpa), though most of this was made available somewhat later, in 1980 and 1981. Among bilateral lenders, Mexico has been quite important. Like most governments of oil-exporting underdeveloped countries, the Mexican government established a discriminatory selling policy, with extremely "soft" terms for governments of some countries in Latin America, including two as different as those of El Salvador and Nicaragua. The precise concessionary element in the Mexican oil sales to Nicaragua is difficult to calculate, but the total would certainly qualify the Mexican government as an important bilateral lender to Nicaragua.[6]

Our intention is to avoid, if possible, obfuscating ideological considerations, but political commentary current in North America does require a brief assessment of the role of loans from Eastern Europe. A glance at Table 55 shows that in quantitative terms, the new Nicaraguan government relied about equally on loans from the Soviet bloc and loans from private banks. In qualitative terms, however, the latter were considerably more important. As in the case of most bilateral lenders, the Soviet bloc countries are loathe to pay out free foreign exchange. The loans involved are "tied"; i.e., must be used to purchase commodities from the country making the loan, and in many cases are specific to the product level. While the ideologically oriented tend to preoccupy themselves with the political impact of Eastern European aid in Nicaragua, the influence that less than $130 million a year in tied aid can buy is not great. Nicaraguan industry and agriculture is based on Western (largely North American) technology, so tied aid from the Soviet bloc was (and is) of little help in financing imports of either inputs or spare parts, and these were the major bottlenecks for economic recovery. For this reason, private bank loans and credit lines from multilateral agencies proved much more important to the Nicaraguan government both quantitatively and qualitatively. Indeed, for balance of payments support, official bilateral loans are not much help, which explains in part why governments of underdeveloped countries—including Nicaragua—have had little choice but to rely heavily upon private bank loans at high interest rates. As we saw in the previous section, the war resulted in considerable destruction of inventories, including inputs. This, combined with excess capacity after the triumph, meant that the urgent need was for free foreign exchange for current inputs, not project aid, and almost all bilateral aid is of the latter type.

The loans from the multilateral organizations were quite flexible, including major components for "working capital" (financing for current inputs). This allowed for an initially impressive recovery of the manufacturing sector, whose output rose by over 15 percent in 1980, and an increase of almost 100 percent in construction. Agricultural output fell again in 1980, due to the low level of planting the year before; but the expansion of the other sectors seemed to support optimism about rapid recovery. In the event, the 1980 recovery—to slightly over 75 percent of the 1977 peak GDP—not only was a harbinger of things to come, but itself proved unsustainable. Two fundamental difficulties slowly became obvious: 1) the capacity to export, in terms of both production (supply side) and markets (demand side), had fallen by as much as 30 percent from 1978 to 1980; and 2) the import requirements of the economy had risen by as much as 20 percent for a given level of national income. The implication of these two structural changes was catastrophic in terms of economic management.

Before considering why these shifts occurred, we can demonstrate their consequence. If we omit the years affected by the earthquake, the balance of commodity trade for Nicaragua was about minus $4 million a year from 1971 to 1977, very close to equality between exports and imports. For these years, gross domestic production averaged $1,350 million in current prices. Let us assume that for these years, the relationship between exports and imports was a necessary condition for achieving the average level of national production. In other words, we are assuming that the output level of $1,350 million required imports of $382 million, and in turn, that level of imports required a more or less matching level of exports. We further simply by assuming that the proportional relationship between imports and national production is constant.[7]

We can now proceed to ask what are called counter-factual questions. Given the conditions set by our assumptions (that exports and imports be balanced and imports are a constant proportion of national income), what level of national income could have been sustained in the prewar years if the postwar import intensity had prevailed during those prewar years? A simple calculation suggests that average annual national output would have been 20 percent lower. In other words, the same level of imports as actually prevailed would have generated 20 percent less national production because of the increase in the import requirements of that production. This calculation presumes that the level of exports (needed to pay for the imports) does not fall. As we asserted above, export capacity after the war was 30 percent lower than before the war. When we take this into account, the sustainable level of national income for the hypothetical case falls to about 55 percent of the actual average for 1971–1977. We can thus conclude that a balance in exports and imports in 1980 would have required depressing national production to that same 55 percent of the average for 1971–1977. Since population grew at about 2.5 percent a year in the 1970s, the sustainable level of per capita income in 1980 would have been less than half of the earlier level.

To put the case succinctly, after the war the Nicaraguan government could meet import requirements with export receipts only if it enforced a Draconian depression upon a population already debilitated by a war of tremendous cost and suffering. In fact, the government sought to reactivate the economy, not depress it. National product in 1980 was 87 percent of the level of the 1970s, not the hypothetical trade-balancing 55 percent. In consequence, Nicaragua ran a trade deficit of $350 million, and in 1981 a deficit of over $400 million.

The decline in the export capacity of the economy was rooted in both social and economic causes. On the economic side, we have seen that the slaughtering of cattle during the last months of the war devastated the livestock industry. Beef exports were $95 million in 1979, up from less than $40 million in 1977, then dropped to $59 million in 1980, and to $21 million in 1981. Because of the war, little cotton was planted in 1979, and exports fell to $30 million in 1980, down from an average of $130 million for 1974–1977. Cotton production and exports made a dramatic recovery in 1981, but still remained below the prewar levels. Overall, the social effect of the collapse of the old regime proved much more disruptive to capitalist agriculture than anyone had anticipated. In the long term, the collapse of the repressive Somoza system may call forth the productive initiative of the peasantry, but in the short run, the effect on exports was negative. On the one hand, the new government granted the agricultural labor force the right to organize itself. But on the other, it opposed wage increases, inhibited by fear of inflationary pressures and the necessity to maintain profit margins for private producers. As a consequence, severe labor shortages resulted and much cotton went unpicked in 1981. The labor shortage was greatly reduced in 1982, when higher wages were paid. In the public sector, management of the state farms (Area Propriedad del Pueblo) proved more difficult than anticipated. As to be expected, the managers of the Somocista estates for the most part fled with their masters, so the state farms were initially run by inexperienced administrators. Problems also developed with the private sector, and these are considered in the next section.

For all of the problems of agriculture, the most disastrous fall in export possibilities came in the manufacturing sector. The manufacturing sector developed in an extremely import-using pattern, but despite this proved to be a relatively small drain on the balance of trade. Agriculture-based manufacturing, which included sugar refining, milk-processing, instant coffee, and meat packing, was mainly oriented to the world market, and this subsector exported far in excess of its imported inputs. In the 1970s, this subsector ran an annual excess of exports over imported inputs of about $25 million. For the rest of the manufacturing sector imported inputs exceeded exports, but only to a small extent. If we omit petroleum refining, with annual imports of more than $60 million, non-agroindustry had a deficit of imported inputs over exports of only about $8 million a year from 1970 to 1977. Thus, in the Somoza period the manufacturing sector as a whole was a net earner of foreign exchange even excluding import substitution effects; that is, excluding the replacement of imports by domestic production. And when we exclude agroindustry, the manufacturing sector still came quite close to generating sufficient foreign exchange to purchase its inputs.

But this balance between exports and imported inputs was wiped out in the late 1970s, partly due to the war and partly due to changes independent of the war. It must be stressed that the CACM was an extremely large market for Nicaraguan manufactures. From the 1960s to the 1970s, manufactured exports more than tripled, to an average of over $250 million in 1976 and 1977. About 40 percent of these manufactured exports went to the regional market. Some sectors—clothing, shoes, building materials, and chemicals—were almost totally dependent upon the CACM for their export sales. In the late 1970s, the CACM virtually collapsed, as we discussed in previous chapters. This collapse affected Nicaraguan manufacturing the most of all CACM countries, for in addition to the general causes of the collapse, the other governments of Central America began to look upon the new Nicaragua with growing hostility. Despite repeated bilateral and multilateral meetings involving the five governments, Nicaraguan manufactures found fewer and fewer regional buyers. As a consequence, even in 1980, the recovery of the Nicaraguan manufacturing sector had to be based largely on the internal market. In 1980, industrial production was about at the level of 1974, yet manufactured exports to the CACM were 15 percent lower in value and down 40 percent measured in constant prices. In 1981, Nicaragua's regional exports fell by another 10 percent in value terms. The decline in regional exports implied that instead of the manufacturing sector as a whole running a surplus of exports over the pre-war level imported inputs of about $20 million as in 1974, the same level of production in 1980 would involve a negative balance of over $10 million.

But the actual negative balance was considerably larger than this. Due to the effect of the war, many inputs had to be imported which formerly had been supplied domestically. With the commercial dairy sector decimated, Nicaragua passed from being a powdered milk exporter to an importer, a net change of almost $10 million. Because of the drop in cotton production, there was insufficient cotton seed for the vegetable oil factories (the largest of which was owned by Alfonso Robelo, member of the first government). Instead of exporting vegetable oil to Central America, Nicaragua became an importer of inputs just to satisfy domestic demand. Many more examples can be given: imports of quality hides for shoes, a reverse of the prewar trade pattern, again the result of the destruction of the cattle herds. As a consequence of these effects, the average import-intensity of manufacturing, which had been 25 percent according to the 1976 manufacturing survey, rose to 35 percent in 1980.

As we noted, manufacturing output in 1980 was approximately the same as 1974. While in 1974 the sector as a whole had exported $20 million more than its imported inputs, in 1980 imported inputs exceeded exports by $60 million. But the situation was even worse when viewed dynamically. In the 1960s and 1970s, an expansion of manufacturing generally resulted in manufactured exports rising more than imported inputs; i.e., expansion of the economy tended to improve the trade balance. But in 1980, with the Central American economies in decline, the world market growing slowly at best, and with new domestic supply constraints (particularly in agroindustry), further expansion of manufacturing would have meant an even larger foreign exchange deficit for manufacturing and a worse balance of payments problem.

In fact, manufacturing output did increase in 1981, and the consequence was a larger balance of payments deficit than in 1980. In this situation it was extremely difficult to decide what policy to follow. Economic expansion would worsen the balance of payments, but ending the recovery would be an additional burden upon a population already ravaged by war. Further, it was not at all clear that reducing production would improve the balance of payments, though this issue lies outside the scope of this chapter.[8] Given this dilemma, it is not surprising that the new government pursued various, even contradictory, policies, in hopes of finding the policy mix that would improve the balance of payments and maintain at least modest growth.

Response of the Private Sector

Of all of the economic problems of the "new Nicaragua," the most delicate and difficult to resolve proved to be the relationship between the state and the private sector. It is true that many of the capitalists who remained in Nicaragua after the fall of Somoza—and most did—had been anti-Somoza and participated to some degree in his overthrow. As is well known in Nicaragua, the FSLN received considerable financial support from the country's wealthy families. However, it was also true that the anti-Somoza (or non-Somocista) capitalists had at least indirectly benefited from the economic policies of the old regime and certainly accustomed themselves to the extremely pro-business framework prior to the revolution. And it was precisely this anti-labor, anti-peasant, pro-*laissez faire*, pro-North American framework which the Sandinistas proceeded to dismantle in rapid strokes. While the Sandinista leaders represented quite diverse ideological orientations (the three factions had only united in March 1979), on at least two issues they were firmly united: 1) that Nicaraguan independence was not negotiable, and 2) the revolution should primarily benefit the peasantry, working class, and middle class—not the wealthy.

As a practical matter, maintaining Nicaraguan independence meant conflict between the governments in Managua and Washington, particularly as economic pressures on Nicaragua from North America expanded into military confrontation. This growing confrontation profoundly disturbed the wealthy families of Nicaragua, who had always maintained close cultural and political ties to the United States. From the outset, the elite tended to blame conflict with Washington on the inflexibility of the Sandinista leadership. Since their enterprises were so closely tied to the North American economy through inputs, equipment, and spare parts as well as markets, the Nicaraguan capitalists viewed the issue of national autonomy rather differently from the Sandinistas, to say the least.

On the question of who would benefit from the revolution, Nicaragua's capitalists were again at odds with the government. The wealthy opposition to Somoza had looked forward to formal democratic institutions, protection of human rights, and guarantees of basic freedoms, such as freedom of press. But the businessmen had also wanted these changes to occur in the context of a state in which business held the dominant position and an economy organized in the interest of capital.

With regard to economic policy narrowly defined, the Sandinista-dominated governments were in fact relatively favorable to private capital. Foreign capital, for example, was allowed to repatriate profits, under the same law which had applied in the Somoza period. The government pursued a policy of wage restraint in the private sector, holding money wage increases below the rate of inflation (while trying to reduce the gap between the lowest and highest paid). A number of potentially strong incentives were extended to the private sector. Credit policy was quite liberal, particularly to the agricultural sector in 1980 and 1981—too liberal, many feel. In January 1982, a multiple exchange rate system was introduced which in effect raised export prices for the private sector. Conciliation with the private sector was pursued in some cases by bringing the capitalists into direct policy making—the former manager of the

Pellas estates, the largest sugar producer in Central America—was made a vice-minister of agrarian reform. Spontaneous land invasions by peasants and agricultural workers prompted a decree guaranteeing property in land (with no ceiling on land holdings) to reassure the large landowners. This decree was judged by a World Bank report to be "a major step forward" in the process of achieving "a major reduction in private sector uncertainty." Foreign capital was particularly concerned that the new government guarantee its property against nationalization and set forth clearly "the rules of the game." After considerable deliberation, debate and delay within the Sandinista leadership, a law of foreign investment was announced in early 1983, which overall was quite favorable to foreign capital by Latin American standards. However, given the growing threat of a major military conflict in Nicaragua, the law probably had no effect.

Despite these specific policies, it quickly became obvious to the wealthy families of Nicaragua that they did not hold dominant political power and had no prospect to do so in the foreseeable future. The new government clearly intended to change the balance of power between landlord and peasant and between capital and labor, as well as to institute limitations upon private capital unheard-of in Central America. Thus, the specific policies designed to favor the private sector did not change the basic context: before the revolution capital had had free rein and now the state intended, if possible, to assume leadership in the mixed economy. Foreign exchange, to which the private sector had free access in the Somoza days, was monopolized and distributed by the Central Bank (except for the growing black market, of course). In practice, the distribution of foreign exchange tended to favor private enterprise compared to state enterprise, but there was decreasingly less to distribute. Since the private sector did not agree with the state priorities, the allocation of foreign exchange increasingly became a source of conflict.

Equally abhorrent to the private sector was the fact that until January 1982, companies received *córdobas*, not dollars, for their exports. The private sector bitterly resented this as a bureaucratic infringement upon its privileges, while the government suspected, with reason, that export earnings paid in foreign exchange would quickly find their way to Miami, or even into the war chest of the exiled anti-Sandinista groups training in Florida and Honduras.

But it was the general reorientation of capital-labor relations that profoundly antagonized private capital. Under Somoza trade unions had in effect been illegal; no employer needed to concern himself with any legal challenge when firing workers. After the revolution, the Ministry of Labor, headed by a non-Sandinista, pursued the narrow economic rights of workers zealously and rapidly, with little bureaucratic delay. In late 1981 the government banned strikes as part of an emergency decree (reacting to terrorist bombings in the north of the country), but it remained the case that private employers could not treat labor relations in the old way. Private capital both resented this and saw the social democratic treatment of capital-labor relations by the government as a sign of worse things to come. In practice, the revolutionary government repeatedly took steps to reduce left-wing influence in the trade unions, occasionally jailing militant leaders and closing their publications. Nonetheless, the wind was now blowing the other way in capital-labor relations, and the private sector was not pleased.[9]

In the broader context, private capital perceived itself as caught in a process of mass awakening and radicalization. The Nicaraguan population had risen en masse in the urban areas to overthrow Somoza. In this process, the population—particularly the urban poor—had discovered its power. And it was clear that the Sandinista leadership was doing nothing to reverse this discovery. This mass awakening without doubt caused profound disquiet among the wealthy, who saw no steps being taken to channel the spontaneous, insurrectionary spirit into tame political institutions. Under Somoza, there had been a professional mercenary army,[10] largely divorced and isolated from the population which it was employed to control. In the new Nicaragua the army had a mass base: it was a citizen army, and the change was as dramatic and epoch-marking as the similar change in the nature of the military after the French Revolution. The new government created a separate national police force[11] which could not be relied upon to take the side of privilege against the poor, as the National Guard had done. Further, the neighborhood defense committees (Comités de Defensa Sandinista), which had begun during the war, continued to play a large role after the triumph. Whatever the Sandinista leadership meant by "Popular Power," the wealthy in Nicaragua were not pleased with it.

It is interesting to speculate as to what might have happened had the political disequilibrium created by the fall of Somoza been allowed to play out its internal dynamics. Certainly objective circumstances gave reason for the Sandinista leadership and the private sector to continue their uneasy alliance of 1979. From the government side, there was a strong incentive to reach an understanding. For example, in 1981, Jaime Wheelock Román, Minister of Agrarian Reform and member of the National Directorate of the FSLN, stressed that further land confiscation would occur only under extreme necessity, for the state lacked the administrative capacity to run what it already held. This reflected a general recognition in the government that if there was to be a recovery, it would necessarily involve private sector cooperation. The private sector, for its part, might have come to grips with the new social and political context had it perceived no alternative but slow extinction.

All of this remains at the level of counter-factual hypothesizing, however, since external pressures quickly overwhelmed the internal dynamic of Nicaraguan politics. Armed interventions and growing hostility from Washington stilled any emerging tendency for conciliation.[12] By 1982 and perhaps before, another war in Nicaragua became a distinct possibility. Nicaraguan capitalists, whatever their political orientation, were loathe to invest in factories that might be destroyed. Those capitalists who had never been sympathetic to cooperation with the Sandinista leadership began to consider seriously the return of a Somocista government to reestablish the old rules of the game. However, some capitalists did speak out against the North American intervention.

Partly in response to President Campins of Venezuela, the Sandinista leadership initiated new talks with the opposition in the last few months of 1982, but by this time both parties knew that the opposition of practical significance was in Honduras, raiding across the border, not negotiating. Further, growing economic pressure from North America made economic expansion difficult at best, so the government could not hold out to the private sector any gains to be made from cooperation. On the contrary, it was a question of sharing out the losses. Even given this bleak picture, most Nicaraguan capitalists were still in Nicaragua in 1983, no foreign subsidiaries of any note had pulled out, and well over a majority of production was in private hands. Thus, the objective situation calls for a reconciliation, but in the context of armed intervention it is hard to see how this might occur.

NOTES

[1]Throughout Central America the fall of Somoza is referred to as "the triumph," with differences of opinion as to the nature of that triumph. We shall follow common usage and employ the term to refer to the date July 19,1979.

[2]See Chapter 1 for a discussion of Zelaya's overthrow.

[3]The standard work on Sandino is Selser (1978).

[4]In quite cautiously bureaucratic language, this point is made by a report of the Economic Commission for Latin America. See ECLA (1979, 6–7).

[5]Until only a few months before the triumph, the FSLN was divided into three factions, and the differences among the three were often bitter indeed. For a chronology of the evolution of the FSLN, see Black (1981).

[6]Any calculation would require assumptions about what the Nicaraguan

government would have paid in absence of the aid from Mexico. The Venezuelan government also made concessionary sales to Nicaragua, but on a smaller scale.

[7] We are assuming that the marginal and average propensities to import are equal.

[8] In our counter-factual analysis, we assumed that all economic relationships were symmetrical. In practice this might not be the case. Attempts to achieve balance of trade equilibrium by depressing the level of national output might create dynamic effects such as falling profit rates which would reduce export production also.

[9] The Sandinista government seemed to confirm the worst fears of the upper classes in late-1981 by jailing three businessmen. The fact that a larger number of left-wing trade unionists were jailed at the same time did not soften the impact of this move on the business community.

[10] Unlike those of most Latin countries, Somoza's National Guard had no draftees and its members were highly paid (Millet 1977).

[11] Under Somoza, there had been no separate police force, with the National Guard performing the police functions as well as military ones.

[12] In early 1983, the Reagan Administration publicly admitted that it was financing the anti-Sandinista armed forces in Honduras and Costa Rica. Officially, the policy intended to "put pressure" on Nicaragua, not overthrow the government. Particularly in Congress skepticism was expressed over this distinction.

REFERENCES

Banco Central de Nicaragua, División de Industria. 1979. *Encuesta Anual de la Industria Manufacturera de Nicaragua 1976.* Managua.

Bell, Belden, ed., 1978. *Nicaragua: An Ally under Seige.* Washington: Council on American Affairs.

Black, George. 1981. *Triumph of the People: The Sandinista Revolution in Nicaragua.* London: Zed Press.

Booth, John A. 1982. *The End and the Beginning: The Nicaraguan Revolution.* Boulder: Westview Press.

Dore, Elizabeth. 1983. "Nicaragua: The Experience of the Mixed Economy and Political Pluralism." Nashville: Center for Latin American and Iberian Studies, Vanderbilt University.

Economic Commission for Latin America (ECLA). 1966. *El Desarrollo Económico de Nicaragua.* New York: United Nations.

——— 1979. *Nicaragua: Economic Repercussions of Recent Political Events.* Santiago de Chile: United Nations.

——— 1982 (July). *Nicaragua: Las Inundaciones de Mayo de 1982 y sus Repercusiones sobre el Desarrollo Económico y Social del País.* Mexico: United Nations.

———— 1982 (July). *Notas para el Estudio Económico de América Latina, 1981, Nicaragua*. Mexico: United Nations.

Fondo Internacional de Desarrollo Agrícola. 1980. *Informe de la Misión Especial de Programación a Nicaragua*. Rome: FIDA.

Leiken, Robert S. 1984. *Central America: Anatomy of a Conflict*. Elsford, N.Y.: Pergamon.

Millett, Richard. 1977. *Guardians of the Dynasty*. Maryknoll, N.Y.: Orbis Books.

Organization of American States, Inter-American Commission on Human Rights. 1981. *Report on the Situation of Human Rights in the Republic of Nicaragua*. Washington: OAS.

Republic of Nicaragua. 1974, 1977. *Encuesta de Población* (Managua)

Republic of Nicaragua, Ministry of Planning (MIPLAN). 1980. *Programa de Reactivación Económica en Benefício del Pueblo*. Managua: MIPLAN.

Selser, Gregorio. 1978. *Sandino*. New York: Monthly Review, 1981.

Weeks, John. 1981. "Determinación y analisis de la satisfacción de las necesidades básicas en los sectores urbanos de Nicaragua." Mexico: CEPAL.

World Bank. 1981. *Nicaragua: The Challenge of Reconstruction*. Washington: World Bank.

8

Economic Crisis in
Central America

The cycle of boom and contraction is a fundamental characteristic of the world economic system. The extent to which any particular country is affected by the world trade cycle depends in part upon the extent and manner in which it is integrated into the international market. The consequences of changes in the world market are also related to two other factors, the size of the economy in question and the efficiency of production compared to production in other economies. Large economies tend to determine the tempo of the world economy, while economies as small as those of the Central American countries are largely passive reactors to world market conditions.

In most general terms, an economic crisis may be defined as a situation in which conditions are such that the economy can no longer expand, for further expansion would create tensions which could not be sustained or resolved. In developed capitalist countries in the last two decades the unresolvable tension associated with economic expansion has been inflation. In underdeveloped countries, the expansion of economic activity is almost always limited by the balance of payments, a constraint important for advanced economies, but not such an overwhelming factor. It is not uncommon for advanced countries to experience recessions when the economy's external balance is positive; this is almost unknown for underdeveloped countries.

In underdeveloped countries there are always unutilized resources which potentially allow for increased production. The most important of these resources is labor, either unemployed or engaged in extremely low productivity employment. Land may also be potentially available, as in Nicaragua and Honduras. However, the utilization of these idle and semi-idle productive resources is invariably dependent upon complementary imports. In Central America this is particularly the case. Manufacturing production requires imported inputs as well as spare parts and machinery which are not produced in the region. But agriculture also is import-using, especially export agriculture. As long as foreign exchange is available, output can expand, for the protected domestic and regional market if not for export. When foreign exchange is scarce, domestic production necessarily suffers a slow-down or contraction. Thus, a recession or economic crisis in the Central American countries has always been triggered by a foreign exchange crisis (deficits in the balance of payments).

Concrete conditions are more complex, though the basic relationship between economic expansion and the balance of payments remains. A deficit in commodity trade, imports exceeding exports, need not in itself provoke an economic crisis. In the first instance, a trade deficit may be the result of temporary or even random factors which make the value of exports or the demand for imports atypical. Unusually bad weather, as Nicaragua suffered in 1982, can have a dramatic impact upon the production of primary products. Natural disasters can also increase the need for imports, as occurred after earthquakes in Guatemala and Nicaragua in the 1970s. If a government can convince its trading partners or international lenders that the trade deficit is temporary, loans can be obtained to cover the short-term foreign exchange problem, imports maintained, and the growth rate of the economy need not suffer.

At the other extreme are what are sometimes called "structural imbalances," trade deficits which result from long-term trends undermining the capacity to export and/or increasing the demand for imports. It is frequently argued that the more developed countries of Latin America, principally Chile and Argentina, suffer from structural imbalance in trade, resulting from a long-term decline in agriculture and the high import-intensity of manufacturing. In such a case, short-term credit to cover trade deficits is more difficult to find and is frequently obtained by the borrowing government pledging to implement some program of "structural adjustment."

Between these two extremes lies a gray area in which each case is open to interpretation. The dramatic increase in the world price of petroleum in the 1970s is a case in point. Throughout the world, non-petroleum-exporting countries ran large trade deficits as a result of the sharp rise in oil prices. Whether these deficits were "temporary" or "structural" depended on one's view of the dynamic consequences of the price increases. If the relative price change (of petroleum compared to other traded commodities) was viewed as permanent, then the deficits were structural, requiring long-term adjustment to other sources of energy and programs of conservation of energy use. If the price increases were judged as transitory, eventually calling forth greater oil production, then the deficits were temporary. In fact, the world's multinational banks treated the problem implicitly as a temporary condition, rushing to extend loans to governments of underdeveloped countries initially without any associated programs of structural adjustment. The external government debt of the countries of the Caribbean and Latin America rose from $22 billion in 1972 to $94 billion in 1978, largely financed by private banks and stimulated by petroleum imports. Foreign debt increased substantially for the Central American countries over the same period, from $700 million to $3.3 billion. Events of the early 1980s proved the boom in petroleum prices to be transitory, but the foreign debt contracted by governments of Latin American countries during 1973–1980 was enormous.

To this point we have considered only trade and capital flows specifically contracted to finance imports when export earnings are insufficient. Whether or not a government can sustain a balance of trade deficit depends upon not only trade-related credit, but also non-trade-related capital flows. The most important of these are profit remittances, short-term capital movements, and long-term capital movements.[1] Except for extremely rare cases, net profit remittances from underdeveloped countries are always positive, representing an outflow of foreign exchange which must be countered by exports or some other balancing item. The most important of these items are short-term and long-term capital flows. Short-term capital flows are those which are not directly intended for any productive investment and are usually in response to favorable interest rates. Except for Panama, this type of capital flow is not very important in the Central American region. Long-term capital flows include government to government lending, multilateral lending (World Bank, Inter-American Development Bank, etc.), private direct investment, and private bank lending.

These and other less important complications imply that a government can maintain economic growth with a trade deficit if that deficit is covered by a variety of capital flows. This is what occurred in the Central American countries during the 1960s and early 1970s. The creation of the common market and the profitability of agribusiness drew in foreign investment, as well as concessionary loans from multilateral agencies. Despite the fact that commodity trade was in deficit for all of Central America during 1960–1972, and the current account deficit (including "invisibles")[2] was on average $170 million each year, all five countries enjoyed respectable to impressive growth rates. This was made possible by private investment flows, multilateral borrowing, and modest borrowing from private banks. By all indications, the deficits were sustainable, not harbingers of crisis.

With the increase in petroleum prices, the current account deficits multiplied in size to unsustainable levels given the capital inflows of the

1960s and early 1970s. These deficits were partly offset by concessionary oil sales from Mexico and Venezuela, but only in part. As shown in Chapter 4, prices rose dramatically for all petroleum-based imports into Central America, particularly industrial chemicals, fertilizers, and insecticides. Notwithstanding these deficits, economic growth was maintained in the Central American countries through the mid-1970s by foreign borrowing, to a great extent from private banks. The largest debts were accumulated by the governments of Costa Rica and Nicaragua, with Guatemala and El Salvador borrowing, but to a modest degree. These latter two countries remain relatively and absolutely unburdened by foreign debt at present. Honduras had a borderline debt problem in the mid-1970s, though it would later become serious.

Thus, the expanded deficits of the 1970s did not in and of themselves undermine the growth of the Central American economies. Available international liquidity, on rather hard terms, provided a financial bridging of the petroleum price boom in anticipation of an adjustment in relative world prices. Had this adjustment occurred in the context of an expanding world and regional market, the debts accumulated in the 1970s might have been manageable with continued economic growth. However, the period of high petroleum prices was followed by a contracting or stagnant world market for primary products and a collapse of the Central American Common Market agreements. At the same time, revolution and civil war exploded in El Salvador and Nicaragua, and insurrection waxed and waned in the highlands of Guatemala. In addition to the direct economic losses due to the fighting, the armed struggles in Central America discouraged foreign private investment and stimulated capital flight.

With the world demand for primary products down and the CACM in ruins, trade deficits increased despite the relative cheapening of petroleum. For a decade and a half the economies of Central America had been able to live with and thrive on trade deficits, but by the late 1970s, the necessary capital flows were not forthcoming to balance the external account for the reasons given above. These points are considered further below. The current economic crisis of Central America is basically the result of regional and world economic and political changes which transformed trade deficits from being sustainable characteristics of growth into unmanageable, structural burdens which had to be eliminated.

Regional Foreign Exchange Crisis

In Chapter 4 it was pointed out that the trade of the Central American countries had two distinct components in the 1970s, intraregional trade and extraregional trade. To a great extent, the commodities traded in each case could not be switched to the other market. The manufactures exported had to stay within the Central American Common Market or not be exported at all from their country of origin. With some exceptions, the manufactures were and are too high-cost to compete in world markets without the capitalists involved suffering low profit rates or losses. In the case of the primary products, the regional market was too small or the complementarities among the countries' production too great.

During the early 1970s and the period of rapidly rising oil prices, extraregional trade grew considerably faster than CACM trade. The value of Central American exports to the rest of the world increased fourfold from 1971 to 1977, while the value of intraregional trade rose less than threefold. There are a number of reasons for this. First, the prices of Central American exports improved substantially from 1971 to 1977, increasing by at least 100 percent for all of the countries and by over 200 percent for El Salvador. The rise in the general price index for exports reflected large increases in the prices of cotton, coffee, and meat, exported outside of the CACM. However, for every country but Honduras, the years after 1977 have been ones of unfavorable prices for extraregional exports. El Salvador was the hardest hit, with export prices during 1978–1981 averaging 25 percent below 1977, followed by Nicaragua with an average decline of about 15 percent for the same period. For Costa Rica and Guatemala, export prices rose somewhat after 1977, but nothing like their increases during the first seven years of the 1970s.[3]

Had world primary product prices continued to rise after 1977, it is possible that the Central American countries, with the exception of those embroiled in armed struggles, would have generated sufficient foreign exchange to satisfy their debt burdens and maintain a level of imports to sustain growth. But primary product prices did not rise, while import prices continued their upward trend. After more or less stable export prices from 1978 to 1980, a deterioration followed. From the end of 1980 to early 1982, the world price of cotton fell by 25 percent and the price of sugar by 75 percent, and the two commodities together represented 15 percent of Central American exports. Coffee, representing a third of regional exports, did better, with its world price relatively stable in the early 1980s. Of the five major export commodities, only bananas enjoyed a significant price rise. But banana exports are of no importance in three of the five Central American countries. The fall in the price of cotton was particularly detrimental to export earnings. In El Salvador and Nicaragua one can attribute the fall in cotton production to the armed struggles there. But cotton production also fell sharply in Guatemala in 1981 (the largest producer in the region), to a great extent because low world prices made the commodity relatively unprofitable. The falling world prices of primary products resulted in a stagnation in the value of Central American extraregional exports. From 1973 to 1977, the value of these exports increased by an average of 27 percent a year, and in the next four years by an average of less than 1 percent, with all of the increase in one year, 1979. In 1981, extraregional exports were actually lower than they had been in 1977.

Trade among the common market countries continued to grow in value in the late 1970s, but this was the last gasp of a collapsing system. Central American regional trade reached its peak in 1980, over $1 billion for the first time, but this peak represented extraordinary circumstances. Nicaragua had imported only slightly over $100 million from the other four countries in its war-ravaged year of 1979. The following year, momentarily enjoying a large inflow of credit including bilateral loans from Guatemala and Costa Rica, its regional imports jumped to $300 million, and subsequently declined sharply. In 1981, for the first time in the twenty year history of CACM, every member country had lower regional exports and lower regional imports than the year before, and this dramatic shift proved to be a signal of things to come, for in 1982 regional trade fell below $800 million.

The combination of declining world market prices and the collapse of the CACM had a devastating effect on the balance of payments of the Central American countries. From 1974 to 1977, the trade deficit (exports minus imports), had been improving. In 1974, the shock of oil prices[4] generated a trade deficit of over $500 million dollars, up from $22 million the year before. But the deficit declined in 1975, 1976, and was zero in 1977. In 1978 deficits returned, to $400 million, over $600 million in 1980, and almost $1 billion in 1981.[5] The huge trade deficit for the region in 1981 was made all the more alarming because the value of imports had actually declined by over $100 million compared to 1980, and in terms of constant prices imports were lower than they had been since 1976. The effect of world market prices on Central American trade can be summed up by noting that in 1977, the value of exports had achieved equality with imports; in 1981, the volume of exports was 11 percent *higher*, the volume of imports 11 percent *lower*, but the trade deficit close to $1 billion.

This growing crisis in trade was made worse by changes in capital flows. During the years of rapid petroleum price increases, the Central American countries taken together had accumulated international reserves despite their trade deficits. That is, short-term and long-term capital inflows had been more than sufficient to offset the trade deficits (and the deficits on "invisibles"). From 1968 until 1977, the net reserves of the five countries rose in every year but one, 1974. From 1978 onwards, net reserves declined in every year. Comparison of 1977 and 1979 is instructive. In both years, the regional trade deficit was virtually zero, but international reserves rose by $270 million in 1977, and fell by $190 million in 1979.

The failure of capital flows to fill the trade deficit is almost entirely explained by private capital abandoning Central America as a bad risk. From 1974 through 1978, the net flow of private investment and loan capital into Central America averaged almost $400 million a year, and for 1979–1981 was a negative $50 million a year. These totals refer only to private capital flows whose source could be identified. The balance of payments data compiled by the secretariat of the CACM includes a category called "capital not determined," a residual category.[6] In the first half of the 1970s, this category had been relatively small, about 5 percent of all net capital inflow and positive, averaging $25 million a year. For 1978 to 1981, this item averaged a negative $290 million, or − 30 percent of all net capital flows and was almost $450 million in 1982. "Capital not determined" cannot represent government to government or government to private bank capital movements, since these would be duly recorded. Simple deduction leads to the conclusion that private capital was not only cutting back on new investments and loans after 1978, but was sending foreign exchange out of Central America at a rapid rate.

With this point in mind, one can put in context the much publicized "mini-Marshall Plan" of the Reagan administration, announced in early 1982 ("Caribbean Basin Economic Recovery Act"). Nicaragua was excluded from participation due to the conflict with Washington (see previous chapter). Preliminary versions of the plan included aid to Guatemala, but the human rights record of the Guatemalan government was such that the plan had to be limited to El Salvador, Costa Rica, and Honduras in Central America if it was to achieve congressional approval. For 1982, the total allocation for these three countries was to be $432 million. Of this total, $119 million was military aid. Of the remaining $233 million, over half ($128 million) was assigned to El Salvador, $70 million to Costa Rica, and $35 million to Honduras (Inforpress 1982).

While $128 million may appear considerable for a country the size of El Salvador, about $30 dollars per capita, it represents only a small part of the capital being expatriated by the private sector in recent years. In 1979, the sum of net private capital flows and "capital not determined" was a massive *minus* $340 million and a negative $500 million for 1980–1981. Thus, the economic aid within the "mini-Marshall Plan" to the private sector of El Salvador in 1982 might have been insufficient to compensate for the decapitalization of the private sector in question. In the case of Costa Rica, private capital inflows have exceeded outflows (though not by much), but $70 million in aid is considerably less than the annual loss of international reserves for 1979–1981, which averaged $107 million a year. This is also the case for Honduras, which lost reserves at a rate of $42 million for 1979–1981, and would receive only $35 million under the program in 1982. In conclusion, the prefix "mini" on "Marshall Plan" is well advised: the economic aid involved is insufficient to stabilize the balance of payments situation of the three governments involved, much less allow for economic recuperation. The obvious inadequacy of the Caribbean Basin plan in part prompted the much larger financial aid recommendations of the Presidential Commission on Central America (Kissinger Commission) which we consider below.

Multilateral lending to Central American governments has declined. From mid-1979 to mid-1980, the World Bank and the Inter-American Development Bank loaned $423 million to Central American governments, and for the next twelve months this total fell to $310 million, a drop of 27 percent (Inforpress 1982). Loans from these organizations were also becoming conditional in a way that they had not been for at least a decade, so that successful negotiations of multilateral loans increasingly restricted the policy options of Central American governments. This point is pursued below, along with consideration of the International Monetary Fund's role in the Central American economic crisis.

After this somewhat involved discussions of changes in trade and capital flows, the basic elements of the Central American economic crisis should be summarized. During the 1960s and early 1970s, the Central American countries generally imported more than they exported, but this was sustainable along with relatively rapid growth because of capital inflows. With the rise in petroleum prices, the gap between imports and exports increased, but growth continued, achieved through foreign borrowing. However, subsequent declines in primary product prices and the collapse of the CACM made the trade deficits and balance of payments situation untenable. Capital flows, both "official" (government to government and from multilateral agencies) and private, declined, in great part due to the political uncertainty in the region. Thus, the Central American countries entered the 1980s with large trade deficits and no apparent means to finance them. In all of the countries, the governments had no alternative but to accept a decline in economic activity, since they lacked the foreign exchange for the inputs necessary to maintain national production.

All of the Central American countries were negatively affected by the factors explained above, but the timing of the impact varied somewhat. Table 56 gives the movement in gross domestic product and per capita product for the 1970s and early 1980s. For all of the countries except Nicaragua, 1978 was a year of expansion, continuing the trend of

TABLE 56
Economic Indicators, 1971–1983
A. Gross Domestic Product in Central America

Year	Costa Rica	El Salvador	Guatemala	Honduras	Nicaragua	Central America
1971	68	67	68	76	76	69
1972	72	71	73	77	78	72
1973	77	74	77	82	82	78
1974	82	81	83	84	92	84
1975	82	84	84	82	94	83
1976	89	90	93	89	99	90
1977	100	100	100	100	100	100
1978	107	105	105	108	93	103
1979	111	101	108	117	70	102
1980	111	88	110	121	76	103
1981	100	79	110	114	78	100
1982	91	73	106	112	77	96
1983	90	71	104	112	79	95

B. Per Capita Personal Consumption in Central America

Year	Costa Rica	El Salvador	Guatemala	Honduras	Nicaragua	Central America
1971	83	81	86	101	93	86
1972	86	82	89	97	93	91
1973	87	87	91	97	94	92
1974	89	87	91	94	101	92
1975	88	87	93	96	100	92
1976	90	91	96	98	101	95
1977	100	100	100	100	100	100
1978	105	97	102	103	90	98
1979	106	88	104	103	65	94
1980	103	80	102	104	70	97
1981	92	72	100	100	69	90
1982	76	67	96	98	67	83
1983	74	64	93	97	65	81

Source: SIECA, July 1982 and country sources.
Note: Per capita consumption differs from per capita GDP due to variation of the share of consumption in national product.

the 1970s. Nicaragua's decline was the result of war, not economic conditions, as was the decline in 1979 for El Salvador, when the other three economies continued to expand. But in 1980, Costa Rica's growth was zero, Guatemala's fell to less than 2 percent, and only in Honduras did production increase faster than population. In 1981, the crisis was being felt across the board: real output fell in three of the five countries, Guatemala had zero growth and Nicaragua's postwar recovery was clearly at an end. It has been the war-torn countries, Nicaragua and El Salvador, which suffered the greatest economic disasters, with national production in both countries over 20 percent lower in 1981 than in 1977. The distribution of that decline has been quite different in the two countries, however. Not even the most severe critic of the Sandinistas would deny that income distribution has become substantially more equal since 1979.[7] And given the failure to implement land reform in El Salvador, even avid supporters of the government would make few claims for improved distribution (*Washington Post* October 3, 1983, 1).

After 1977, per capita consumption ceased its growth in the Central American countries. From 1970, there had been no growth of note in Honduras and only very modest in Nicaragua, concentrated in the latter case in the year of recovery from the earthquake (1973–1974). But in the other three countries improvement was almost continuous from 1971 to 1977, at 2.5 percent or better per year. In 1983, however, consumption per head had dropped to below the 1977 level in Guatemala, and to the level of the 1960s in El Salvador and Costa Rica.

Costa Rica

The Costa Rican economy had enjoyed continuous and rapid growth until the late 1970s. From 1974 to 1977, it seemed to weather the shock of oil price increases, with the balance of payments improving each year. However, the current account deficits (trade plus "invisibles") were quite large and had been financed by extensive foreign borrowing. In 1971, Costa Rica's foreign debt had been about $200 million and rose to over $800 million in 1977. This did not necessarily foretell disaster, since export earnings were growing and the annual debt payments still modest. The situation became untenable as a result of the crush of international prices, with export prices falling by a third relative to import prices from 1977 to 1981. The balance of payments pressure which resulted required further foreign borrowing, making the increase in debt during the first half of the 1970s look modest indeed. From just over $800 million in 1977, the foreign debt rose to almost $1.5 billion in 1979, and to $2.7 billion in 1981. Despite the highest export earnings in Costa Rican history in 1981, debt service payments consumed 27 percent of these earnings, up from 11 percent in the mid-1970s. Another 20 percent went to pay for petroleum imports, so half of Costa Rica's export earnings were claimed by two apparently irreducible items.

Some writers make much of Costa Rica's "welfare state" as a cause of the country's economic collapse, seeing the basic problem to be large government budget deficits. These allegedly caused rapid inflation, undermining the profitability of exports and generating excessive imports. This implicitly was the reasoning of the IMF stabilization program of 1981. In fact, the evidence is sufficiently contradictory to allow for alternative interpretations. Through the 1970s, state expenditure on current goods and services rose at the same rate as national income in real terms. In 1980, public consumption expenditure was the same in constant *colones* as it had been the year before, and fell by 7 percent in 1981. It is true that deficits were high, but this was because real tax revenues did not increase, a common consequence of reduced levels of economic activity. In any case, the Costa Rican deficits were no higher than those in Guatemala and Honduras, countries never accused of excessive social expenditure. The Costa Rican economic collapse can be explained as a straightforward case of a mounting debt burden combined with unfavorable international prices. It could be argued that of all the Central American countries, it was Costa Rica which was most characterized by a transitory economic cycle and least required structural adjustment.

In the view of the IMF, however, Costa Rica in the early 1980s was a case of a country "living beyond its means" and a prime candidate for the bitter medicine of economic deflation. This austere prescription found a receptive audience in President Monge. With some exceptions, IMF loan packages tend to be based on a rather fundamentalist and largely pre-Keynesian reading of neoclassical economic doctrine and the conditions they embody reflect this.[8] The IMF conditions for a loan to the Costa Rican government included:

(1) eliminate ceilings on interest rates;
(2) eliminate quota restrictions on imported commodities;
(3) devalue the *colón* and eliminate multiple exchange rates;
(4) end subsidies to industry and agriculture;
(5) reduce government spending and raise taxes; and
(6) raise the prices of government services (Inforpress 1982).

The economic consequences of these measures should be fairly clear. The last three have the effect of restricting domestic demand, depressing production, and thereby reducing imports of both consumer commodities and producers' commodities. The necessity for such a depression of demand is hard to contest in the Costa Rica context. By the late 1970s, the government no longer had the foreign exchange to maintain imports at their prevailing level, and sources of additional foreign loans had been exhausted. Imports had to be reduced, and a severe contraction of the economy could achieve this. There are two ways in which the necessary contraction could be managed. One would be to maintain state services and subsidies and have the burden of the contraction born by the private sector and personal consumption.[9] If demand falls sufficiently, both inflation and imports should reach target levels. Alternatively, the burden of reduced demand could be placed upon state expenditure and personal consumption. Personal consumption must suffer in either case, since both courses of action imply less domestic production, employment, and earned income. The distributional consequences of the alternatives are potentially quite different, particularly in the case of Costa Rica. Since the state had no military budget of consequence, cutting government expenditure would mean and did mean reducing health care, funding for education, etc. These are choices involving distribution of losses and of equity.

Not so from the IMF viewpoint. The pivotal impact of world prices was stressed little, and Costa Rica's economic crisis attributed to certain "distortions" in the economy. Import restrictions, tariffs, and subsidies had allegedly created a non-competitive manufacturing sector. The national currency was "overvalued" (too few *colones* per dollar), discouraging exports and encouraging excessive use of imported inputs. The government budget deficit bred inflation, which made all of these "distortions" worse. A fervent adherent to this doctrine would go as far as to say that eliminating the "distortions" could correct the situation relatively quickly with minimum pain. For example, devaluation would stimulate capitalists to export, providing employment for the workers laid off due to a fall in domestic demand. Eliminating the budget deficit would reduce inflation and thereby raise private savings and investment, and so on. The critics of this position would argue that the basic problem in Costa Rica's case and similar cases is the depressed condition of the world market, and that the consequence of eliminating "distortions" is to redistribute real income away from the lower classes with the effect on economic recovery either insignificant or negative.

The distributional impact of measures is an empirical question, but it should be clear that such policy debates have moved out of the realm of technical arguments into the territory where ideology and politics are dominant. Very much at issue in the debate is the faith one has in private capital, a faith that has to have been shaken by the rate at which the private sector in Costa Rica has sent capital abroad in recent years. Pointing out the political and value-laden nature of economic policies is not a criticism, but a necessary recognition of the fact that economic growth and economic decline embody a struggle within society over how the gains and losses will be distributed.

Honduras

Honduras also found it necessary to reach an accord with the IMF, but the conditions imposed were fewer and less austere. In order to receive additional IMF funding, in April 1981, the Honduran government introduced what it called the "Anti-Inflation Plan." The title of the plan is somewhat surprising, since it suggests that inflation was the major economic problem at the time. In fact, the consumer price index had risen slightly less than 10 percent for the twelve months from March 1980, to March 1981, the lowest rate for any other Central American country or Panama. Few countries in the hemisphere could have boasted an inflation rate so low. As it turned out, the rate of inflation in Honduras was slightly higher in the twelve months after the plan was announced than for the previous year.

The major economic problem facing the Honduran government in the early 1980s was the balance of payments. Unlike Costa Rica, Honduras was not hard-hit by changes in international prices. Honduras was the only country in Central America to enjoy more favorable world prices during 1978–1980 than in 1977. It was also the only one of the Central American countries to experience a substantial increase in private foreign investment in the late 1970s. We have said that Costa Rica was a case of an economic crisis generated by unfavorable terms of trade. Honduras during the same time period was a case of a balance of payments crisis caused by rapid growth which drew in imports beyond the economy's capacity to export. The Honduran economy grew at almost double the rate of its closest Central American competitor from 1977 to 1980, at 6.6 percent a year. Imports measured in constant prices grew at over 10 percent a year and at 20 percent a year in current value. Exports also grew, but slower, about the rate at which national product was growing. As a result, the trade deficit increased, from $20 million in 1977 to over $100 million in 1980. The Honduran government then began to engage in heavy foreign borrowing to finance the balance of payments deficits, but in the context of rapid growth as opposed to Costa Rica's declining growth rate. In 1976, the external debt had been a modest $550 million, and by 1981 rose to $1.4 billion. This brought debt service payments to over 20 percent of exports, a burden comparable to Costa Rica's.

To the extent that it was appropriate anywhere, the IMF package for

Costa Rica was probably more appropriate for Honduras. The Honduran balance of payments crisis was an excess demand phenomenon, resolvable by reducing the growth rate, while in Costa Rica the problem was one of unfavorable export and import prices. Further, the Honduran state was running large fiscal deficits, 64 percent of tax revenues in 1980. While the IMF conditions for Honduras did not ignore the deficits, it put less emphasis on them than in the Costa Rican loan conditions.

Guatemala

The remaining three Central American countries were all torn by internal armed conflicts in the late 1970s, though the bitter struggle in Guatemala had not reached the point of seriously affecting production. Tourism has been substantially reduced by the insurrection and the extremely brutal repression of all opposition to the various military governments. Many human rights groups judge the Guatemalan situation to be the worst in Central America, a striking conclusion with El Salvador as competition. Precise data on the drop in tourist revenues are not available,[10] but this factor is less important than other economic problems that developed in the late 1970s. These problems give the Guatemalan economic crisis a long-run character to a much greater extent than for Honduras or Costa Rica.

Like Costa Rica, Guatemala was seriously affected by changes in world prices. Import prices rose relatively to export prices in every year after 1977, and by 1980 a unit of Guatemalan exports bought fewer imports than it had for ten years. Only El Salvador suffered more from the deterioration of the terms of trade after 1977.

The deterioration in the terms of trade was to a great extent the result of stagnation in the world price of coffee, Guatemala's most important export. The problems for coffee exports and other primary products went beyond low prices. In the 1970s Guatemala, like other countries of the region, suffered from plant blight, with coffee exports stagnating after the middle of the decade. Production of cotton, the second most important export, declined sharply, by 8 percent in 1980, and a staggering 23 percent in 1981. The decline in cotton production could merely be a consequence of world prices dropping below the break-even point for capitalist producers, in which case the problem is transitory. More likely is that the heavy use of chemical fertilizers (see Chapter 5) and related methods of raising yields have affected the soil. Indeed, this ghost of over-exploitation of the soil haunts agribusiness throughout Guatemala.

More serious problems arose in the extractive sector. In the early

1970s, the Guatemalan government had anticipated development of petroleum and mining which would reduce dependence on agricultural exports, particularly coffee. Oil reserves appear to be quite modest, however, and it is unlikely that domestic production could offset imports of petroleum for the foreseeable future. But great hopes had been held for the exploitation of nickel. The EXMIBAL nickel project, a consortium of International Nickel and Hanna Mining, had involved investment of over $200 million. The company received a number of extremely favorable concessions from the government, including exemption from import duties. Exports of nickel were expected to reach about $60 million in 1978. In fact, export earnings from nickel did reach this level (in 1980, not 1978), but then disaster struck. In late 1980 International Nickel and Hanna Mining suspended operations in Guatemala, and in 1981 announced that production had been terminated. Why this decision was made is unclear, since there is evidence that the world price of nickel in 1981 was above what the company itself had identified as the price which would give it an acceptable rate of return. Circumstantial evidence indicates that the EXMIBAL venture was terminated due to the political instability of the country, and that the parent corporations decided to concentrate their efforts elsewhere, where costs were lower. Whatever the case, the decision dealt a fatal blow to hopes that Guatemala would diversify into mineral exports. The decision also negatively affected the credit rating of the Guatemalan government with private multinational banks.

The Guatemala crisis eludes the type of straightforward characterization possible for Costa Rica and Honduras. The sting of relative prices was a major element in the crisis, but other elements add considerable complexity. If the recent decline in the production of export crops has been the consequence of plant blight and low prices, then a more robust world market will bring prosperity back to agriculture. It may be, however, that the agricultural decline represents more deep-seated difficulties. Further, the foreign exchange lost by the ending of nickel mining must somehow be replaced from other sectors. Finally, Guatemala in the early 1980s had a larger portion of its trade with the CACM than any other country in the region, almost 30 percent for 1980–1981 (an average of $380 million for these two years). The prospects for maintaining that level of regional exports is extremely bleak. A favorable element in this otherwise dark picture is that the Guatemala foreign debt is extremely modest. Debt repayments and other debt-servicing were less than 4 percent of export earnings in 1981. This fact does not fundamentally change the conclusion that one cannot anticipate a strong economic recovery in the near future.

El Salvador

The economies of El Salvador and Nicaragua have been overwhelmed by war since 1978, and in both cases the most profound pessimism is justified, though for different reasons. Civil war and its ramifications brought virtual economic collapse to El Salvador, with the worst effects yet to come. From 1978 to 1981, manufacturing production in constant prices fell by one-third and agriculture by 12 percent. For total national production the decline was 33 percent from 1978 to 1983 (see Table 56). In 1983, per capita income was 40 percent below its peak of 1977, or a return to the level of the early 1960s. Destruction of productive assets has not been insignificant in El Salvador, but much less than occurred in Nicaragua in 1978–1979.

The collapse of the Salvadoran economy has been more a result of the dynamics of a society in civil war than war destruction as such. At least since early 1981, victory by the insurgents has been a real possibility, and this has generated massive capital flight, over $800 million for 1979–1981. The prospect of land reform—whose slow pace of implementation makes it largely a prospect—has also contributed to the large-scale decapitalization. Perhaps even more debilitating than capital flight has been the consequence of US financing of the Salvadoran balance of payments. The effect of this aid has been to sustain the commercial sector while the productive sectors decline. This is a familiar syndrome which reached its fullest expression in South Vietnam in the early 1970s. Civil wars by their nature disrupt production, if for no other reason than that the authority structure which regiments the labor force is weakened or even swept away in parts of the country. Foreign finance in the form of grants or low-interest loans serve to maintain the level of imports or cushion their fall. This process began in El Salvador in 1981 and 1982. As production declines and foreign finance increases, it becomes more profitable to engage in trade than in production. The syndrome is a case of "the tail wagging the dog," with commerce and banking losing their secondary role as derivative from production and taking on an independent life fed from abroad. In such circumstances fortunes can still be made and consumption maintained—elite consumption at any rate— while agriculture and manufacturing sink deeper into depression. The Salvadoran economy may be well into such a vicious cycle.

The accumulating difficulties of the Salvadoran economy promoted three requests for credit from the IMF, in 1979, 1980, and 1981. The disbursed total is small: $63 million with $36 million to follow if the government manages to meet IMF economic targets. The most recent IMF lending to El Salvador has been part of a program of "structural adjustment," which we consider in the final section. The intent of the policy changes is to stimulate exports within a general plan of improving resource allocation. As indicated above, one can debate whether such programs are remedial in any circumstances. In the case of El Salvador, more efficient resource allocation could hardly touch the basic problems, which are derivative from the civil war. The Salvadoran economy is indeed undergoing profound "structural adjustment," in which (1) the productive sectors are withering and commerce asserting itself as dominant, and (2) capital flight so overwhelms the balance of payments that import and export policies are largely marginal.

Nicaragua

The previous chapter treated in some detail the problems of the Nicaraguan economy. These problems are of three types. First, there are the economic factors common to all of the Central American countries: the collapse of the common market and declining primary product prices. Nicaragua has suffered less from the deterioration of the terms of trade than any of the other four countries except Honduras, but has been severely affected by the drop in regional trade. Political conflict with the other countries, the general decline of regional trade, and domestic supply constraints caused Nicaragua's exports to Central America to fall from $146 million in 1978 to $71 million in 1981. Second, the Nicaraguan economy is in the process of major structural change. Third, and overwhelming the first two, Nicaragua is again at war. What makes this war so debilitating is that while there is little prospect that Nicaragua will lose it, there is also little prospect that the Sandinista government can end it militarily. As long as Washington is prepared to finance harassment and invasion of Nicaraguan territory and the governments of Honduras and Costa Rica co-operate, the war will continue. When defeated militarily, as during April–June 1983, the invaders can retire to Honduras and prepare their next venture.

This continuous state of war has had a profound impact upon the Nicaraguan economy. Direct destruction has been modest compared to the fighting during 1978–1979, and it is unlikely that the invading army has the capacity to go beyond acts of sabotage, lacking as it does popular support. However, the constant harassment along the border has forced the Nicaraguan government to divert considerable resources to national defense. This has involved not only foreign exchange to purchase arms from France and Eastern Europe, but also the call-up of reserve units has drawn skilled men and women out of the government ministries. The state social programs have had to be cut back due to scarcity of foreign exchange, particularly medicine for health clinics and books for schools. A further casualty of the new war has been economic policy, for the leadership of the Sandinista movement is so preoccupied with military matters that little time and consideration can be given to crucial economic decisions.

Confronted with the economic problems common to the other countries of the region and a growing military threat, the Nicaraguan government began in late 1981 to implement an austerity program, the most important goal of which was to correct an increasingly serious balance of payments deficit. In 1980, the current account deficit was $400 million; it would rise to one-half billion in 1981. The "Emergency Plan" contained little but a statement of intent with regard to economic policy, and it was in 1982 that significant steps were taken to bring the economy under control.

The Nicaraguan emergency plan was essentially a deflation package designed to depress aggregate demand and thereby reduce the demand for imports and contain the inflationary pressures in the economy. The reduction of aggregate demand had two parts. First, the fiscal deficit had to be reduced. Due to the disruption of the fiscal system caused by the fighting in 1978 and 1979, real tax revenues had declined. The demand for government services had increased dramatically, due to human suffering described in the previous chapter and to the aspirations of a mobilized population. The fiscal deficit therefore increased considerably in 1980, though it remained the lowest in Central America, far below either Guatemala's or that of Honduras. A virtual freeze was placed on the civilian budget, and real expenditure was the same in 1981 as 1980 (SIECA July 1982, 5) and fell slightly in 1982.

Second, because of the import intensity of Nicaraguan production, output had to be reduced if the total import bill was to be significantly affected. This was achieved through the direct allocation of foreign exchange to public and private enterprises. Beginning in late 1981, an inter-ministerial committee began to assign foreign exchange directly to enterprises on the basis of priorities. At the outset, the priorities reflected studies done on consumption habits of the population, with the intention that the declines in output would affect the standard of living as little as possible. As the military threat increased, national security criteria were added, such as clothing for the army. The allocation of foreign exchange was the most effective economic policy tool the government had, since it de facto determined the level of output company by company. During 1982 and early 1983, perhaps as many as 50 of the manufacturing firms hiring twenty or more employees had to close from lack of imported inputs. These closings were distributed proportionately between the state and private sectors. Manufacturing plants were closing down throughout Central America, of course, but only in Nicaragua did it occur as part of a coherent plan and with explicit intention to minimize the drop in the standard of living.

Preliminary estimates by the Central Bank of Nicaragua indicated that the deflationary program had considerable success, with imports falling from $900 million in 1981, to less than $750 million in 1982. The current account deficit did remain unsustainably large, however, over $300 million in 1982. Attempts to finance the balance of payments deficit by foreign borrowing proved difficult to impossible when the Reagan administration brought pressure on private banks not to lend to Nicaragua. This balance of payments pressure prompted the government to expand its rationing system, which through mid-1982 had been limited to sugar. The previous policy of supplementing domestic supplies with imports of basic consumer commodities could no longer be maintained. The rationing remains limited in scope in 1984, restricted to a half-dozen essential items such as rice and soap (Republic of Nicaragua 1983). In mid-1982, gasoline was rationed through a separate program, though this had little foreign exchange impact until the following year.

A major source of instability in the balance of payments since the fall of Somoza has been illegal capital flight. Immediately after the triumph, the government instituted a dual exchange rate system in which the state allocated foreign exchange to companies and individuals at the official exchange rate (10 *córdobas* to the dollar) and allowed a parallel free market in foreign exchange for those not receiving official allocations. In the third quarter of 1981, this free market rate stood at twenty-seven *córdobas* to the dollar. As the political situation became more tense internally and the threat of U.S. intervention increased, this parallel market in effect became a free market for capital flight. The free parallel market, similar to what was allowed in Costa Rica at the same time, was abandoned in late 1981 when its rate was fixed by the state at twenty-seven *córdobas* to the dollar. Whether or not this and other steps reduced capital flight is open to debate, but a black market in the *córdoba* developed, with a rate more than double that in the regulated parallel market.

The policies of the Nicaraguan government to combat the country's economic crisis stand in sharp contrast to those pursued elsewhere in the region. Whether a deflationary policy based on minimizing the effect on the standard of living of the masses of the population can in practice guide an economy through a crisis and facilitate eventual recovery cannot be known from the Nicaraguan experience. By 1982, the economy was being overwhelmed by the military situation. A poor country by any standards, Nicaragua had suffered a catastrophic war during 1978–1979, was facing increased economic isolation, and confronting armed invasion. Economic recovery remains dependent upon a less hostile environment, and there seemed little likelihood of this in the mid-1980s.

Panama

Compared to the five countries to the north, Panama has had rather mild economic difficulties, at least on first inspection. After 1979, all of the five Central American countries had negative growth rates. Panama's GNP, after a three-year stagnation from 1973 to 1976, has grown continuously, if not robustly. The absence of growth during the mid-1970s is explained by the high proportion of imports accounted for by petroleum, over 30 percent. But once the shock of oil prices had worn off, the economy apparently weathered the regional crisis much better than its neighbors. To a great extent this is the result of the unique structure of Panama's foreign exchange earnings. As shown in Chapter 4, by the second half of the 1970s, commodity exports were less than 20 percent of foreign exchange earnings, and a mere 12 percent in 1980. As a result, the fall in primary product prices on world markets affected the balance of payments relatively little. And after 1976, the deposits of short-term capital in banks of the International Financial Center rose rapidly: $11 billion in 1976, $20 billion in 1978, and $30 billion in 1981 (Inforpress 1982). Largely as a result of the earnings from banking services, Panama was able to sustain trade deficits twice as large as those for any Central American country and maintain growth. In terms of volume, commodity exports fell by 16 percent from 1976 to 1981, while foreign exchange earnings rose over 250 percent.

Panama did experience balance of payments pressure in 1978–1979, in part due to debt-service payments. The Torrijos government sought an accord with the IMF, receiving a credit line of $80 million in 1979 in return for agreeing to meet certain economic targets. The IMF was particularly concerned with the government budget deficit. In 1978, total state expenditure had exceeded tax revenue by over 60 percent, and in 1979, the proportion reached 90 percent. Reform of the taxation system and a reduction of state subsidies to agriculture resulted in considerable improvement. The deficit fell to slightly over 50 percent of tax revenues in 1980 and held at the same proportion in 1981. The growth rate of national income did decline, but the 5 percent rate in 1980 and 4 percent in 1981 were in sharp contrast to negative rates in all of the Central American countries for these two years and also for much of South America and the Caribbean.

Closer inspection raises doubts about the economic health of Panama. What is normally meant by the word "production" has hardly grown at all over the last decade in this economy, despite the quite respectable rate of growth of national income. For the ten years from 1972 to 1981, national income grew at 4 percent per year, and only Guatemala of the Central American countries grew faster. However, the growth rate of all of the goods-producing sectors was extremely low: barely 1.5 percent for agriculture and manufacturing, and negative growth for construction. In 1981, this strange pattern of growth reached its *reducto absurdum*. Measured national income rose by 4 percent despite declines in all goods-producing sectors: a negative 2.5 percent in agriculture and manufacturing and negative 7 percent in construction. The positive overall growth rate was the result of an 8 percent increase in transport and communications, and an 11 percent increase in commerce and banking. Normally one expects these sectors to grow because there are more commodities to be transported, exchanged, and financed. In fact, there were fewer. Domestic production of goods fell and imports also fell, implying that the supply of commodities was 5 percent lower in Panama in 1981 than 1980.

It would appear that much of the growth of the Panamanian economy in the last decade is an illusion of measurement, for per capita consumption of goods (domestic production and imports) has fallen slightly. Urban real wages, for example, were lower in the early 1980s than the mid-1970s, despite a measured rise in per capita income and despite the fact that in the earlier period the economy was in recession. Agriculture has particularly suffered. From 1976 to 1980, the production of basic staples—rice, corn, and beans—fell by 14 percent. Some of this decline is explained by government removal of the producer support price for corn in 1979, part of the IMF package, but the stagnation of agriculture appears to be long term.[11]

The growth of international banking in Panama seems to have generated no dynamism outside of that sector itself. While the growth of the banking sector has prevented the type of severe balance of payments crisis suffered by the Central American countries, it has not been associated either with a rise in private consumption nor investment in productive activities, which presumably are the goals of economic growth. It may be that these goals cannot be achieved in the context of an economy increasingly based on banking, commerce, and services.

"Structural Adjustment" in Central America

In the 1970s, a consensus emerged in the international development community that foreign assistance to underdeveloped countries should be directed toward the elimination of poverty. This current of thought can be found in the working papers and reports of the US Agency for International Development (AID), the World Bank, the Inter-American Development Bank, and various UN agencies. This view of how development assistance should be oriented came to be called "the basic needs approach" (Weeks and Dore 1982). The World Bank and Inter-American Development Bank both practiced a policy of giving preference to the least developed countries among their members. Subject to geopolitical considerations (e.g., aid to Israel), AID followed a similar principle. While one should not exaggerate the reorientation of policy, the World Bank, for example, moved away from its strong emphasis on lending for roads and other infrastructure into financing social programs such as health and education to a greater degree than before.

In the 1980s, this philosophy has virtually disappeared in the multilateral agencies in favor of a return to the orthodoxy of two decades ago. Once again, the problem of poverty is seen as secondary to, or its solution derivative from, achieving a more efficient allocation of resources. Overwhelming emphasis is placed on "market forces," and the key phrase is "structural adjustment to the new macro environment" (Wright 1980 and Landell-Mills 1981). In this view, the economic problems of underdeveloped countries, particularly the balance of payments problem, must be solved by internal policy changes which have the effect of reducing state regulation of economic activity. The term "structural adjustment" is somewhat misleading in as far as it suggests planning. The implicit adjustments would be achieved by market forces once tariffs are reduced, qualitative controls on imports eliminated, subsidies and price supports to producers terminated, and a myriad of other state regulations phased out. The underlying philosophy is that the vast majority of state regulations on capital's operation have the effect of artificially maintaining inefficient production. Most at fault here is the package of policies associated with import substitution,[12] which is judged to discourage exports while creating a heavy burden of import-intensive, inefficient production. To a great extent, the major bilateral and multilateral foreign assistance agencies have come around to the IMF point of view, for the latter agency had been extremely skeptical of the basic needs approach from the outset.

The change of orientation is demonstrated in a loan program for industry created in 1982 by the IDB.[13] The new program provides foreign exchange to Latin American and Caribbean countries for the import of inputs and machinery to manufacturing. The rationale for the program was that in many countries the manufacturing sector operated at low capacity due to the shortage of foreign exchange. Clear priorities with regard to industries that would qualify for loans were given: (1) that the industries involved either exported a major part of their output or that it could be demonstrated that they would do so with the help of the credits; and (2) that in the case of industries producing for the local market, it be shown that these are internationally competitive. Further, the evaluation of loan requests would take into account such considerations as the government's exchange rate policy, method of allocating foreign exchange, tax policy toward industry, and subsidies and price supports to agriculture in as far as they affect industry. Never before had the IDB made loans conditional on the macroeconomic policies of a borrowing government. The IDB also proposed to maintain close working contact with other multilateral agencies to keep the program consistent with policies of those agencies. One of the first governments to receive a loan under the program was that of El Salvador, and the conditionality of this loan is quite similar to what one would get from the IMF, with stress on establishing a "free market" exchange rate, deregulating the interest rate, and evaluating profitability of industry on a company by company basis. A similar emphasis appears in recent World Bank statements (World Bank 1983).

The return to an emphasis on unregulated markets and less state involvement in the economy is of questionable relevance to the countries of Central America, for it is difficult to see how this policy package would remedy the region's economic problems, which are political as well as economic. The economy of Nicaragua is a victim of military conflict and of attempts by Washington to isolate that country from multilateral agencies, multilateral banks, and world markets. El Salvador, too, is a country whose social and economic dynamic is determined by war and increasingly distorted by large infusions of foreign exchange from Washington. Honduras may soon be caught up in the same maelstrom of war.

But even if Central America were not destined for a regional conflict in the 1980s, a policy based on more use of market forces and less state intervention seems singularly inappropriate. All of the Central American countries and Panama have had a history of the type of open, "outward-looking" economic policy implicit in the structural adjustment remedy. By the standards of Latin America and the Caribbean, government has played a relatively small role in economic life, with the exception of Nicaragua since 1979. In the last few years, exports have averaged about 30 percent of national income in Central America, higher than the proportion a decade earlier. Thus a remedy based on orienting the economies more to international market would not be a change of policy, but pursuing more of the same. Central America is not like Chile in the 1960s or Peru in the 1970s, with histories of vigorous and single-minded pursuit of import substitution and its high levels of protectionism and state involvement in production.

Whatever economic program is followed by the Central American governments, successful capitalist development requires an increase in world commodity prices, foreign investment and access to international borrowing. World commodity prices may recover in the 1980s, though this is far from certain. But there can be little prospect for increased foreign investment or international borrowing on more attractive terms. Central America is a region of capital flight, not capital inflow. The growing military hostilities in the region are unlikely to inspire investors, foreign or domestic, to venture their capital no matter what policies the various governments pursue. The international liquidity situation is even worse. In the 1970s, the large balance of payments surpluses of the oil-exporting countries generated an enormous flow of funds into multinational banks. This provided the liquidity for loans to governments of underdeveloped countries. These same countries, Saudi Arabia being a prime example, also increased their quotas in the IMF, expanding the lending capacity of that institution. The large foreign exchange surpluses of oil-exporting countries are now a thing of the past, and most experts predict a continuation of the present world liquidity shortage. Private banks are notoriously overextended in countries such as Brazil, Mexico, and Chile, and are likely to be extremely cautious in lending even if funds were available. At the same time, all of the multilateral agencies have less to lend. Both the IMF and the World Bank have had difficulty obtaining from the Reagan administration the normal level of funding, much less increased funding.

This bleak assessment of the economic prospects of the isthmus is shared by the governments of the Central American countries. In 1983, at a meeting of representatives from private and multilateral financial institutions in Brussels, officials from the five governments predicted economic collapse for the region unless financial aid were forthcoming rapidly and in large amounts (Central American Governments 1983). It was the prospect of such a collapse, along with military successes by the left in El Salvador, that prompted the Reagan administration to create a special presidential commission on Central America in mid-1983.[14] The commission, headed by former Secretary of State Henry Kissinger, issued its report in January 1984.

The commission's highly controversial report divides itself into two parts: an analysis of the political turmoil in Central America, placed clearly in the context of US-Soviet rivalry; and an economic program to reactivate the economies of the area. The report sees the foreign exchange crisis in the region to be the most pressing economic problem, and estimates the balance of payments support required by El Salvador, Guatemala, Honduras, and Costa Rica for 1985–1990 to be $20.6 billion,[15] and recommends $8 billion as the US bilateral contribution. In February

1984, the Reagan administration sent a proposal to Congress to implement this recommendation. A close reading of the commission report indicates that the aid is to have a clear economic and political orientation. A number of policy steps are strongly encouraged for adoption by the Central American governments, which include: 1) "the greatest possible involvement of the private sector", 2) an effort "to create favorable investment climates", 3) reduction of public investment so that resources can be "diverted to the private sector", and 4) improving economic policy to encourage exports (US Government 1984, 54–58).

In other words, the commission foresees a recovery of the four Central American economies based upon less government initiative, fewer regulations on private capital, and liberalization of trade policy. These recommendations fit well with the "structural adjustment" philosophy of the multilateral agencies. Without doubt, exports have to be fostered in all of the Central American countries, but one can question whether a program so oriented to the private sector can achieve this. The issue is not an ideological one, but practical. Historically, the Central American governments have placed fewer restrictions on the private sector than any governments in the hemisphere, so it is hard to see how further catering to private business interests will qualitatively improve either the "investment climate" or growth performance. Indeed, for the last twenty years foreign investors have judged Costa Rica to have the most favorable investment climate in the region, and it is the Costa Rican governments which have placed more restrictions on capital than any others in Central America.

The fact that foreign capital has judged Costa Rica to be the most fertile ground for investment indicates that the favorability of an investment climate is considerably more complicated than a government's economic policies narrowly defined. What has made Costa Rica so attractive is the political stability of that country and the absence of major civil strife. Questions of tariff policy, export incentives, and so on, become pivotal in private sector decision making only when there is a general context of political stability.[16] In the present context of Honduras, El Salvador, and Guatemala, political conditions are so unstable that still fewer restrictions on the private sector will probably have the effect of permitting easier capital flight, not capital inflow. Thus, the balance of payments support suggested by the Kissinger Commission is likely to finance disinvestment from Central America in the 1980s.[17]

Further, encouraging "private sector initiative" and "participation" would seem to conflict with the commission's judgment that the benefits from past growth "were distributed in a flagrantly inequitable manner," and its warning that in future growth must be "more equitably shared" (US Government 1984, 24, 40). While a strategy of relying upon a relatively unfettered private sector has resulted in impressive growth performances in certain countries during particular historical periods, few would argue that such a strategy tends naturally to reduce economic inequalities. Indeed, the present economic inequalities in Central America are in part the result of rapid growth during the 1960s and early 1970s, which was based upon private sector initiative and limited government regulation. It is more of this experience which the US bilateral aid would seek to foster.

With or without financial aid from the United States, some form of restructuring of the Central American economies is unavoidable. The collapse of the CACM in itself makes this a necessity. These economies developed a pattern of production over the last three decades oriented to agroindustry and a regional market, in the context of political stability based on repressive, dictatorial governments overwhelmingly oriented to private sector economic interests (Costa Rica being a partial exception). This pattern of production cannot sustain growth in the 1980s. Commodity prices are down, the regional market a thing of the past, and the fuel of expansion—foreign investment—not forthcoming. Further, there is little prospect for the type of foreign borrowing that financed the trade deficits of the 1970s, except from the US government with political strings attached. And most profoundly, the rule of dictators has been seriously weakened, and in a majority of the countries of the region who shall hold political power in the future is in doubt, which has shaken the confidence of private investors.

In this context of economic and political uncertainty, a restructuring of the various economies of Central America will be forced upon the region. It is likely to occur through negative growth rates, falling standards of living, and significant economic disintegration, not through a smoothly managed adaptation to the "new macro environment."

NOTES

[1] See Chapter 4 for the data on these variables for Central America.

[2] See Chapter 4.

[3] Costa Rica's export price index for 1978–1981 averaged 5 percent above 1977, but this increase disappears to zero if 1980 is omitted. The increase is also 5 percent for Guatemala.

[4] The Managua earthquake of 1972 also contributed to the large regional trade deficit in 1974. Nicaragua had run a surplus in 1972, and a combined deficit of over $300 million for 1973–1975, with over half of this in 1974.

[5] The regional trade deficit almost disappeared in 1979, only $2 million. This was due to the collapse of internal demand in war-torn El Salvador and Nicara-

gua. Perversely enough, war was coincidental with a combined trade surplus of over \$500 million for the two countries in 1979. Export earnings fell sharply in both countries in 1980.

[6] This category, *capital no determinado,* is the difference between the sum of measured net capital flows and the total net capital flows which can be deduced independently from the trade and "invisibles" balance on the one hand and the end of the year change in international reserves on the other.

[7] For evidence on distribution in Nicaragua since the triumph, see Weeks 1981.

[8] Each member country of the IMF has a "quota," reflecting its contributions to the organization. A government can borrow up to a portion of its quota unconditionally (about \$75 million for Costa Rica in 1981). To borrow beyond this portion, a government must enter into an accord with the IMF, in which it agrees to fulfill certain conditions, meet specific economic targets in a set period of time, with these stipulated by the IMF. In 1980, the Costa Rican government had exhausted its unconditional borrowing, so further borrowing required a conditional accord.

[9] There are a number of ways this could be done. For example, devaluation would increase the price of imported inputs, forcing the private sector to reduce output. Devaluation would also decrease consumer demand for imports.

[10] One indicator suggests the decline: hotel occupancy rates in Guatemala fell from 79 percent in 1979, to 50 percent in 1981. (Inforpress 1982).

[11] See Chapter 5.

[12] See Chapter 6.

[13] The official name is "Special Program for Industrial Reactivization."

[14] At one point the report comments, "But the outlook [for recovery], even under optimistic assumptions, is not very promising . . . [w]ithout a significant increase in levels of foreign assistance . . ." (US Government 1984, 46).

[15] An estimate was also made of Nicaragua's external financing needs, but the report excluded that country from receiving aid, for explicitly political reasons.

[16] Feinburg and Pastor (1984) offer a program of economic assistance with some elements in common with the Kissinger Commission proposals, but argue explicitly that such a program can be successful only in the context of peace in the region.

[17] The problem of capital flight is summarized in an article in *The New York Times,* February 14, 1984, Section A, 1, 8.

REFERENCES

Banco Central de Reserva de El Salvador. 1983. *Revista Mensual, 1983 (February).* San Salvador.

Central American Governments. 1983a. "Regional Report for Central America"

———1983b. "Statement of the Central American Spokesman at the Meeting in Brussels with the International Financial Community".

Comissión Económica para América Latina (CERAL). 1983. *Apreciaciones sobre los Efectos de la Crisis Internacional en los Paises Centroamericanos.* Mexico City: United Nations.

Development Group for Alternative Policies (The Development Gap). 1983. *Supporting Central American and Caribbean Development: A Critique of the Caribbean Basin Initiative and an Alternative Regional Assistance Plan.* Washington: Development Gap.

Feinburg, Richard and Robert A. Pastor. 1984. "Far from Hopeless: An Economic Program for Post-War Central America." In *Central America: Anatomy of a Conflict,* edited by Robert S. Leiken. Elsford, N.Y.: Pergamon.

Inforpress Centroamerica. 1982. *Centroamerica, 1982.* Guatemala: Inforpress.

Inter-American Development Bank (IDB). 1977. *Latin America's External Indebtedness: Current Situation and Prospects.* Washington: IDB.

———1983 (January). *Economic Report: Honduras.* Washington: IDB.

———1983 (June). *Economic Report: Guatemala.* Washington: IDB.

———1983 (July). *Economic Report: Costa Rica.* Washington: IDB.

———1983 (July). *Economic Report: Nicaragua.* Washington: IDB.

———1983 (August). *Economic Report: El Salvador.* Washington: IDB.

Landel-Mills, Pierre M. 1981. "Structural Adjustment Lending: Early Experience. *Finance and Development* 18, no. 4. Washington.

Newfarmer, Richard. 1983. "US Latin American Economic Policy." In *From Gunboats to Diplomacy: New US Policies for Latin America,* edited by Richard Newfarmer. Baltimore: John Hopkins University Press.

República de Nicaragua, Ministerio de Comercio Interior. 1983. *Sistemas de comercialización: Productos Básicos de Consumo Popular.* Managua.

Secretaría Permanente del Tratado General de Integración Económica Centroamericana (SIECA). 1982 (July). *Estadísticas Macroeconómicas de Centroamérica, 1970–1980.* Guatemala: SIECA.

US Government. 1984. *The Report of the President's National Bipartisan Commission on Central America.* New York: Macmillan.

Weeks, John. 1981. "Determinación y analisis de la satisfacción de las necesidades básicas en los sectores urbanos de Nicaragua". Mexico: CEPAC.

Weeks, John and Elizabeth Dore. 1982. "Basic Needs: Journey of a Concept." In *Human Rights and Basic Needs in the Americas,* edited by Margaret E. Graham. Washington: Georgetown University Press.

Wright, Peter. 1980. "World Bank Lending for Structural Adjustment." *Finance and Development* 17, no. 3. Washington.

World Bank. 1983. *World Development Report 1983.* Washington: World Bank.

Index

Italicized page numbers refer to material in tables.